D0525244

Pedagogies of Religious Education

CASE STUDIES IN THE RESEARCH AND DEVELOPMENT OF GOOD PEDAGOGIC PRACTICE IN RE

EDITED BY MICHAEL GRIMMITT

McCrimmons
Great Wakering, Essex

Dedicated with love to Carol, my wife.

First published in the United Kingdom in 2000 by
McCRIMMON PUBLISHING CO LTD
Great Wakering, Essex, England
Email: mccrimmons@dial.pipex.com
Website: www.mccrimmons.co.uk

ISBN 0 85597 621 7

British Library Cataloguing in Publication Data.
A catalogue record for this book is available from the British Library.

Cover design by Brendan Waller
Typeset in Palatino 10pt roman
Printed and bound by Thanet Press Ltd, Margate, Kent   G/00

Contents

PREFACE

The last forty years have seen the emergence of a range of pedagogies of Religious Education (RE) which have taken the subject forward from a form of Christian confessionalism to an educational study of religion and religions capable of stimulating pupils' interests in issues of belief and value and encouraging them to relate whatever insights they have gained from the great spiritual, religious and cultural traditions of the world to the circumstances of their own lives.

Many of these pedagogies have emerged as a consequence of the work of research projects, sometimes funded by money from government-related agencies or charitable trusts and located within universities and colleges of higher education. While there has been considerable sharing of insights between these projects, each in its own way has sought to make a distinctive contribution to our understanding of the nature of RE in a multicultural, pluralist society and to the development of ways of learning and teaching appropriate to the demands of the subject and the needs of the pupils.

In this book those who have been responsible for undertaking, with their colleagues, some of the most important and influential research and development work in RE in the UK during the last twenty five years provide an overview of the pedagogical features of their projects. Individual contributors write in their own name and in their own style but do so on behalf of a project which in most cases they have directed or co-directed. The fact that their contributions are, for the first time, set alongside those of other professional and academic colleagues in the field, recontextualises their contribution within a wider debate about what constitutes good pedagogic practice in RE.

I hope that bringing these accounts together within a single volume will provide both trainee and practising teachers of RE in secondary schools and their primary school colleagues with a valuable resource enabling them to become better informed about the rich variety of styles of teaching and learning which are available to them. I hope too that those who read this book, perhaps as required reading during their PGCE year or as part of a Continuing Professional Development course, will be sufficiently inspired by it to want to read the original texts of the projects and gain first hand experience of trying out their ideas. For this reason I have asked contributors to provide comprehensive bibliographies of their project's publications and classroom texts and resources.

I would like to record my gratitude to all those who have contributed to this volume and to Joan McCrimmon for her enthusiastic interest in publishing it.

Michael Grimmitt,
University of Birmingham,
January, 2000

CHAPTER 1

INTRODUCTION:
THE CAPTIVITY AND LIBERATION OF RELIGIOUS EDUCATION AND THE MEANING AND SIGNIFICANCE OF PEDAGOGY.

Michael Grimmitt

THE CAPTIVITY OF RELIGIOUS EDUCATION

Following the 1988 Education Reform Act, RE in non-denominational schools in England and Wales has increasingly become the victim of ideological agendas which have had the effect of deflecting teachers' attention away from the innovatory and creative pedagogies available to them and encouraging them to adopt narrow and limited styles of teaching which are politically safe but educationally regressive. An overview of these agendas provides an important backcloth against which to set the discussion of pedagogies of RE which are the subject of this book.

How RE has fallen victim to a technicist and standards-related political ideology of education.

The agenda for re-shaping education, schools and the curriculum for the final years of the twentieth century and beyond was set by the Conservative government in the late eighties and early nineties and consisted of the imposition of a market-led, output and assessment orientated, centralised education system and a National Curriculum upon the country. There can be no doubt that these radical changes in the English and Welsh educational systems were politically motivated. It would have been wholly feasible for the government to have introduced a system of education which gave prominence to assessment while drawing upon an extensive and respectable body of educational theory. Equally they could have also established a unified national curriculum grounded in well established theories of learning and teaching. Instead they chose to prescribe a framework of content and outcomes for the national curriculum which was deliberately free of curriculum theory and made no attempt to address the characteristics of the learner or identify what the underlying principles of education should be.

The national curriculum was seen as a commodity which the government could *deliver* to teachers in schools who, subsequently, would *implement* and *deliver* it to pupils. Its structure reflected the government's view that traditional subjects were the most suitable means by which knowledge should be acquired and that subject knowledge could be commodified into discrete statements of attainment. The concept of *curriculum* as process was ignored as this would have undermined the view that pupils' learning can be measured quantitatively in accordance with the pre-determined levels of attainment, of which for most curriculum subjects eight were identified. The testing of all pupils' attainment through the administration of *Standard Assessment Tests* (SATs) in literacy, numeracy and science at 7, 11 and 14 years and the national examinations in all curriculum subject at 16 years would provide evidence of how well schools and teachers were *delivering* the national curriculum. These results would be used to create league tables of all primary and secondary schools in the country, so enabling parents as consumers to compare the efficiency of different schools in their locality. Additionally, an *Office for Standards in Education* (OFSTED) with widespread powers would inspect and report on all schools and teacher education courses using a *framework* of inspection based on extensive criteria of effectiveness. The *evidence* collected by inspectors would be used to reassure the public that the government's commitment to *raising standards* was being rigorously pursued. As a consequence, the influence of teachers, educationists, academics and local education authorities on all aspects of the system would be decreased while their accountability for its successful or unsuccessful implementation would be increased.

A significant feature of the government's strategy for putting this new system of education in place was the development of a new language of education. It functioned in such a way as to suggest that the new system was fully integrated and more coherent than any system in the past and would give pupils an *entitlement* to a much better education than ever before. The new language of education, as indicated earlier, reflected the language of economics, especially that of the free market beloved of the then Prime Minister, Margaret Thatcher. It was characterised by words like *competition, product, consumers, purchasing power, freedom of choice for parents, value for money, entrepreneurialism*, etc. Within the new system schools would now thrive or decline according to their ability to meet the needs and demands of the educational market. Consequently the language of commercial and business management was imported into education. Schools were part of the *enterprise culture* and were expected to compete with each other in *marketing* their *product* and attracting *consumers*. Headteachers were required to *manage* their schools in ways which took efficient business management as its model; school governors were charged with the need to show that expenditure could be justified by reference to worthwhile returns, such as the school's achievement of good standards of performance by all pupils in national tests. Teaching staff, in the new language of education, became responsible for *managing* and *delivering* the curriculum rather than *teaching* it.

Finally the traditional language of *learning* and *teaching* was absorbed and lost within a framework dominated by the notion that by clearly stating the *intended outcomes* of any educational or training programme this would enable objective judgements to be made about the success or otherwise of pupils or students, and, by implication, the success or otherwise of schools and the teachers which they employed. The notion of identifying *attainment targets* and *levels of attainment* and of expressing these in terms of *learning outcomes* and of *recording and reporting attainment* reflected the importation of the mainly American concept of *competence-based assessment*. This concept was first adopted as a style of assessment used in all courses leading to the awards of the National Council for Vocational Qualifications (GNVQs and NVQs) and latterly as the basis for the award of Qualified Teacher Status by the Teacher Training Agency (TTA). Within a culture which gave more and more importance to breaking down skills and abilities into their component parts it was eventually translated into the language of *Standards*. It is this word that has come to dominate all government rhetoric about education, both as a substitute for an articulated theory of education and as providing the ultimate criteria for determining the success or otherwise of what schools and teachers achieve.

The all pervasive influence of this outcome, objectives-led, competencies or standards driven educational ideology has persisted despite the fall from power of the Conservative government in May 1997. It is true that there was an expectation on the part of many teachers and academics that this market-led, managerial approach to education and its technicist view of teaching would be liberalised by the incoming Labour government. In the New Labour educational policy it was anticipated that, consistent with Socialist principles, schools would be given a new vision of their role in restoring the democratic ideals of social justice, inclusion and human transformation to a central place in personal, community and national life. If anything, however, the present Secretary of State for Education, Mr David Blunkett, is even more committed to a *standards-driven* and *performativistic* approach to education than his Conservative predecessors and has tied his own political future to 'delivering' a significant rise in the national standards of literacy and numeracy by this means by the year 2002. A central plank in his policy to achieve this is that primary schools are now required to devote at least two hours per day of curriculum time to this task. With the introduction of new optional tests in English, maths and science for pupils aged 12 and 13 in the year 2000, it could mean that from 7 years onwards a child will need to face formal tests of literacy, numeracy and science in almost every year of their school lives (1).

Even though RE is not a subject within the national curriculum and is not required by the 1988 Education Reform Act to conform to its framework of attainment targets, programmes of study and levels of attainment, it has come under enormous pressures to do so. In a survey that I undertook in 1990 on behalf of the government-controlled Schools Council Curriculum Authority (SCAA), almost half of the 150 Local Education Authorities (LEAs) of England and Wales had begun to bring RE into line with the national curriculum, outcomes and assessment related framework. Today there is no LEA which has not done so. This means that RE in the schools of England and Wales has now been accommodated to exactly the same *assessment* and *standards* driven ideology as all other curriculum subjects. Initially the pressure to bring RE within this managerial style of learning stemmed from a desire to prevent the subject's marginalisation from the rest of the curriculum. If pupils were subject to certain forms of assessment in all other subjects but RE, what did that say about the importance of RE? Later, as we will see, other government initiated pressures made it even more difficult for RE to remain outside the framework which, by the mid nineties had become normative within the education system.

How political and religious alliances conspired
to allow RE to be captured.

So far my account has avoided reference to the religious clauses of the 1988 Education Reform Act. While much has been written about their impact upon the development of RE in Britain, few commentators have attempted to assess their influence within the wider educational ideology which I have been describing. Instead they have tended to restrict their account to an exposition of the conservative and often reactionary views of RE expressed by individual members of the House of Lords during the passage of the Education Bill, to the processes whereby the wording of the clauses came to be agreed during the Parliamentary debate, or to the reactions of the faith communities to the eventual implementation of the Act. In a sense, how the clauses came to emerge from Parliamentary debate is largely immaterial. What has been much more decisive is the way in which these clauses have been subjected to even narrower interpretations within further government circulars, guidelines and Education Acts during the nineties and, most particularly, in the production in 1994 of the *Model Syllabuses for Religious Education* illustrative of what the Conservative government broadly required and expected of all LEAs. It is this process of how the Conservative government gradually tightened its hold on RE, despite the subject being legislatively outside the influence of the Secretary of State for Education and a matter for LEAs to decide, that explains how it has become a victim of ideological manipulation, religious domestication and further marginalisation from other curriculum subjects and reached its present state of relative powerlessness as a humanising influence within and upon the whole curriculum. The fact that the Labour government from August 2002 intends to introduce into all secondary schools compulsory lessons (equivalent to 5% of curriculum time) in *Citizenship Education* and a new curriculum in *Personal, Social* and *Health Education,* further undermines the educational contribution that RE is making and suggests that this government, like the previous one, has little belief in RE's personal and community value other than as a means of appeasing the faith communities and maintaining the concordat between state and church which has been reflected in all educational legislation since 1870.

Turning to the religious clauses of the 1988 Education Reform Act, how have these been used to buttress the educational ideology I have described? Initially, the Conservative government, in putting forward legislation to introduce a National Curriculum had hoped to avoid any entanglement with religious bodies by leaving the 1944 Education Act's religious clauses intact and unchanged. Unfortunately a lobby by academics (myself included) in support of RE becoming a national curriculum subject misfired and acted as the catalyst for a considerable backlash against multi-faith RE from the Christian Right. Desperate to prevent this from affecting the passage of the whole Bill, the government was dependent upon the good offices of the former Bishop of London in the House of Lords to effect a compromise between those wanting the restoration of Christian confessionalism as a basis for RE and those mindful of the impact of such legislation on community relations in a multi-faith society. The eventual agreement of Section 8 (3) of the Act was seen to hold the balance of interests between the Christian lobby and those of other faiths, namely that *'all new syllabuses must reflect the fact that the religious traditions in Great Britain are in the main Christian whilst taking account of the teaching and practices of the other principal religions represented in Great Britain.'* In actual fact, the agreement of this clause was a far from satisfactory outcome and, in my view, put back the cause of educational RE some thirty years – a state from which the subject will not recover unless the specific naming of Christianity is removed from Section 8 (3) of the Act.

Almost immediately the inherent inequality of the provision led to increased tension and competitiveness between members of different faith communities anxious to ensure that they secured maximum exposure of pupils to their religion in RE. They placed pressures on LEAs to ensure that RE agreed syllabuses reflected the application of a numerical formula in the development of the RE curriculum; 51% of the syllabus to be devoted to the study of Christianity and 49% to the other religions. Worse still, the religious clauses led to an almost universal emphasis in agreed syllabuses upon pupils studying religions in isolation from each other by means of the *systems* or *systematic* approach. This was in opposition to the use of thematic approaches which enable pupils to develop some appreciation of how religion as a generic concept provides a unique means of critiquing secular, materialistic, mechanistic and pragmatist approaches to values and the human condition and offers an alternative way of formulating the goals to which human consciousness may aspire. Furthermore, the Act's use of the phrase *'whilst taking account of the teaching and practices'* of the different religions led to these becoming the essential criteria for the selection, organisation and structuring of content within agreed syllabuses.

Taken together, the combination of applying a market-led ideology to education and implementing the restrictive interpretation of clause 8 (3) of the Education Reform Act, has led, despite a change of government, to the captivity of RE by the joint forces of politicians and religionists each pursuing their own self-interests. (2) This is in sharp contrast to the liberal and humanistic concerns that had gradually evolved and established a consensus for the study of religion in the curriculum of the state schools in England and Wales during the thirty or more years before the Act – a consensus which was widely admired by countries as far apart as the USA, Australia, South Africa and Northern Europe. In short, in the space of less than a decade, liberal educational ideals and a well established and a respected educational consensus for RE teaching has been progressively dismantled by both Conservative and Labour government educational policies.

The part played by the faith communities in the captivity of RE

A strange and disturbing feature of the last decade or more has been the part played by the faith communities in the captivity of RE. The two or three years following the 1988 Education Act were dominated by renewed tensions among and between the faith communities, religious educators and local government officers over the interpretation of its religious clauses. For example, there was widespread concern about the requirement for collective worship in schools to be *'wholly or mainly of a broadly Christian character'* (Section 7 (1)). Some local mosques instructed parents to exercise their right to withdraw their children from school worship. There was also an increase in the number of Muslim parents prepared to become school governors in order to safeguard their children's religious interests. On the other hand, supporters of the legislation, such as right wing Christians, were anxious to press their advantage and ensure that the religious clauses of the Act (both Sections 7 (1) and 8 (3)) were rigorously implemented, even in schools where 95% or more of the pupils were Muslim. On several occasions Christian parents were prepared to take an LEA to court for failing to ensure that its agreed syllabus or RE curriculum in schools accurately reflected these requirements.

In the light of widespread attempts (3), especially on the part of LEAs, to adopt a liberal and creative interpretation of the clauses and to reach a more judicious balance between the religions in the RE curriculum, the government used a number of means to make clear what it expected to be taught in RE, and how Christianity should be predominate in the curriculum at all stages. These included Government Circulars (3/89 and 1/94), a letter from the Secretary of State to Chief Education Officers (18 March, 1991), another Education Act (1993) and, under the guise of providing *Exemplary Material*, '*a range of model syllabuses to help LEA Agreed Syllabuses Conferences in their work.*' It was through inviting faith communities to play the major role in deciding upon the content of the Model Syllabuses that the government effectively persuaded the faith communities to drop their opposition to the religious clauses of the Act. With hindsight this overtly political decision can be seen to have set in motion a series of events which, collectively, have probably exacted more damage upon the development of RE in England and Wales than any legislation, both before or after the 1988 Education Act.

Firstly, in setting up six separate working groups each representing a religion and asking them to 'set out the key areas of knowledge about their faith which they considered appropriate at different stages of study', the government could more or less guarantee that the syllabus would be content rather than process led and that each religion would be studied separately and in isolation from the rest. In other words, RE would become the *study of religions*, not the *study of religion*. Secondly, while purporting to provide a 'range of model syllabuses' which would help LEA Agreed Syllabus Conferences in their work of producing their own syllabuses, the two models that resulted were so similar that they did in effect impose a view of RE and its curriculum content upon LEAs. Thus, despite the existence of legislation requiring LEA RE agreed syllabuses to reflect local concerns and circumstances, the production of the model syllabuses came very near to establishing, if not in name but in practice, a national RE curriculum reflecting the broader educational ideology explained earlier combined with the specific expectations of faith communities.

In a surprisingly audacious move to reinforce the government's influence on, if not control of the subject at local level, three years after their publication 'a detailed knowledge of the Model Syllabuses' was made a compulsory requirement for all teacher trainees in RE. In bringing in this requirement the government treated the model syllabuses as the equivalent in RE of the centrally determined content which it had imposed upon all subjects within the national curriculum. This elevation of the Model Syllabuses from a model to a compulsory curriculum for training RE teachers gave the model syllabuses considerably more influence upon classroom practice in RE. A document which was originally intended as a model in syllabus design, through its influence on teacher training, quickly began to acquire significance in determining how RE would, in future, be taught in schools.

The effect of applying the model syllabuses to classroom RE, despite their adoption of *learning about* and *learning from* religions as the two attainment targets, has been to encourage teachers to fall back on a predominantly descriptive approach to the study of religions in which *learning about religions* is dominant. Where teachers attempt to encourage pupils to *learn from religions* it falls far short of the pedagogical strategy which the original concept involved, namely that pupils should evaluate their understanding of religion in personal terms and evaluate their understanding of self in religious terms (Grimmitt, 1987, 213). In other words, the evaluative process of *learning from religion(s)* should be fully integrated into how, within a secular educational context, pupils are *learning about religions* in the first place.

THE LIBERATION OF RELIGIOUS EDUCATION

The first step in liberating RE from its captivity by self-interested politicians and religionists is to ensure that the subject's very rich repository of pedagogical research and development is made available to both trainee and practising teachers of RE. The notion that by having a detailed knowledge of the Model Syllabuses for RE and a few Agreed Syllabuses RE trainee teachers can acquire an appreciation of their subject's educational potential and develop the skills and abilities required to fulfil it is far from credible. On the whole, these official documents do not capture the extent to which the subject's educational vitality is dependent upon teachers being able to understand and use effectively the different methodologies and pedagogies which have been devised to address the perennial issues and difficulties which arise from bringing religion and education into a relationship within the context of a secular education system serving the needs and interests of pupils who are members of a diversely plural society. It is essential, therefore, that teacher training courses provide trainees with a sound conceptual understanding of these matters so that they enter the profession recognising that teaching RE is an exacting and complex process which requires approaches to teaching and learning to be informed by pedagogical principles which draw upon psychological theories of learning and human development.

This is to contradict the current tendency – a by product of the competence-based model of learning – for teaching to be seen as a relatively simple skill that can be learned by imitation and improved by practice.

But acquiring such understanding is not just a theoretical matter: it must be linked to practice. Opportunities for trainee teachers of RE to try out a variety of pedagogies of RE in a classroom setting and so add to their understanding of them are increasingly difficult to guarantee during the PGCE training year. When it is claimed by OFSTED subject inspectors that 'standards in RE are improving' one must look carefully at the criteria that are being used to make such a judgement. Standards or competence-related criteria rarely if ever relate to trainees' pedagogical understanding, only to evidence of certain forms of practice being applied, such as whether clear teaching objectives are identified, whether appropriate targets for pupils' learning are set, if teaching and learning builds on prior attainment, etc. The formulation of competence-related criteria in an assessment schedule can mean that an impoverished model of learning and teaching which addresses the criteria superficially is given tacit approval. If that is the case, where is the stimulus for improving the quality of pupils' learning, and what meaning is being given to that overworked term 'quality' if judgements are made within a framework in which mechanistic forms of teaching and learning are regarded as normative? Is it little wonder that so many practising teachers of RE, who are the mentors of trainee teachers of the subject, use such a limited range of pedagogical strategies in their teaching and expect trainees to do the same?

THE MEANING AND SIGNIFICANCE OF PEDAGOGY

Establishing a basis for thinking about pedagogies of RE.

Fortunately, after a long period of neglect, the term pedagogy is re-establishing itself in educational parlance and thinking. This book, hopefully, may contribute to the ongoing debate about its meaning as well as encourage an interest in achieving a greater variety of good pedagogic practice in RE. A first step is to begin to be clear about how the term can be defined and then applied in RE.

A possible working definition of a *pedagogy* is: *a theory of teaching and learning encompassing aims, curriculum content and methodology.* Another is: *a science of teaching and learning embodying both curriculum and methodology.*

Whatever the definition, the fundamental concern of pedagogy is *to relate the process of teaching to that of learning on the part of the child* (Simon, 1981, 95)

Even though it may not be a term that RE research projects have used much in the past to describe how they have understood the basis for learning and teaching in RE, there is no doubt that what projects advocate are *pedagogical models* or, where they provide a fully integrated theory of teaching and learning in RE which includes aims, methodology and curriculum content (but not all do), *a pedagogy of RE.*

As indicated earlier, each of these models attempts to address and resolve some of the perennial issues and difficulties which arise when education and religion are brought into a relationship within the context of a secular education system serving the needs of children and young people who are members of a religiously diverse and predominantly secular society.

All pedagogical models of RE are expressions of certain assumptions about how education and religion can be brought into a relationship within the context of a secular educational system. These assumptions are based upon a particular view of religion and of education; indeed they *combine* a particular view of religion(s) with a particular view of education. How this relationship is conceived sets the parameters within which *pedagogical judgements* are made. Let us consider this process.

A view of how religion(s) and education can be brought into a relationship will reflect a view of why and how pupils will benefit from their study of religion(s). Both views will find expression in the choice of *aim* for RE, the *selection of curriculum content* thought appropriate to achieving this aim and *the choice of methodology (or methodologies)* thought capable of bringing about the learning outcomes necessary to fulfil the aim. These are the component parts of a *pedagogy of RE* and there will be points of similarity and difference between what each pedagogical model proposes and the assumptions upon which these proposals are based.

At the heart of a pedagogy of RE, however, lies an intention to promote a particular kind (or several different kinds) of *interaction* between the pupils and the religious content which they are studying. The nature and scope of the kinds of interaction that are considered appropriate and desirable also reflect the assumptions about the nature of religion and education which underlie each pedagogical model. These interactions may be grouped into two broad categories: those which contribute to pupils *learning about religion* and those which contribute mainly to pupils *learning from religion*. In the former category are included *instructional, conceptual, empathetic interactions* (i.e. where pupils assimilate and accommodate the content as understood within its faith context), and in the latter category *reflective, interpretative, critical, and evaluative interactions* (i.e. where pupils assimilate and accommodate the content as understood within its faith context but then re-contextualise it within their own self-understanding for the purposes of values clarification, existential analysis, illumination of personal constructs, etc., or subject its truth claims to critical evaluation using criteria from a variety of disciplines – philosophical, scientific, ethical, psychological, etc.). Most of the pedagogies of RE which have been developed in the last fifteen or twenty years seek to promote interactions in both categories, but not in relation to all the components of each category listed here.

In order to actualise the kinds of interaction deemed important each pedagogical model deploys certain *pedagogical procedures or strategies* which determine how pupils will *experience, engage with, and respond* to the content. The choice of these pedagogical procedures or strategies reflects whatever *pedagogical principles* the model is applying to the specific problems of teaching and learning in RE, given its particular view of religion and education and how they are related. In those pedagogical models in which pedagogical judgements reflect the application of specific theories of learning or of human development to the task of teaching RE (and not all models do so), these principles constitute general laws or substantive hypotheses about how optimal, or at least the intended learning outcomes may be achieved. It is to actualise whatever form of interaction or interactions that these principles require that *pedagogical principles and procedures* are employed.

To summarise, *pedagogical principles* are general laws or substantive hypotheses about teaching and learning which inform the process of devising *pedagogical procedures or pedagogical strategies* which, in turn, determine how pupils will *experience, engage with and respond to the content*. Ideally in designing a pedagogical model pedagogical principles should first be expressed in generic terms (i.e. as Piaget or Bruner might formulate a principle about assisting concept development) and then expressed in terms specific to RE. To take a simple example from my own work:

Grimmitt (1973): What Can I do in RE?

Generic pedagogical principle: through the interplay of the mental activities referred to as *assimilation* and *accommodation* the child builds up *schemas* and all new experiences are brought within and interpreted by existing schemas acting as a unitary mass. By abstracting what is new from each new experience the child *reconstructures* the existing schemas. To do this new elements will need to be *assimilated* and this process in turn will require the abandonment of some former elements (i.e. the process of *accommodation*). The *reconstructuring* will be complete when the new learning is mastered (*Piagetian constructivism*).

RE- related pedagogical principle 1: encouraging pupils to build conceptual bridges between their own experiences and what they recognise to be the central concepts of religion assists them in understanding religious concepts.

RE- related pedagogical principle 2: learning is enhanced when the selection and presentation of content takes account of and is related to the child's feelings, acts, experiences, needs, questions, opinions, beliefs, values and developmental stage.

RE- related pedagogical procedure or strategy applying both principles 1 and 2: the combination of the *Existential Approach* and the *Dimensional Approach*, the former consisting of *Depth Themes, Symbol and Language Themes*, and *Situation Themes*, and the latter consisting of presenting selected religious concepts by way of the six dimensions of religion. Work on themes within the *Existential Approach* precedes work on the explicitly religious concepts within the *Dimensional Approach*.

Here the *pedagogical procedure or strategy* is designed to implement the *pedagogical principle* and in so doing fulfil or contribute to the stated aims of RE. However, different kinds of pedagogical procedure or strategy could be devised which are just as capable of implementing the same principle (as indeed they have been by other writers and projects). However, in a sense, the pedagogical principles are more important than the pedagogical procedures or strategies because the principles are transferable and invite teachers to invent their own pedagogical strategies for implementing them. It is when teachers are unaware of the importance of applying pedagogical principles in their work, or have a limited understanding of them, that pupils' potential for learning in RE is rarely actualised.

It is not always easy, however, to distinguish between *pedagogical principles* and *pedagogical procedures or strategies*. For example, when I argued the case in *RE and Human Development* (Grimmitt, 1987) *for learning about and learning from religion* as expressing an appropriate and desirable *interaction* between the pupils and the religious content which they are studying, I saw this distinction as providing a *pedagogical procedure or strategy* capable of implementing several pedagogical principles concerned with how pupils can accommodate educational value from studying religion and religions. Since the distinction was incorporated into the SCAA Model Syllabuses it seems to have become a *pedagogical principle*! I, however, continue to see it as a *pedagogical procedure or strategy* as the following examples show:

Grimmitt (1987): RE and Human Development

RE- related pedagogical principle 1: if religions are studied in such a way as to juxtapose the content of the *religious-life worlds* of adherents with the content of the *pupils' life-worlds*, pupils become informed about religious beliefs and values and are able to use them as instruments for the critical evaluation of their own beliefs and values (141)

RE- related pedagogical principle 2: the structure of the curriculum, its content and learning experiences should be specifically designed to assist pupils to develop the skills and abilities of being able to apply religious insights to an understanding of their own situations and experiences (241)

RE- related pedagogical principle 3: in order for RE to make a contribution to promoting pupils' personal, social, spiritual and moral development pupils need to be helped to translate insights gained from an exploration of religious education's field of enquiry (i.e. *Human Givens, Core Values, Substantive Religious Categories, Shared Human Experience and Traditional Belief Systems*) into personal terms (213).

RE- related pedagogical procedure or strategy applying principles 1, 2 and 3: the interactive process of learning about and learning from religion.

RE- related pedagogical principle 4: the process of growing in self-knowledge involves continually keeping in focus the interplay that must exist between self and others (207-238)

RE- related pedagogical procedure or strategy applying principle 4: the loci of interaction between self and others – *Family, Faith Community, Plural Society and World-Wide Community* – provide *organising categories* for subject matter drawn from *Traditional Belief Systems and Shared Human Experience.* (P.238). (e.g. pupils explore the theme of Christians celebrating together in the family, in the faith community, in the plural society, in the world-wide community.) (238)

Understanding and evaluating the pedagogies of RE described in this book:

This basis for thinking about pedagogies of RE may, at first sight, seem extremely complicated and unnecessarily prescriptive. A reason for this is that, so far, there has been very little discussion between religious educators and researchers about the theoretical basis upon which pedagogies can and should be devised, developed and evaluated in RE. As evident from the contributions to this book, experienced researchers have difficulty in distinguishing between the *pedagogical principles* underlying their project and the *pedagogical strategies* implementing them, even when they have been asked to do so. Indeed, in the case of some contributions, it is far from easy to identify either principles or strategies from their descriptions of what the project sought to do and how it did it! This is because their original research was not necessarily conceptualised in terms of the exacting pedagogical criteria that I asked contributors to apply to it. But without a common basis for thinking about pedagogies of RE how can the all important task of comparing and contrasting their procedures and proposals be understood, let alone evaluated?

While, as I tried to show earlier, during the last fifteen or more years there have been extraneous factors limiting the effect that research projects have had on pedagogic practice in RE, there have also been reasons internal to those projects which have limited their impact. One reason is a tendency for projects to be insular, isolationist and intent on maintaining their independence and distinctiveness from other research projects. For example, over the years, projects have resorted to extending their influence by developing their own networks of supporters and practitioners – *disciples* would not be too strong a word in some instances – through mounting in-house training courses, conferences and workshops, and, in the case of University researchers, attracting research students to undertake further work to extend the research beyond the model's immediate parameters. While the causes for this may be found quite justifiably in the need for individual and institutional research profiles to be safeguarded and for publishers to be assured that the project materials they have agreed to publish are unlike anything else in the field, the down side is that trainee and practising teachers, as a result, find it extremely difficult to integrate the pedagogical insights of different projects eclectically into their practice.

The present book is a deliberate attempt to break down this isolationism between projects. Although individual contributors write in their own name and on behalf of a project which in most cases they have directed or co-directed, the fact that their contributions are, for the first time, set alongside those of others who, professionally and academically, they may have considered as rivals as well as colleagues, recontextualises their contribution within a wider debate about what constitutes good pedagogic practice in RE. It is my hope that, as a consequence, readers, whether trainees or practising teachers, will be better placed to compare and contrast each project's assumptions and concepts, be better able to identify points of similarity and difference between them, and feel better prepared to incorporate some of their pedagogical principles and strategies into their own teaching. The inclusion of comprehensive bibliographies of each project's publications and resources is intended to encourage and support those who wish to investigate a project in more detail and try out its ideas in their own classrooms.

But a final word about evaluation is needed. It is quite remarkable that to date there have been no extended, independent evaluations of any of the pedagogies of RE represented in this book, other than as pilot studies undertaken during the life of the projects themselves. This is a serious deficiency because it means that there is no *empirical* evidence of the reasonableness or otherwise of the claims that each project both implicitly and explicitly makes about the viability of the pedagogical procedures or strategies that it adopts in accordance with its central pedagogical principles in order to meet its aims. While this same charge may also be made against other contemporary pedagogies adopted in other curriculum subjects, it is especially important that attempts to evaluate the quality of pupils' learning in RE is supported by the application of research methodologies which enable the reliability of certain pedagogical strategies to fulfil pedagogical principles and meet stated aims to be tested. A carefully conducted research project directed towards these ends would do far more than rhetoric to secure the liberation of RE from its current captivity within the technicist and standards-driven vacuum which continues to subvert the subject's educational potential.

NOTES

1.   There are now statements of attainment for pupils at age six years, compulsory tests at seven, eleven and fourteen years, optional tests at eight, nine, ten, twelve and thirteen years and public examination (i.e. GCSE) at sixteen years. The TTA is now introducing compulsory literacy, numeracy and ICT tests (additional to compulsory passes at Grade C in GCSE English, Maths and Science) for all trainee teachers seeking QTS from 2001 onwards.

2.   It is in the self interest of the politicians to maintain centralised control of the curriculum (including RE) and so avoid divergent interpretations being applied at the local level which would undermine and subvert its centrally determined, ideological intentions. It is in the self interest of the faith communities to ensure that RE in schools is restricted to a descriptive study of religions using texts approved by themselves and limiting the freedom of teachers to use religious content in an instrumental manner. The assumption here is that each faith community *owns* or has *custodial rights* over its religion and only *loans* its content to schools on the condition that it is treated in a sympathetic and uncritical manner. For an example of this view and criticism of my own position see Cooling (1996).

3.   For a deliberately positive response to the 1988 Education Reform Act within a liberal religious and educational framework, see Hull, J.M. (1989). With hindsight the strategy of welcoming the Act's official endorsement of a broad multi-faith approach to RE was, in my view, mistaken. The Act should have been opposed on the basis of its failure to meet the principles of equal opportunities and for discriminating against non-Christian religions.

REFERENCES

Cooling, T. (1996) 'Education is the Point of RE – not Religion?', in Astley, J. & Francis, L.J. (Ed.) *Christian Theology and Religious Education: Connections and Contradictions* (London, SPCK) pp.165-183.

Grimmitt, M.H. (1973) *What Can I do in RE?* (Great Wakering, Essex, Mayhew-McCrimmon).

Grimmitt, M.H. (1987) *Religious Education and Human Development* (Great Wakering, Essex, McCrimmons).

Hull, J.M. (1989) *The Act Unpacked: the meaning of the 1988 Education Reform Act for Religious Education*, Birmingham Papers in Religious Education (University of Birmingham and the Christian Education Movement).

Simon, B. (Ed.) *Education in the Eighties: the central issues* (London, Batsford) p. 95.

CHAPTER 2

CONTEMPORARY PEDAGOGIES OF RELIGIOUS EDUCATION: WHAT ARE THEY?

Michael Grimmitt

What choices of pedagogy do RE teachers have? Where are they to be found? Are they all equally effective? Are more pedagogies needed? This chapter is concerned to address these questions, particularly for the benefit of trainee teachers of RE, but also in order to argue the case that pedagogical knowledge and skill provide the foundation upon which all successful RE teaching depends.

CONTEMPORARY PEDAGOGIES OF RELIGIOUS EDUCATION

For the purpose of this discussion, eight types of *pedagogical model* for use in non-denominational and non-confessional RE have been identified from the scholarly literature that has been produced by religious educators in the UK during the last forty years. The eight types of pedagogical model with their contributors are:

1. *Liberal Christian Theological, Experiential, Implicit Models:*
    (Hubery, 1960; Loukes, 1961,1965; Goldman, 1964, 1965; Hull, 1970, 1975a, 1975b, 1975c).

2. *A Phenomenological, Undogmatic, Explicit Model:*
    Smart, 1968; The Schools Council Lancaster Secondary RE Project, 1971, 1972, 1977a, 1977b, 1978; Smart & Horder,1976; The Chichester Project, 1982, 1984, 1986, 1987, 1989, 1991, 1993, 1995, on going,);

3. *Integrative Experiential and Phenomenological Models:*
    (Grimmitt, 1973; Holm, 1975; The Schools Council Lancaster Primary RE Project, 1977c; The Religious Experience and Education Project, Hammond, Hay et al.,1990; Nye & Hay, 1996, on going);

4. *Human Development, Instrumental, Learning About, Learning From Models:* (Grimmitt & Read, 1977; The Westhill Project, Read et al , 1977; Read et al, 1986: Revised 1992; on going; Grimmitt,1987; The Religion in the Service of the Child Primary RE Project, Grimmitt et al ,1991a; Grimmitt 1991b; Hull 1996);

5. *An Ethnographic, 'Interpretive', Multifaith Model:*
(The Warwick RE Project, Everington, 1993; 1996, 1998; Everington, Jackson et al 1995; Jackson 1997, on going;);

6. *A Revelation-Centred, Concept-Cracking, Trinitarian Christian Realist Model:*
(The Stapleford RE Project, Cooling, 1993, 1994a, 1994b, 1996, 1997, on going);

7. *A Literacy-Centred, Critical Realist Model:*
(Wright 1993, The Spiritual Education Project, 1997a, 1997b, 1998a, 1998b,1999, on going);

8. *Constructivist Models of Learning and Teaching in RE:*
(The Children and Worldviews Project, Erricker, C & J, 1994; Erricker et al 1997; Erricker, 1998, 1999, on going; The Constructivist Pedagogies of RE Project, Grimmitt, 2000, on going).

Between the nineteen sixties and the present there has been a tendency for pedagogies to become increasingly complex and sophisticated and to be closely inter-related and inter-dependent. Each pedagogy owes much to those that have preceded it and while significant shifts of focus or orientation have occurred and re-interpretations of former insights and principles have been frequent, there is a sense in which each new pedagogy is a direct response to, and therefore a successor of, those that have gone before it. This is as true of those pedagogies which have emerged from a determination on the part of an individual or group to contest earlier proposals (e.g. Cooling's critique of Grimmitt and Hull) as of those which came about as a result of a conscious decision to build upon and extend a model which was widely recognised to be strong and influential (e.g. the evolution of integrated and human development models from experiential models, and of the incorporation of insights from human development models within an ethnographic model). While it is not possible within the compass of a single chapter to compare, contrast and evaluate these models in detail, some indication of their main features, how they have evolved and the pedagogical principles that they endorse should serve to highlight the pedagogical options and principles into which trainee RE teachers need to be inducted. Readers seeking to engage in a more detailed comparison of these eight models, especially in the light of how they are described, amplified and justified by their authors in the following chapters of this book, may like to consider how each is broadly responsive to the following three questions:

1. What kind or kinds of interaction between the pupils and religious content does the model seek to promote?

2. What pedagogical procedures or strategies does the model deploy in order to achieve the kind or kinds of interactions identified above?

3. What pedagogical principles inform the model's pedagogical procedures and strategies, including its approach to the choice of curriculum content?

THE ORIGINS OF CONTEMPORARY PEDAGOGIES OF RELIGIOUS EDUCATION

The origins of the main agendas which have largely determined the evolution of the different pedagogies of RE over the last forty years can be found in two fundamentally different and seemingly opposing models of why and how RE should be taught. These are the Liberal Christian, Theological, Experiential, Implicit Models, particularly associated with Hubery, Goldman and Loukes in the middle and late nineteen sixties and with Hull in the early nineteen seventies, and the Phenomenological, Undogmatic, Explicit Model associated with Smart and The Lancaster Projects in the late nineteen sixties and seventies and subsequently with the work of The Chichester Project.

With hindsight it is now possible to see that the problem of attempting to reconcile the phenomenological and experiential approaches within an integrated pedagogical model of RE has proved to be the stimulus for the development of nearly all other pedagogical models of RE for the last twenty five years. The discussion of the eight pedagogical models which follows concentrates mainly on identifying the pedagogical principles which have emerged from a consideration of this issue.

1. A Phenomenological, Undogmatic, Explicit Model:

Of the two types of model – the Liberal Christian,Theological, Experiential, Implicit Models and the Phenomenological, Undogmatic, Explicit Model – the influence of the latter model is the more evident in classrooms today, although not in the form in which it was originally advocated in *Schools Council Working Paper Number 36* in 1971. Because of the way in which the approach has become so severely truncated and misrepresented in practice it is worth summarising its main features as developed by the *Schools Council Lancaster Secondary RE Project.*

As presented in *Schools Council Working Paper Number 36* (1971) and elaborated six years later in *A Groundplan for the Study of Religion* (1977c), the model envisages pupils engaging with religious content with three broadly different intentions each requiring a different kind of interaction:

- to study the tradition's *self-understanding* in an empathetic and non-evaluative manner *bracketing* their own presuppositions and opinions;

- to acquire certain capacities to *understand* (i.e. an awareness of religious issues and of the contribution of religion to human culture, a capacity to understand beliefs and practices, and an awareness of the challenge and practical consequences of religious belief – such awareness and understanding being founded on accurate information, rationally understood and considered in the light of all relevant facts (*SCWP* 1971, 44-45)), and to *think* (philosophically, sociologically, psychologically, historically, ethically and aesthetically) *about religion* (*Groundplan* 1977, 22-24);

- to engage in a reflective process whereby the outcomes of engaging in a 'dialogue with experience' are brought into a 'dialogue with living religions, so that one can interpret and reinforce the other' (*SCWP* 1971, 43).

Broadly speaking, if there is a pedagogical principle which should inform the model's pedagogical procedures and strategies it is that:

- learning and teaching in RE should promote both academic and personal forms of knowledge and understanding.

In the event the model fails to provide pedagogical procedures and strategies which are adequate for supporting pupils in any of the three types of interaction. In its original form, its advocacy of Smart's six-dimensional typological model of religion as a means of studying religion is the closest that it comes to suggesting a *pedagogical strategy*; but this is limited to supporting the first type of interaction and the strategy remains undeveloped (*SCWP* 1971, Chapter 5). Furthermore, its use and justification is more to do with the importance that is attached to the model providing a broad conceptual framework of religion which emphasises the similarities between religions and a starting point for the study of any religion than with any pedagogical principle that it might reflect.

In like manner the model provides no pedagogical support at all for pupils to engage in the second and third kinds of interaction. What is meant by the dialogue with religion and experience being brought into a relationship with each other 'so that one can interpret and reinforce the other' is never explained and never translated into a pedagogical procedure or strategy. No criteria for the choice of content are provided. It is not surprising, therefore, that in popular understanding of 'the phenomenological approach', the broad, liberal educational value that the model attributes to the study of religion, including its capacity to address the personal and existential concerns of the pupil, is largely absent and that it has become a by word for a narrowly descriptive and content-centred approach to teaching RE.

From its inception in 1977, The Chichester Project, while distinct from the Schools Council Lancaster Projects, has shared their commitment to applying a phenomenological model to the teaching of world religions, but has concentrated on illustrating how the approach can be applied to the teaching of Christianity. In 1987, John Rankin, the project's first director, commented on the unresolved tensions associated with the use of the phenomenological model.

'It was the Schools Council Secondary RE Project based at Lancaster
   which popularised the use of the words 'implicit' and 'explicit'.
   'Implicit' RE was concerned with the pupils' search for meaning and
   'explicit' RE was concerned with the detailed phenomena of
   religion. Religious Education was to be a dialogue between implicit
   and explicit, a dialogue between the quest for meaning and the
   'meaning giving' phenomena of religion. In fact this has never quite
   worked out and there is an uneasy relationship between the
   protagonists of each type. Of course, it is a matter of degree.
   Nevertheless teachers of RE can usually be divided according to
   whether they see their prime task as being to lead their pupils to

find their own religious interpretation of life, or whether they place greater emphasis on *understanding* the beliefs and practices of religion.' (Erricker, 1995, 4.)

Interestingly, the Chichester Project, which in 2001 will have been in existence for 25 years, has not attempted to formulate or develop a distinctive pedagogy of RE which addresses this tension. On the contrary, it has encouraged a range of authors to develop their own creative responses to the tension by producing classroom texts and materials which will enable pupils to be better informed about Christian beliefs and practices. But even when the texts are pupil-related and encourage reflection on personal experience in order to stimulate a dialogue with, for example, Christian religious and community experience, the methodology serves the intention of promoting the pupils' understanding of the phenomena rather better than it serves to enable pupils to interpret their own experiences in the light of their studies. By insisting that Christianity is a 'world religion' the project has undoubtedly done a great deal to redress a tendency for Christianity to be treated differently from other faiths in the classroom, but the absence of a clearly identified and articulated pedagogical framework which teachers can apply when selecting their own content from Christianity (or any other religion) has limited the project's overall influence on the development of RE. As a consequence, the generally high quality classroom materials it has produced have not been sufficiently influential to counter the tendency in practice for the phenomenological model to be reduced to that 'mere description' which John Rankin, Alan Brown and their colleagues have been so anxious to avoid (Erricker, 1995, 8).

2. Liberal Christian Theological, Experiential, Implicit Models:

In contrast to the phenomenological model, evidence of the presence and direct influence of the Liberal Christian Theological, Experiential, Implicit pedagogical models in contemporary classroom practice is much less apparent. However, despite the dominant influence of the phenomenological approach from the nineteen seventies onwards, it is arguably the case that these early experiential pedagogies have continued to exert an influence on the development of pedagogies of RE in the UK which has been at least equal to that of the phenomenological model. This is particularly remarkable considering that in their original form the views upon which the experiential pedagogies were predicated could not have been more directly at odds with those of the phenomenological approach. But many RE teachers in both county and denominational schools responded with considerable enthusiasm to the inventive and creative styles of experiential learning that emerged from the pedagogies of Goldman and Loukes in the late nineteen sixties. The publication of a number of classroom resources broadly in line with their approaches also ensured their continued popularity. It was, however, work by other religious educators in developing the educational potential of the Liberal Christian Theological, Experiential, Implicit Models which prevented them from being lost beneath the rising tide of interest in world religions and safeguarded their wholesale abandonment in favour of the newly proposed Phenomenological, Undogmatic, Explicit Model. An essential part of this process was to demonstrate that experientialism could be disconnected from Christian confessionalism while retaining its capacity to assist pupils in understanding religious concepts and religious beliefs and contribute to their personal development.

Between 1970 and 1975 Hull made a significant contribution to this process by refining the theological and educational basis of Christian experientialism. He indicated the need to distinguish between religious experience as 'ordinary experience', 'ordinary experience understood at depth', and as 'specific or sui generis experience', and to consider how each has a different methodological implication for RE teaching. Initially he worked out the beginnings of a new rationale and methodology for theme teaching in relation to teaching the Christian faith and the Bible, but by 1975 he was showing interest in exploring world religions through life-themes. Although he did not extend this work into a fully developed pedagogy of RE he published several influential articles arguing why establishing an educational basis for teaching RE which is secular and pluralistic need not be in conflict with a Christian view of faith or education. This analysis remained influential for almost twenty years until his liberal/radical Christian theological interpretation came under attack from evangelical Christians for distorting Christian truths and allowing them to be absorbed within a perspective reflecting the values and constructs of a secular ideology, within which liberalism itself was included (Cooling, 1994, 53-63). The issue continues to be influential in determining the current course of pedagogical development in the subject, as indicated by the emergence of both Christian realist and critical realist pedagogical models of RE in the late nineteen nineties.

3. Integrative Experiential and Phenomenological Models:

During the nineteen seventies and early eighties interest in the process of transforming Christian experientialism so that it could be integrated more successfully with the phenomenological approach continued. Grimmitt, Holm and Hay each provided a different way of interpreting and responding to what proved to be the central problem of pedagogical development during that time, namely demonstrating that it is possible for ordinary experience and religious experience, as a sui generis experience specific to the religions, to be brought into a mutually informing relationship.

Grimmitt (1973) saw the problem as needing to be addressed from both theological and educational standpoints because without both it would be difficult to formulate a pedagogy which did not appear to undermine the religious integrity of the religious content being studied or the academic integrity of the educational process within which the study was taking place. Theologically, he argued that if, as Tillich suggests, religion and human experience are inextricably connected, the starting point for the exploration of religion can be either human experience of every day life (provided it is examined at depth) or human experience of religion as discerned through its 'experiential' dimension. His educational perspective involved seeing the process of reflection on life at depth as promoting a form of *existential analysis* which enabled pupils to develop skills, sensitivities and perceptions which enhanced their ability to empathise with and understand the subjective religious consciousness of religiously committed people. The central pedagogical principle of his model involved encouraging pupils 'to build conceptual bridges between their own experiences and what they recognise to be the central concepts of religion'(Grimmitt, 1973, 49). His strategy for implementing this involved combining what he called an *Existential Approach* with a *Dimensional Approach*, the latter drawing upon Smart's multi-dimensional model of religion but modifying it in order to take account of pupils' learning and developmental characteristics. He envisaged that the learning sequence would normally be from existential analysis to phenomenological investigation because of the significance of the former in laying the conceptual foundations for understanding the latter.

Holm (1975), while not wishing to abandon the use of children's experience in her developmental structure for RE, wanted to disassociate experience-based teaching from any suggestion that it involved a

31

theological agenda or had neo-confessional intentions. Her response to the issue of how ordinary experience and religious experience can be linked was to provide a *sociological* account of how religion is a universal phenomenon and embraces all aspects of human life and experience. Accordingly experience-based learning through *Human Experience Themes* was limited to fulfilling two related educational purposes. The first purpose was to encourage pupils to reflect on those significant human experiences which raise questions about life and its meaning. Like Grimmitt's *Depth Themes*, their learning outcomes were identified as pupils gaining a greater understanding of themselves, others, the natural world, human relationships, etc. The second purpose stemmed from Holm's view that 'religions suggest answers to the ultimate questions which man (sic) asks about his (sic) existence.' (Ibid, 7). Thus by reflecting on human experience pupils are prepared for understanding how religions address ultimate questions and provide 'a coherent interpretation of the whole of human life and experience.' (Ibid, 7) In Holm's view, therefore, the use of children's experiences in RE is to be primarily concerned to fulfil a preparatory and foundational function for the later phenomenological study of world religions, introduced mainly from the age of 13 years (Ibid, 58). She made no further suggestions about how the phenomenological approach should relate to experience-based work and, once again, the learning sequence envisaged was from reflection on ordinary experience to using these insights to understand religion and religions.

The recommendations of the *Schools Council Lancaster Project on RE in Primary Schools* (Schools Council, 1977c) were very similar to those which had already been proposed by Holm, with the possible exception of its recognition that the relationship between reflecting on experience and exploring religion was more interactional than she had envisaged within her pedagogy. The project took care to identify the *capacities* and *attitudes* that should result from pupils' engagement in a dialogue between exploring human experience and exploring religion. This emphasis became more prominent and significant in the pedagogies of the nineteen eighties and nineties as they gave increasing importance to the concept of RE contributing to the human or personal development of pupils.

The work of Hay and *The Religious Experience and Education Project* based at the University of Nottingham represented as much an attempt to restore the fundamental principles of the phenomenological approach, as an extension of the meaning of experiential learning. In Hammond, Hay *et al*

(1990) we are told, '...Phenomenology' has come to mean, in the minds of many, a concentration on external, public 'phenomena' as part of an 'objective' study of religion. But it is not what was meant by the authors of Working Paper 36' (Ibid, 6). (Whether it had 'become' this or never been anything other than this is a moot point.) Hay and his colleagues set themselves to devise a pedagogy which took seriously the need to help pupils to learn to feel empathy with the experiences of religious people, not by *bracketing* their own experience but by helping them 'to learn to be aware of and take seriously their own inner experience and their potential to be aware' (Ibid,17). There was, then, a clear assumption that ordinary and sui generis religious experience are part of the same continuum, a view which the project accepted on the basis of evidence of *religious experience* being reported to be a common phenomenon among 'half or more of the adult population of this country' (Ibid, 15). However, although not necessarily true of more than a small proportion of pupils, 'many pupils are for the most of the time radically divorced from either the ways of perceiving or the areas of ordinary human experience that are of central interest to religious people' (Ibid, 13). Enhancing pupils' self-awareness in order to increase their abilities to connect with the experiences which religious people take seriously can not, however, be achieved unless the child's secularised consciousness is also challenged. The project therefore devised a number of exercises in *experiential learning* which were designed to focus on personal, inner experience, in order to 'assist young people to explore silence, to centre themselves, to be aware of the here-and-now of their experience, to discover awe and wonder in themselves...and to reflect on these realities in the light of the metaphors and expectations of the (religious) believer' (Hay, 1986, 23). Consistent with this intention, an *active learning* approach was advocated with value being accorded to developing pupils' intuition.

The pedagogy which Hay and his colleagues developed was widely seen as 'a methodology to explore the "spiritual".' As well as laying the basis for understanding 'the experience which lies at the heart of faith' (Hammond, Hay et al 1990, 21), the method was also concerned with 'helping pupils to develop their own individual responses to the spiritual dimension' (Ibid, 22). Like other attempts to integrate the experiential and the phenomenological approaches, encouraging pupils to explore their own *inner space* was seen as being logically prior to attempting to relate this to the experiences of religious believers. It is interesting, however, that despite the close association of the two approaches through religious experience the transition from reflecting on personal experience to exploring its equivalent within the religious traditions was not really supported by clear pedagogical procedures or principles. It is noteworthy that in the project's main teaching resource, out of 231 pages only 12 refer to the use of explicitly religious material. That the transition can be made is illustrated in only one article (Ibid, 178-182). While the weakness is not insurmountable, it does confirm the project's tendency to give too little importance to the place of learning about explicit religious traditions in RE and to neglect the structuring power of religious content in determining the RE curriculum. This, however, is an issue which the project is continuing to address in a constructive and creative manner.

4. Human Development, Instrumental, Learning About, Learning From Models:

A significant shift in understanding the relationship between experiential and phenomenological approaches occurred in the second half of the nineteen seventies as a result of the collaborative work of Grimmitt and Read at the RE Centre, Westhill College, Birmingham. In their *Christians Today Project* (1975-1977) they placed a new emphasis upon using the religious content of RE to illustrate what it means for human beings to make a *faith* response to those 'fundamental, inescapable questions about the human condition' which arise from reflection on shared human experience. It was to emphasise and express the interactional nature of the relationship between studying content and responding to it in a reflective manner that they introduced the concept of *learning about* and *learning from religion* (Grimmitt and Read 1977, 7-8). *The Westhill Project* (1980 -1986 and beyond) and Grimmitt's book, *RE and Human Development* (1987) both have their foundations in the educational rationale and pedagogical principles which underpinned this early research project.

Although sharing a common origin, however, the elaboration of the human development model took place independently over a period of ten or more years (1977-1987). There is, however, close agreement between The Westhill Project's model and Grimmitt's model, especially on how education and religion can be related, what benefits pupils can derive from the study of religion and what kinds of interaction between pupils and the content they are studying are best able to produce those benefits. Their pedagogical principles and procedures are also broadly similar. The analysis which follows, therefore, does not attempt to differentiate between the two models but tries to sketch the *pedagogical features* of a generic human development model designed to promote pupils' personal development through the study of religion.

In its statement of educational aims the model endorses the importance of presenting the beliefs and practices of religions to pupils accurately and in a manner which enables them to empathise with and understand the subjective religious consciousness of religiously committed people. In taking this view it endorses and advocates the use of the phenomenological approach. However, it also stresses the *instrumental* value that the study of content should have to pupils' spiritual, moral, social and cultural development. This instrumental view is reflected very clearly in The Westhill Project's principal aim of RE which is:

- to help children mature in relation to their own patterns of belief and behaviour *through* exploring religious beliefs and practices and related human experiences (Read et al, 1992, 2).

Grimmitt expresses a very similar notion as a fundamental pedagogical principle:

- If religions are studied in such a way as to juxtapose the 'content' of the religious life-worlds of adherents with the 'content' of the pupils' life-worlds, pupils become informed about religious beliefs and values and are able to use them as instruments for the critical evaluation of their own beliefs and values (Grimmitt 1987,141).

Consequently, the model places considerable stress on the importance of devising and applying pedagogical procedures or strategies which support pupils in translating insights gained from their study of RE's field of enquiry into personal terms.

While in the work of The Westhill Project the distinction between *learning about* and *learning from religion* is only implicit, it is developed by Grimmitt as a formula for determining the application of a number of distinctive pedagogical strategies, some intended to support the pupils' understanding of religion and religions and others intended to enable that understanding to contribute to the pupils' personal development. For example, *learning from religion* involves encouraging pupils to ask *autobiographical questions* and to engage in both *personal and impersonal evaluations* of religious beliefs, values and practices. But the kinds of interaction that constitute *learning from religion* are not just seen as requiring pupils to ask a few personally-related questions, engage in a few moments of reflection, or express a few opinions about religious beliefs etc., all tacked on at the end of a lesson when they have been *learning about religion*. Such an approach is too superficial to realise the intention of encouraging pupils:

- to evaluate their understanding of religion in personal terms and evaluate their understanding of self in religious terms (i.e. in terms of the religious beliefs they have learned about) ' (Grimmitt 1987, 213).

But any pedagogical principle which informs the choice of pedagogical procedures cannot be implemented only by introducing a technique of questioning; it requires a much wider and more pervasive application. The model that is developed is derived from the view, therefore, that the *structure of the curriculum and the choice of content and teaching methods* must *all* be specifically designed or chosen to enable pupils to develop the skills and abilities of being able to apply religious insights to an understanding of their own situations and experiences and to their own self-concept.

Thus the model is innovative in so far as the RE curriculum's religious content is not chosen or structured in accordance with *phenomenological principles* (i.e. by using typological themes like founders, festivals, sacred places, etc., by reference to the 'logic' of religion or by incorporating content identified by the faith communities), but in accordance with *pedagogical principles, informed by a theory of human development*. For example, in Grimmitt's version of the model, the 'essential minimum of key concepts' from each religion are identified in relation to the way in which they interpret eight universal 'Core Values' (Grimmitt 1987, 121-132). These concepts are then explored within the structure of themes which have particular significance to human development – *experience of group membership, of celebrating common beliefs and values, of sharing a common language, of identifying with human models, and of holding beliefs in common* (Grimmitt 1987, 231). And because the process of growing in self-knowledge involves keeping the interplay between self and others continually in focus, the curriculum content selected from both shared human experience and the religious traditions is further contextualised within the main loci of interaction between self and others – *family, faith community, plural society and world-wide community* (Grimmitt 1987, 238-246). It is only when there is *coherence* between the component parts of the model, with each part playing its role in implementing one or more pedagogical principles, that its educational intentions become realisable. Even then, the complexity of the model can count against it and its strength can be considerably diminished when some of its features are transplanted within a curriculum structure which, in other respects, reflects a rationale for RE which is alien to its intentions (as, for example, in the SCAA 1994, *Model Syllabuses for Religious Education*).

The pedagogical model endorsed by the University of Birmingham research project entitled *The Religion in the Service of the Child Project* (RISC: 1989-1992) is a variant of the human development model. While endorsing an *instrumental* view of the place and role of religion in RE, the project's distinctive contribution, however, arose from researching the effects of introducing very young children to the direct study of religion. As a consequence of close observation of how young children interact with religious items taken into a classroom, the project totally rejects the view that pupils need to be prepared for their encounter with religious content through investigating human experience or by using their own experiences in some preliminary, sensitising manner. Instead the project takes as its central pedagogical principle that:

- through encouraging pupils to interact with certain carefully selected religious items they will receive 'gifts' from their encounter which may contribute to their personal development, and in the case of 'believing children', may affirm them in their own faith and enrich their understanding of their own religious and cultural tradition (Grimmitt *et al* 1991, 8-15).

This principle is translated into a four-stage pedagogical strategy involving *engagement, exploration, contextualisation, and reflection*. The strategy is designed to stimulate and support children's interactions with the religious items in order to help them to develop a number of competencies each having a wide transfer value but also having particular relevance to the development of spiritual awareness. (The competencies are identified as: *communicating, questioning, imagining, empathising with, identifying with, valuing and believing*). Consequently any reflection on human experience and any attempt to connect what has been learnt with children's own experiences occur as a result of pupils encountering explicit religious phenomena. The project's view that the direct study of religious content can encourage pupils to address significant questions of personal experience and its meaning represents a realisation of the Lancaster Project's vision of RE stimulating a dialogue between experience and living religions which the narrowly prescribed educational outcomes of a strictly phenomenological approach is unable to deliver. Furthermore, the pedagogy advocated by the project confirms that the concept of *learning from religion* is the essential educational device which enables pupils to apply and personalise their *learning about religion and religions* to their own lives and circumstances and so benefit beyond the limited educational outcomes of the phenomenological approach. The project also recognises that the ability of pupils to identify and empathise with religious concepts, beliefs and practices and to learn from them is greatly enhanced when these are presented in the context of the daily lives of children who are members of a faith community – a view subsequently endorsed and adopted by the ethnographic, interpretative, multifaith pedagogical model.

5. An Ethnographic, 'Interpretive', Multifaith Model:

In the late nineteen eighties and early nineties Jackson and his colleagues at Warwick University undertook a series of ethnographic investigations into the transmission of religious culture from parents and faith communities to children. The research team later applied their experience of using interpretative anthropology and the data obtained to devise a pedagogy of RE which would enable pupils to relate to a way of life that was different from their own. The pedagogic model they devised incorporates and builds upon some of the pedagogical principles already discussed. For example, it encourages pupils 'to focus upon personal knowledge and experience which can be related (by analogy) to material from the religious tradition'; it emphasises the interactive nature of the pupils' engagement with the content – what the project refers to as *oscillating* between the pupils' world and the world of the 'insider' (Everington, Jackson et al, 1995, 4); its materials depict the lives, experiences, views and religious membership of children and young people with whom pupils are invited to identify and relate; and it encourages pupils 'to use material from a religious tradition as a stimulus to reflecting upon matters of personal significance or concern' – a process which owes much to the concept of *learning from religion* but which the project calls *edification* (Ibid, 4, Jackson 1997, 11-12, 130-134).

There are, however, several features of the work of the project which are distinctive and innovative and represent significant contributions to the evolution of effective pedagogies of RE. These relate to the application of important insights from 'interpretive' anthropology to how religions are represented in RE, to how *personal faith* and *tradition* are shown to operate, and to the role that interpretation plays both on the part of *insiders* in holding to a faith and on the part of *outsiders* in trying to understand it (Jackson, 1997). The project's presentation of each religion as a relationship between individuals, the religious (and sometimes ethnic) groups to which they belong, and the wider religious tradition, releases religions from the over-systematised and homogenised presentations from which RE has suffered since the nineteen seventies.

The process of *learning about religion(s)* has always been more narrowly circumscribed, pedagogically, than the process of *learning from religion(s)* or of exploring shared human experience or the *implicit* side of religion. The project breaks new ground and contributes new understanding to what is involved in *learning about religion* when it concludes that:

- coming to understand how religious people and religious groups within the same religious tradition interpret and express their understanding of faith in a variety of different ways, requires pupils to become active *interpreters* of religious meaning making, not just passive observers or recipients of information about a tradition (Everington, Jackson et al, 1995).

The adoption of this pedagogical principle meant that the project team had to devise pedagogical procedures or strategies which would encourage pupils to engage in a *hermeneutical activity* similar to that of the religious believer in order to gain further insights into their way of life. The application of this principle is particularly evident in the third stage of the model's four stage pedagogical strategy for *Interpreting Religions* which is called *Working it out*. What underlies this stage is the idea of pupils learning to bring 'two pieces of (religious) material together (one, perhaps, being an example of personal testimony and the other a credal statement) so that each sheds light on the other.' (Ibid, 4). The process, though complex, is particularly well illustrated in the three pupil textbooks designed for use at Key Stage Three.

The materials designed for use with younger children – *Bridges to Religions* – also conform to the same pedagogical principles but are more dependent on the teacher having the skills to help pupils 'to build bridges between the experiences of children in the stories and the children using the materials in school.' Teachers are supported by a comprehensive strategy for doing this which, while mapping key ideas and routes for exploring them, is sufficiently flexible to allow them to plan their own RE topics, but the central emphasis is on 'using bridging discussions to compare and contrast ideas, feelings and attitudes of children in pupils' books with your pupils' (*Teacher's Resource Book* p.9).

6. A Revelation-Centred, Concept-Cracking, Trinitarian Christian Realist Model:

In several articles and a book published in the early nineteen nineties, Cooling, Project Director of the Association of Christian Teachers' Stapleford Project, raised a number of objections to the epistemological and methodological bases upon which pedagogies of RE have been developed in the previous twenty years. The central feature of his work is his concern with the dominant influence of secular educational criteria and an *instrumental* view of religious content in determining both the aims and outcomes of RE and methods of teaching it. He sees this as imposing upon the presentation of religions a liberal religious ideology which misrepresents the more traditional forms of religious belief, both Christian and non-Christian. He is also concerned 'that an overly descriptive approach to religion has concentrated on giving information about the world's religions at the expense of exploring its meaning for believers and of showing its relevance to modern children' (Cooling 1994b, 3-4). The principles – not all pedagogical – which he puts forward are intended to meet these objections. Although he hopes that members of other religious traditions who share his concerns will be able to contribute to the wider application of these principles, he scrupulously avoids generalising his arguments to include other faiths. It is, therefore, a *hermeneutical programme* for teaching Christianity that he advocates and, to date, this is what it has remained.

Cooling's pedagogical proposals derive from his position as a Christian Realist, namely that the theological beliefs of the Christian faith community constitute an objective and authoritative revelation of God as disclosed through scripture and tradition, and that such beliefs cohere within a theological framework and are interpreted and understood by reference to Christian doctrine (Cooling 1996, 170). Pupils have a right to an understanding of these beliefs and of how Christian people come to hold them as a claim upon their lives. The procedures for constructing the RE curriculum and deciding upon the methods for teaching it must, therefore, ensure that the 'integrity of the religious material' is preserved (Ibid, 168). This means that 'Teachers are not, therefore, free to make whatever use they like of Christian texts' (Ibid, 173). 'In planning a syllabus they should always use the content in ways that reflect, and are consistent with, the religious community's interpretation of that material' (Ibid, 180). The faith communities must, therefore, have a decisive role in choosing the religious content for inclusion in RE and in ensuring that 'the key teachings which should form the interpretative framework for teaching Christian content are clearly identified.' (Ibid,174). For this reason he is fully supportive of the *Model Syllabuses for Religious Education*, especially Model 2 (SCAA, 1994), to which he, as a member of the Christianity working party, contributed.

Although the phenomenological approach, properly applied, can promote the accurate knowledge and understanding of a religious tradition's self-understanding that Cooling is seeking for pupils, he advocates an approach which, surprisingly, incorporates many of the pedagogical principles previously discussed, including the notion of *learning from religion*. This is a consequence of his recognition of the conceptual difficulties that pupils have with understanding Christian beliefs which are alien to them and which do not form part of their every day experience (Cooling, 1994b, 8). Pedagogically, he finds the solution in a hermeneutical process called *concept-cracking* which is applied to the way in which Christian beliefs are taught. The approach, endorsed by The Stapleford Project, involves finding parallels between Christian beliefs and pupils' experiences and is reminiscent of the Christian experientialist, developmental approach to concept formation first proposed by Hubery in the nineteen sixties (Hubery, 1960, chapters 3 and 4) and developed by Grimmitt in the nineteen seventies (Grimmitt 1973, chapter 5).

While, for Cooling, achieving accurate understanding of Christian beliefs is the most important learning outcome of RE, he is prepared to recognise that pupils will gain in different ways from understanding Christian beliefs. For example, the process of *learning from religion* is acceptable to him because he recognises that it is about promoting the spiritual development of pupils. This can include religious conversion, which he describes as 'a very radical form of learning from Christianity' (Cooling 1996, 177) but it can also occur when pupils 'have learnt something about themselves from Christianity without themselves having to be Christian' (Cooling 1994b, 23). Usually this is seen as pupils being engaged at a personal level with the challenge of religious belief. It is a characteristic of Cooling's thinking that any kinds of interaction that teachers encourage between pupils and religious material should result in pupils' understanding becoming more closely accommodated to the doctrinal meaning of the text. This reflects his view that both educational and religious outcomes of RE are achieved when the subject provides children with an *accurate* understanding of what religious adherents believe, not when some personal, existential insight occurs which is not directly related to a tradition's self understanding.

7. A Literacy-Centred, Critical Realist Model:

In the second half of the nineteen nineties Andrew Wright provided a penetrating, critical analysis of the ways in which pedagogical models of RE during the last forty years have been shaped – apparently by default rather than by design – by accommodating themselves to the presuppositions of either romantic or post-modern hermeneutics. He considered that both provide highly contentious perspectives on religion and education and, therefore, questionable bases for the development of pedagogical principles and procedures for teaching and learning in RE.

In his analysis Wright argues that romantic hermeneutics applied to religion stress the centrality of human experience and require that 'any authentic religious understanding must pass beyond the external shell of religious language and culture and engage with the inner core of numinous experience' (Wright 1997b, 204-205). Accordingly, religious language (including narrative, symbol, metaphor and doctrine) is not seen in itself to embody realist truth but to function only as a signpost to the experiential, pre-linguistic spiritual dimension which is seen to be before and beyond language. When this 'romantic theological hermeneutic of translation' is transferred to an understanding of experientialism within RE, (as, for example, by Goldman and later by Hammond, Hay *et al*), it follows that 'only when children's experiential sensitivity and cognitive ability are suitably developed are they ready to appropriate religious texts (and phenomena), and only then will they be capable of translating concrete realistic theological statements into abstract experiential ones' (Wright 1997b, 208-209). Similarly, when a 'romantic hermeneutic of transcendence' is applied to an understanding of the phenomenological model pupils ideally 'must learn to transcend the phenomenological surface of religious culture and enter into an appreciation of its noumenal heart if genuine religious understanding is to take place' (Wright 1997b,

209). Thus the particularities of each of the religions take their place alongside others as contingent and culturally relative traditions embracing a universal theology and a common and universal religious experience. Wright is unable to reconcile this view with his critically realist position which contends that absolute truth is discernible within the traditional language of religion and not contingent upon personal experience.

Interestingly Wright does not see the influence of post modern hermeneutical theory as so much in evidence in contemporary pedagogies of RE as that of romantic hermeneutical theory. Post-modernism regards any claim to knowledge as a form of false consciousness and, contrary to Wright's views, affirms the absolute contingency and relativity of interpretation. Indeed it invites a plurality of interpretations of meaning, whether in relation to the meaning of a religious text or the meaning of life, there being no objective criteria for the determination of truth. Wright, in opposing this view, cites as evidence of the influence of this hermeneutical perspective in RE the stress placed by *The Warwick RE Project* (Everington 1996; Jackson 1997) and *The Children and Worldviews Project* (Erricker et al 1994) on children's use of language and their world views as having an authenticity of their own. He could have also cited the process of *learning from religion* as embodied within the human development pedagogical models of RE, especially as it is interpreted within the Gift Approach developed by *The Religion in the Service of the Child Project*. (Grimmitt et al 1991a). Here a plurality of interpretations and respect for, and encouragement of children's imaginative interpretations of all aspects of religion – narratives, symbols, metaphors, – are seen as positive contributions to the enrichment of children's spirituality and personal development.

Wright's work, in contrast, is firmly embedded within the critical realist tradition (which sees religious language as embodying objective truth) and much influenced by the writings of Gadamer and Habermas. While he has not yet fully explicated pedagogical principles which might provide the basis for the construction of a critical realist pedagogical model of RE, the following broad concerns which he identifies are those which such a model would need to incorporate:

- since understanding always proceeds from the forestructures of the interpreter, a genuinely child-centred religious education must begin with the principle that the child's pre-understanding is a vital component to the learning process (Wright 1998a, 67);

- religious education must be willing to encourage children to explore and develop their emergent religious viewpoints, not by expecting them merely to rely on their own individual preferences and inclinations but by actively challenging them to consider other options (Ibid, 67);

- (with regard to the selection of content) the concern will be with the selection of an appropriate range of contrasting narratives that will enable the emergence of religious literacy. (These will include) narratives embodying negative attitudes towards religion and advocating a-theologies that deny the reality and value of religious truth claims. Added to this would be a range of critical narratives drawn from... anthropology, literary criticism, philosophy, psychology, phenomenology, sociology, feminist theory, theology etc., which offer tools for the secondary interpretation of the primary religious narratives (Ibid, 68).

Despite Wright's fundamental disagreement with the philosophical and epistemological bases of earlier pedagogical models, it is interesting that what he envisages as an appropriate and desirable outcome of RE is closely in accord with, for example, the intentions of both human development and ethnographic models, namely that:

'through the encounter with other horizons pupil's perspectives will become progressively refined and clarified, enabling a greater competence in their articulation of their own religious beliefs, coupled with a greater awareness of the nature of their continuity (with) and divergence from the beliefs of others' (Wright Ibid, 68).

8. Constructivist Models of Teaching and Learning in RE:

The pedagogical principles which the research team of *The Children and Worldviews Project* wish to see applied to education in general and RE in particular derive from their carefully conducted research into the experiences and thinking of children and how they engage in the construction of personal meaning in their lives. From its inception in 1993 the project has been driven by a concern to engage with children's minds in both a rational and affective sense; to listen to their viewpoints and opinions; to identify what is important to them by allowing them to determine the direction taken by conversations and discussions both in the classroom and outside it; and to listen to the different ways in which they use language to describe their life experiences and make sense of them.

The team sees such an investigation as a means of finding out how children's own thinking and experiences influence their ability to learn.

But developing a pedagogy which utilises children's natural capacities for *individual storying* and *constructing meaning* and incorporating it into the learning process so that teachers can *deliver* the formal RE curriculum more successfully is not their prime concern. They follow Foucault in holding that the meaning which the individual constructs represents reality and that truth is related to personal narratives constructed out of individual experiences. Clive Erricker expresses the view as follows:

> 'If we accept that children already possess a narrative within which they construct meaning, then it is meaning rather than truth or knowledge that underpins the education of the whole child. To put this simply, we cannot impose a narrative upon them which does not engage with their own, nor a rationality which does not make sense in terms of the way they have constructed meaning from their experience.' (Erricker et al,1997, 9)

Consequently the team sees the process of encouraging pupils to communicate their experiences, to share the meanings that they have given to them, and to reflect upon those meanings in the light of the responses of others as being intrinsically valuable to children's educational and spiritual development, not as being instrumentally valuable as a hermeneutical device to enable them to interpret or understand formal religious concepts. It is not surprising, therefore that the pedagogical principles which are most clearly articulated by the research team relate almost exclusively to what is referred to as the encouragement of the pupils' *life-knowledge* (Ibid, 140), that is, 'knowledge... gained from experience... that... is communicated and refined through selective conversation with others' (Ibid, 139-140). That the project does intend to develop a pedagogy which enables pupils to construct links between their *life-knowledge* and formal religious concepts may, however, be inferred from the following passage, which also provides a good summary of the main features of the project's process model of RE:

> 'What exactly will the children be doing when they are engaged in religious education? Initially, the aim will be to concentrate on the children's own experiences, and the teacher's role will be to allow the temporal and psychological space for children to express these experiences without fear of judgement either by the teacher or by

peers. The sharing of the issues arising from their experiences will result in reflection and a deeper understanding of what is being addressed, still within the context of the worldviews of the children in a particular class, which are being expressed within the narratives they tell. With the skills of identification of the issues and reflection on those issues introduced and to some extent developed, it is possible to apply them to the subject matter of the curriculum, which can then be addressed at a deeper level. This amounts to an engagement of minds rather than simply an apprehension of outward forms and description. In summary, this process can be described as *identification, reflection and application.*' (Ibid, 164 -165)

But the project is ambivalent about the extent to which formal religious knowledge can be accommodated within pupils' personal *meaning structures* or *worldviews* and whether it is desirable that it should be. Certainly no pedagogical procedures or strategies which could be used by teachers to try and bring about such accommodation are provided. It is interesting to speculate on the reasons for this. The most obvious one is the fundamental incompatibility between the postmodern relativist, relationist, constructivist view of knowledge and learning which the project endorses and the so-called 'objective', rationalist, absolutist view of knowledge which is how religious knowledge is mainly understood by religious traditions and how it is presented in contemporary RE syllabuses. In adopting a postmodern constructivist theory of knowledge and learning to explain how children construct meaning from their individual and cultural experience one might have expected the project to have applied the same theory to how children construct meaning from their encounter with religious knowledge, as presented in the RE curriculum. If, as one suspects, pupils accommodate such knowledge within their own meaning structures (in a similar way to that in which, according to The Warwick RE project, religious people accommodate their beliefs and practices of their own faith within their own meaning structures), then this has important pedagogical implications for teaching and learning in RE. The fact that this theory of human learning challenges contemporary orthodoxy, both religious and educational, is no reason for drawing back from applying it to these two significant areas of human experience and endeavour. But this is what the project does (Erricker, 1997, 189). Surely the time has come for religious educators to take seriously the fact that a lively debate about the realist or non-realist nature of religion has been going on among theologians for well over twenty years and that this debate is essentially about the credibility of religious faith in a postmodern age. As such it can no longer be side-stepped or ignored in any serious attempt to construct a pedagogy of RE which purports, as this one does – and justifiably so – to address the contemporary needs of pupils and young people.

Social constructivism provides the theoretical underpinning of a research project, entitled *Constructivist Pedagogies of RE*, which Grimmitt and his research student, Astrid Jeske, at Birmingham University have recently commenced. To date some initial investigations into how secondary pupils construct meaning have led to the identification of a three-stage pedagogical strategy which deliberately seeks to accommodate the formal teachings of religion within the personal meaning constructs of pupils. This three-stage pedagogical strategy consists of:

1. *Preparatory Pedagogical Constructivism (PPC)*
    In the first stage of the strategy pupils are engaged in an enquiry into and reflection upon their own *experience* in order to *prepare* them conceptually and linguistically for an encounter with the item of religious content. The teacher contributes to the pupils' enquiries and reflections through questions and interventions which may include practical, group-focused activities.

2. *Direct Pedagogical Constructivism (DPC)*
    In the second stage of the strategy pupils are confronted with the item of religious content *directly*, but without explanation and instruction, so that it becomes the stimulus for them to begin to construct their own meaning and understanding of it by using observation, formulating hypotheses, and drawing upon their own experience and that represented in the group. Again, the teacher and pupils may contribute to the process through questions and different forms of intervention.

3. *Supplementary Pedagogical Constructivism (SPC)*
    In the third stage of the strategy pupils are provided with additional or *supplementary* information about the item of religious content which enables their constructions to become more complex and embrace alternative perspectives. It is important, however, that this process is seen as inviting pupils to continue to be *constructivist* in their response to such new information. In other words, pupils do not abandon their interpretations in the face of some 'objective'

knowledge which the teacher provides but continue to engage in an *interpretative process* in which new knowledge is considered *critically* and may or may not be accommodated within their own understanding. The teacher plays a significant part in the process by providing information and by supporting pupils in their attempts to consider if and how they might accommodate this within their own meaning structures.

The most important constructivist principles of learning which this three-stage pedagogical strategy embodies are:

- that the item of religious content is *always* brought into a dynamic relationship with critical and reflective thought which pupils undertake as situated or contextualised individuals;

- that any communication of information about the item of religious content on the part of the teacher is *always* related to the constructions that pupils are using, applying and articulating;

- that the sequence of learning is *always* from encouraging egocentric interpretations of experience within *situated thought* (the pupils' life-worlds) through *alternative contextualised interpretations* (as represented by interventions from other pupils or the teacher), to *evaluative judgements* about the interests which each interpretation serves and expresses.

Although the research is in its early stages there are already indications that the concept of *emancipatory constructivism* (O'Loughlin, 1992) has important implications for developing a pedagogy of RE which raises pupils' awareness of the positive and negative effects of religion upon human life, including its intrinsic sexism and racism. This involves the development of an investigatory framework which encourages pupils to *deconstruct* and *reconstruct* traditional and formal religious concepts in the light of their own experience and alternative perspectives, including feminist ones. Consequently the agenda of the realist or non-realist nature of religion is neither side-stepped nor ignored but investigated and addressed.

END PIECE

While this analysis of pedagogies of RE does not claim to be a comprehensive and definitive account of all pedagogies which have been produced in the UK during the last forty years, it does provide an overview of those pedagogies which have contributed during this period to the creation of effective and educationally defensible approaches to the teaching of RE in non-denominational schools. It is, of course, unfortunate and regrettable that as educational policy making has become increasingly centralised and has favoured a mechanistic view of learning and assessment the direct influence on classroom practice of many of these pedagogies has decreased. Those who are in every day contact with pupils and young people and who are committed to encouraging and supporting their development in the broadest possible sense will, however, appreciate the endeavours of curriculum theorists and research teams, both past and present, who set aside the political agenda and work to identify how a subject like RE can provide the best possible educational experience for them. The ability of RE to continue to address and meet the changing needs of children and young people and to make a significant contribution to their development as persons depends on both teachers and researchers being open to exploring new options and possibilities for the subject, however challenging they may be.

REFERENCES

Cooling T. (1993) 'The Use of Christianity in the Primary School Curriculum', *British Journal of Religious Education*, 15:3, pp.14-22.

Cooling, T. (1994a) *A Christian Vision for State Education* (London, SPCK).

Cooling, T. (1994b) *Concept Cracking: Exploring Christian Beliefs in School* (Stapleford, Notts, Association of Christian Teachers).

Cooling, T. (1996) 'Education is the Point of RE – not Religion? Theological reflections on the SCAA model syllabuses', in Astley, J. & Francis, L.J. (Ed.) *Christian Theology and Religious Education: Connections and Contradictions* (London, SPCK) pp.165-183.

Cooling, T. (1997) 'Theology goes to school: the story of the Stapleford Project', *Journal of Christian Education*, Vol 40: 1, pp.47-60.

Erricker, C., Sullivan, D., Erricker, J., Logan, J., Ota, C., (1994) 'The development of children's worldviews', *Journal of Beliefs and Values*, 15:2, pp.3-6.

Erricker, C., (Ed.) (1995) *Teaching Christianity: A World Religions Approach, Revised Edition* (Cambridge, The Lutterworth Press, First Edition, 1987)

Erricker, C., Erricker, J., Ota, C., Sullivan, D., Fletcher, M., (1997) *The Education of the Whole Child* (London, Cassell).

Everington, J. (1993) 'Bridging fieldwork and classwork; development of curriculum-materials within the Religious Education and Community Project', *Resource*, 16:1, pp.7-10.

Everington, J. (1996) 'A Question of Authenticity: the relationship between educators and practitioners in the representation of religious traditions', *British Journal of Religious Education*, 18:2, pp.69-77.

Everington, J., (1998) 'Evolution not Revolution: an examination of the contribution of a curriculum development project to the implementation of a new Agreed Syllabus', *British Journal of Religious Education*, 20:3, pp.144-154.

Everington, J., Jackson, R. et al, (1995) *Interpreting Religions* series (Oxford, Heinemann).

Goldman, R. (1964) *Religious Thinking from Childhood to Adolescence* (London, Routledge & Kegan Paul).

Goldman, R. (1965) *Readiness for Religion: a Basis for Developmental Religious Education* (London, Routledge & Kegan Paul).

Grimmitt, M.H. (1973) *What Can I do in RE?* (Great Wakering, Essex, Mayhew-McCrimmon).

Grimmitt, M.H. & Read, G.T. (1977) *Teaching Christianity in RE* (Leigh-on-Sea, Essex, Kevin Mayhew).

Grimmitt, M.H. (1983) *Religious Education and Humanisation* (Strathfield, N.S.W., Australian Association for RE).

Grimmitt, M.H. (1987) *Religious Education and Human Development* (Great Wakering, Essex, McCrimmons).

Grimmitt, M.H., Grove, J., Hull, J.M., & Spencer, L (1991a) *A Gift To The Child: Religious Education in the Primary School* (London, Simon & Schuster: available from Stanley Thornes, Cheltenham).

Grimmitt, M.H. (1991b) 'The use of religious phenomenon in schools', *British Journal of Religious Education*,13:2, pp.77-88.

Hammond, J., Hay, D., Moxon, J., Netto, B., Raban, K., Straugheir G., & Williams, C., (1990) *New Methods in Teaching RE: An Experiential Approach* (Harlow, Essex, Oliver & Boyd).

Hay, D., (1986), 'Experiential education in religion as de-indoctrination', (*Nottingham, Religious Experience Research Project*).

Holm, J. (1975) *Teaching Religion in School* (London, Oxford University Press).

Hubery, D.S. (1960) *The Experiential Approach to Christian Education* (London, Chester House Publications and Denholm House Press).

Hull, J.M. (1970) 'The Theology of Themes', in Hull, J.M. (1984) *Studies in Religion & Education* (Lewes, The Falmer Press) pp.123-133.

Hull, J.M. (1975a) 'Theme Teaching as a Method of Religious Education', in Hull, J.M. (1984) *Studies in Religion & Education* (Lewes, The Falmer Press) pp.135-147.

Hull, J.M. (1975b) 'History, Experience and Theme in Religious Education', in Hull, J.M. (1984) *Studies in Religion & Education* (Lewes, The Falmer Press) pp.149-161.

Hull, J.M. (1975c) 'Perennial Symbols: preparing to Teach religion through Life-Themes', in Hull, J.M. (1984) *Studies in Religion & Education* (Lewes, The Falmer Press) pp.163-172.

Hull, J.M. (1996) 'A Gift to the Child: A New Pedagogy for Teaching Religion to Young Children', *Religious Education*, 91:2 pp.172-188.

Jackson, R., (1997) *Religious Education: an interpretative approach* (London, Hodder & Stoughton)

Loukes, H. (1961) *Teenage Religion. An enquiry into attitudes and possibilities among British boys and girls in secondary modern schools* (London, SCM).

Loukes, H. (1965) *New Ground in Christian Education* (London, SCM).

Nye, R. & Hay, D. (1996) 'Identifying Children's Spirituality: How do you start without a starting point?', *British Journal of Religious Education*, 18:3, pp.144-154.

O'Loughlin, M. (1992) 'Engaging teachers in emancipatory knowledge construction', *Journal of Teacher Education*, Vol 43, No 5, pp.336-346.

Read. G.T. et al (1977) *Religious Education: its nature and aims* (Queensland, Curriculum Branch, Department of Education).

Read, G., Rudge, J., Teece., & Howarth, R.B., (1992) *How Do I Teach RE? The Westhill Project RE 5-16*, 2nd Edition (Cheltenham, Stanley Thornes; 1st edition 1986)

Religious Experience and Education Project (1986) *Inside Information* (Nottingham, REEP)

Schools Council Working Paper No 36 (1971) *Religious Education in Secondary Schools* (London, Evans/Methuen).

Schools Council Working Paper No 44 (1972) *Religious Education in Primary Schools* (London, Evans/Methuen).

Schools Council (1977a) *Journeys into Religion: Religious Education in Secondary Schools: Teacher's Handbook A* (London, Hart Davis).

Schools Council (1978) *Journeys into Religion: Religious Education in Secondary Schools: Teacher's Handbook B* (London, Hart Davis).

Schools Council Occasional Bulletin (1977b) *A Groundplan for the Study of Religion* (London, Schools Council).

Schools Council (1977c) *Discovering an Approach: Religious Education in Primary Schools* (London, Macmillan).

School Curriculum and Assessment Authority (1994) *Model Syllabuses for Religious Education Model 1: Living Faiths Today; Model 2: Questions and Teachings* (London, SCAA).

Smart, N. (1968) *Secular Education and the Logic of Religion* (London, Faber & Faber).

Smart, N. & Horder. D. (Ed.) (1976) *New Movements in Religious Education* (London, Temple-Smith).

Wright, A. (1993) *Religious Education in the Secondary School: Prospects for Religious Literacy* (London, David Fulton).

Wright, A. (1996) 'Language and Experience in the Hermeneutics of Religious Education', *British Journal of Religious Education*, 18:3, pp.166-180.

Wright, A. (1997a) 'Mishmash, Religionism and Theological Literacy. An Appreciation and Critique of Trevor Cooling's Hermeneutical Programme', *British Journal of Religious Education*, 19:3, pp.143-156.

Wright, A. (1997b) 'Hermeneutics and Religious Understanding. Part One: The Hermeneutics of Modern Religious Education', *Journal of Beliefs and Values* 18:2, pp.203-216.

Wright, A. (1998a) 'Hermeneutics and Religious Understanding. Part Two: Towards a Critical Theory for Religious Education', *Journal of Beliefs and Values*,19:1, pp.59-70.

Wright, A. (1998b) *Spiritual. A Survey, Critique and Reconstruction of Contemporary Spiritual Education Pedagogy in England and Wales* (Abingdon, Culham College Institute).

Wright, A. (1999) *Discerning the Spirit. Teaching Spirituality in the Religious Education Classroom* (Abingdon, Culham College Institute)

CHAPTER 3

THE CHICHESTER PROJECT:
TEACHING CHRISTIANITY: A WORLD RELIGIONS APPROACH

Alan Brown

INTRODUCTION

The Shap Working Party on World Religions in Education began its life with a meeting at the Shap Wells Hotel in 1969. The establishment of Shap marked the growing interest in the teaching of world religions in schools as well as in universities. It may surprise some, therefore, that the Chichester Project on teaching Christianity in English Secondary Schools had its origins in the Shap Working Party.

The growth of interest in the teaching of world religions during the 1970s caused those with a visionary eye to recognise that the style and content of Religious Studies teaching would have a profound effect upon how Christianity would be taught and what the subject content would be. The then Secretary of Shap, Professor Edward Hulmes, wrote a paper for the Shap Annual General Meeting in which he drew attention to the need for a Project on the Teaching of Christianity:

> 'I feel certain that SWP [Shap Working Party] ought to devote some of its time to Christianity as a major world religion, but I know that there are members who feel that Shap's particular contribution has been and ought still to be in the dissemination of information about other world faiths.'

13 December 1976

While some members of Shap may have been ambivalent about a Project on Teaching Christianity in English Secondary Schools (PROCESS), one member of the Shap Working Party, John Rankin, agreed to explore the possibility of co-ordinating such a project and finding funds to support the initiative.

A joint paper written by Edward Hulmes and Ninian Smart on PROCESS was prepared for the Shap Working Party prior to Hulmes' paper for the Shap A.G.M:

'We note the following features of much teaching about Christianity:-

First, the fact that Christianity is often treated on a different basis than, say, Buddhism, seems frequently to lead to a loss of empathy for Christianity among pupils. Different faiths too can seem more attractive, for various reasons.

Second, because of certain traditions in religious education and English theology, the exploration of Christianity can be too selective and restricted for a rounded view of it as a functioning faith to emerge. Different liturgical expressions of Christianity, for instance, cannot be derived solely from a study of Biblical material.

Third, we recognise that questions of teacher commitment to the faith, or some version of it, are naturally more prominent and problematical than in relation to other religions. Positively, commitment may spark enthusiasm and skill in teaching. Negatively, it may get in the way of exploring the facts and feelings of Christianity. It largely is a matter of the temperament of the teacher. This aspect of affairs ought to be explored and openly debated, with a view to helping the process of education concerning Christianity.

Fourth, there is little material suitable for introducing a non-Christian child (e.g. a Muslim or Hindu) to Christianity.'

24 February 1976

Some of these points may resonate with the views and experiences of religious education teachers today and, reading them, one is prompted to reflect on how much has changed in attitude and outlook since 1976. The fourth point ignores the non-religious pupil, the child who has no point of contact with any religion – an issue which has received considerably more attention over the last twenty-five years. That particular issue was touched on in the early years of the Project; could an 11-year-old pupil really have had no contact with religion? The answer would depend upon the type of

54

religious education presented to pupils in their primary schools and whether one believes that contemporary British society is wholly secular.

It was from such seed that the Chichester Project was born. It was and is, in effect, genetically and ideologically related to the Shap approach to the teaching of religion. While the 1970s is recognised by religious educators as the decade when teaching about world religions took off, it really is quite remarkable that those who played a key role in promoting such an approach should have begun to reflect so early on the need for a more effective approach to the teaching of Christianity in English Secondary Schools.

The Project Develops

The first meeting of the Chichester Project took place on 14th and 15th December 1977. The date has significance only because the first publications would not emerge for another five years. The path towards publication was not simply one of deciding appropriate content. The process by which the publications would be arrived at was of the greatest significance, as were the pedagogical approaches which the Project would develop.

The first meetings looked at some of the issues raised by Edward Hulmes and Ninian Smart. Hulmes attended the first consultation meeting, Smart was unable to do so. Discussions centred on the effects of a teacher's commitment to a particular faith when teaching about it and others, the problems of objectivity, which methodologies are appropriate to teaching about Christianity, whether there is a 'mainstream Christianity', and the educational problems which arise from variety and diversity within Christian belief.

The first consultation concluded with five aims being generally agreed upon by the participants:

(1) to extend knowledge of the beliefs, practices and values to be encountered within Christianity;

(2) to encourage appreciation of the importance and influence of these beliefs, values and practices in the lives of Christians;

(3) to develop an awareness of the wide diversity of interpretation contained within the Christian tradition;

(4) to encourage serious reflection on the evidence upon which Christian claims are based;

(5) to develop an understanding of the language of Christian discourses and Christian worship.

The fourth aim was, and remains, the most controversial and would have a marked effect upon the style and approach of the publications as well as upon the movement of personnel in and out of the Project.

THE PERSONNEL

Any project is directed by its personnel and the Chichester Project was no exception. There were the original Trustees, the Director of the Project, John Rankin, then Head of Religious Studies at the West Sussex Institute of Higher Education (WSIHE), David Naylor, RE Adviser for Hampshire, and Alan Brown, then Senior Lecturer in Religious Studies at WSIHE. Alan Brown is currently the Project Director and Mary Hayward has replaced David Naylor.

The Project was created to function in a genuine consultation mode. Individuals, perhaps nine or ten in number, would discuss and present papers, drafts for publication, etc., which would then be open for full debate normally over a 24 hour period. This process, healthy though it may appear and probably was, raised profound theological and educational differences with the result that some people moved in and out of the Project without ever having their work published. Some left of their own volition, others needed encouragement.

The most withering aspect of the Project for would-be authors, however, was the intense, vigorous criticism to which each article or draft manuscript of a book was subjected. It would be hard to imagine a more intensive critique of a writer's work held in their presence particularly as these were not experienced authors but a collection of willing writers stepping into the publishing pool for the first time. The consequence was that, for those who were allowed to stay with the process, the learning curve was steep, painful but hugely beneficial. One just had to be aware that one's colleagues were working to improve one's own work, and that each writer was on the receiving end of very high quality advice and support. It was very humbling and uncomfortable, particularly as the criticism was usually fully justified.

This aspect of the pedagogical approach of the Project was a seminal element in its development. As a result, the pedagogical methodology and the teaching strategies were subject to a critique, presented not by one educational consultant but by a variety of educators concerned with classroom practice. In addition, while the Project was rooted in the ideology of the Shap Working Party (which rarely, if ever, speaks with one mind), and while members of the Consultation each represented different philosophies of religious education, there arose an agreed unity of approach within the Trustees and others who stayed with the Project during the five years of development and subsequently.

Issues Of Content

By 1978, specific areas of content had been decided upon, though some were never to see the light of day.

- Christian Communities
- Foundation Documents
- Christianity in Literature, Art and Music
- What Christians Believe
- Christian Individuals
- Christian Spirituality
- Christian Festivals
- Christianity in non-western cultures
- Christian Ethics

Note the date and the continuing interest of religious education publications today! Some materials were needed then, and are still needed now, but how could they be produced in a suitable format which would attract teachers and students while encouraging them to wrestle with unfamiliar concepts and ideas?

In terms of contributing to the religious education agenda at the time, and probably today, over twenty years later, what was not published by the Project is probably more relevant than what was. It continues to be difficult to find good accessible information for secondary school students which will help them to explore the diversity of Christianity in non-western cultures. Christianity in Literature, Art and Music is still only slowly inching forward. The current emphasis on spiritual development (not, note, Christian Spirituality), may result in some work proceeding along those lines, but Christian Spirituality has not figured largely in the development of religious education since the 1970s. Perhaps the next decade will focus on the spiritual aspects of the different world religions – an enormous task which some have already begun to explore.

Ironically, the most difficult topic was 'Christian Belief'. The variety of interpretations which exist within Christianity means that Christians simply believe different things and, more significantly, believe that other Christians are fundamentally wrong. As soon as an affirmation of faith is made, someone will challenge it on theological, linguistic, philosophical or other grounds. Should one introduce Key Stage 3 students to this complexity within the Christian tradition on the grounds that this is what Christianity is actually like -- full of debate, difference and diversity? Or should one concentrate on very general 'agreed areas' and be safe, sound and secure but in danger of pointing to a monolithic type of Christian belief and practice which does not exist?

In practice, the range of titles published was an attempt to deal with this diversity. Some forms of Christian diversity, however, appear so precious or to be so theologically distinctive that they become meaningless to students who understand little of the rites, beliefs and practices of Christianity and even less of theological niceties and are not motivated to take the study of religion seriously at all.

One sharp indication of this came in a proposed publication (never to see the light of day) which would explore the differences between Roman Catholic and Protestant Christianity. This appeared, initially, to be a straightforward proposal but in practice it raised a whole range of problems, not least about whether students would be able to understand the issues which divide Christians and which they take very seriously but which are likely to have little if any significance to anyone outside the faith. Some Protestants are quite 'Catholic', some Catholics are quite 'Protestant', and then there is the Church of England! Would it be appropriate to explore the transubstantiation / consubstantiation issue with thirteen-year-olds? Did the seminal difference lie in attitudes to the Papacy or in attitudes to the concept of Church? Were such issues important in a society where the observation of religious practices was a minority activity? Would it be more desirable for the focus to be on ecumenism than upon division? While these issues were of undoubted interest and importance to the Churches, were they really of direct significance and importance to students following compulsory RE?

AMIDST THE DEBATE

In 1979 the Chichester Project became a charity in the hope of attracting funds from grant-awarding bodies. Some funds did come in but slowly and not substantially. Lutterworth Press agreed to publish the first four booklets in 1982, with four more to follow if the first batch was successful. There had been a discussion regarding the production of a teacher's handbook and one was, eventually, produced in 1987 (edited by Clive Erricker) but the thrust of the work was predicated upon the assumption that good textbooks, used by students, would have a positive affect upon the way in which teachers taught. In other words, the production of good quality classroom texts embodying sound pedagogical procedures would influence teachers' practice.

But the activities of the Project, as a charity, were not to be solely concerned with publications. Alongside the publications would run a research activity looking at the way in which Christianity was presented in public examinations at G.C.E. and C.S.E. levels. Dr. William Kay was invited to undertake this research and did so in the period 1981/82. A conference was held in December 1981 on Examinations at 16+ and the significance of the new examinations (G.C.S.E.) for the teaching of Christianity.

RESEARCH AND DEVELOPMENT

One of the outcomes of the pilot study undertaken by Dr. William Kay on Christianity in religious education examinations was that 53% of the schools responding to his questionnaire (a total of 145 schools) believed the presentation of Christianity in examination syllabuses to be inadequate and 33% thought Christianity was adequately presented. Dr. Kay's tentative conclusion to the study was:

'Perhaps the best way of reading them (the survey results) would be as giving support for the possibility of a new style of examination syllabus, one which started at the twentieth century and worked backwards rather than starting in the first century and moving forwards.'

(RE Examination Pilot Study, 1982)

The research also provided some indication of how teachers approached teaching Christianity and what were the major influences on them in their presentation of Christianity in Years 7-9 in the secondary school.

Prior to the administration of the questionnaire, those working with the Project envisaged the major influences upon classroom practice would be: initial training, personal conviction, agreed syllabuses, examination syllabuses, educational philosophy, educational research, books available, the religious education adviser and the school tradition. The research, however, indicated the following to be the most influential factors:

Personal conviction:	(mean)	3.44
Professional training:	(mean)	3.069
Educational philosophy:	(mean)	2.855
Educational research:	(mean)	2.490
Books:	(mean)	2.483

It is of interest to note that Agreed Syllabuses were not mentioned and that examination syllabuses came ninth in this list, suggesting that both exercise a fairly minimal influence on classroom practice. However, when personal convictions were correlated with the other factors, significant (usually at .001 level) correlations (Kendall's Tan) were found with:

Professional training;
School tradition;
RE adviser;
Examination syllabuses.

On the face of it the correlations are not easy to explain, though the most obvious way of doing so is to suggest either that the teacher's initial training experience influences their subsequent personal convictions or that personal convictions determine the choice of initial training institute. Similar considerations can be applied to most of the other factors except the influence of the religious education adviser.

It may be time to look again at such influences on teachers to see if the tentative results of Kay's research would be replicated today. In passing it is interesting to note that RE Agreed Syllabuses appeared to have little influence and the suggestion of starting at the 20th century and working back has not received the attention it deserves. One of the more controversial aspects of the Project's work was an internal investigation into how personal commitment could, and did, inhibit the presentation of accurate information about various Christian traditions.

THE AIMS OF THE CHICHESTER PROJECT

It would be correct to say that the aims of the Project evolved from the 1976 paper presented by Hulmes and Smart, through the principles agreed at the first meeting of the Project in 1977, to the aims as formulated and re-produced inside the front cover of the first ten books which the Project published. These are reproduced here in their entirety and represent a summary of the Project's educational philosophy as it had evolved over five years:

The Chichester Project is concerned with the production of material for teaching Christianity in secondary schools. It is a research project supported by many professionals in the field of Religious Education. It tries to foster an open approach to the teaching of Christianity in accordance with the following principles.

The pedagogical principles endorsed by the Project

1. Although Christianity is to be seen as a world religion, it will probably provide the material for the greater part of most RE syllabuses, especially as it figures largely in the cultural life of Britain and in the moral foundation of her government.

2. The pupils' acceptance or rejection of Christian tenets is not the direct concern of the teacher. The material should be capable of being used without offence to pupils of any faith. The aim of Religious Education is to support pupils' understanding. It is of the utmost importance to this country that pupils come to understand Christianity in its many forms. This is educationally important in itself, but it also contributes to the more general expectation that RE will contribute to pupils' capacity for religious understanding in the widest possible sense.

3. The project starts from the assumption that religious sensibility is an essential dimension of human development, and that however diverse its manifestations it is an inherent human capacity. The awakening and educating in each pupil of this sensibility, which is fundamental to the understanding of religion, is the prime task of the RE teacher.

Teaching methods applied by the Project

The first materials produced by the project were in the form of pupils' books. Each book was prepared by an individual who was given the freedom to express their own professional insights and opinions; no attempt was made to impose a uniformity of treatment upon either approach to, or treatment of content. The Project's view remained throughout that the quality of RE teaching should benefit from teachers utilising a variety of approaches informed by examples of good practice.

Each book bears the style of the individual author and is a separate entity within the project. There was no attempt to produce a course or a Religious Education curriculum. It was hoped, however, that the material would be able to fit into the variety of RE syllabuses and schemes of work devised by teachers in schools.

In general, the approach is to begin with an aspect of Christian practice or experience which can be observed, and to proceed to ask questions about it. Too often in the past, Christianity has been approached solely from a study of the New Testament, indeed, usually by way of the Gospels and sometimes only by way of one Gospel! The Project wished to encourage the study of the New Testament, but was aware that this alone would not equip students sufficiently to develop an adequate understanding of the diverse expressions of Christianity that they would encounter in their studies and their lives. The concern was that pupils would discover that religious beliefs and practices are intrinsically interesting and that some might even have meaning for them in responding to the events and circumstances of their own lives.

The role of the teacher

From what has been said about the general principles, some might conclude that the teacher who possesses Christian convictions has to suppress them. This is not the case. Indeed, the teacher's convictions can often become a valuable resource for pupils trying to discover what it means to be a Christian. This should not, however, contradict the principle which leaves pupils free to come to their own conclusions, and it should hardly be necessary to caution teachers against pressing for any kind of religious allegiance on the part of pupils. Any such attempt would be contradictory to the nature and purpose of the materials.

It cannot be emphasised too strongly, however, that material is only material and we confidently expect teachers to enliven and enrich these outlines from their own experiences and resources. Nor is it expected that classes should slavishly follow all the suggested exercises and activities. These should be apportioned according to the teacher's more intimate knowledge of a class and of individual pupils.

Each book has a bibliography which could be useful in pursuing the topic further.

> The Chichester Project is an ongoing research project supported by the Shap Working Party for World Religions in Education and the West Sussex Institute for Higher Education. Grants have been made by the Spalding Trusts, All Saints' Trust, and the United Society for Christian Literature. Further sources of finance are being sought. The project is a registered charity. Teachers are invited to send their comments and suggestions on the material, to assist further development.

John Rankin, Project Director, 1982.

THE LATER YEARS

After the publication of the ten pupil books by 1986, the teacher's handbook, *Teaching Christianity: a world religions approach*, appeared in 1987. Also in 1986 the Project tried to develop a video following the same principles as the book but finances did not allow it to develop beyond the planning stages. The trustees then decided to change publishers from Lutterworth to Longmans and produced two more teacher's books, *RE Topics in the Primary School* (1989) and *RE Topics across the Curriculum* (1991). While much of the content was concerned with Christianity, topics from other world faiths were also included. The process by which these emerged was slightly different from the secondary school materials. In each case drafts of the materials were sent to 20 teachers who then met for a 24 hour conference in order to comment on the material in depth.

After twenty years the Project is currently working collaboratively with the National Society to produce resource material on Christianity for Key Stages 1-3 with a projected publication date of 2001.

TEACHING STRATEGIES

One of the most common failings when discussing Christianity as a World Religion is to misunderstand the intention of the phrase. Of course it would be helpful if students could learn about the different varieties of Christianity throughout the world but the intention of the Project is different. From its outset the Project assumed that students would approach Christianity with very little knowledge or understanding of the structure, practices and beliefs of the religion. What the Project was interested to establish was if teachers and students could be encouraged to approach the teaching of Christianity in the same methodological style and using the same strategies with which they might approach Islam, Hinduism, Buddhism, etc. In other words, could Christianity be seen and understood as a 'world religion' by students growing up in Britain? A parallel case was presented by the Open University's first Religious Studies course, *Man's Religious Quest*, developed in the 1970s and 1980s, which, after a brief introduction, presented students with the challenge of studying Hinduism, a religion totally unfamiliar to many O.U students. These O.U. students bought their residual 'Christian' model to bear on Hinduism and quickly discovered that this would not do. Consequently members of the Chichester Project wondered if teachers and students would it be able to approach the study of Christianity in an open and exploratory manner or whether it was inevitable that they would bring their own prejudices to bear upon it in the classroom. Much would depend upon the approach and quality of the teaching and learning materials which they were using – something which the Project, of course, was concerned to address.

The Project adopted a phenomenological approach to deciding upon the topics and the content to be addressed in its first four publications – *Christian Communities, Christian Experience, Christian Worship*, and *Jesus*. The rationale was for the Project to take its cue from Christian phenomena and religious practice which students would see around them. Starting from their awareness of 'a church', the question arises, what does it mean, and what could it mean, for a church to be a Christian Community? Central to the life and work of Christian Communities is Christian

Worship, and what both Christian Communities and Christian Worship offer to individuals who participate in them is Christian Experience. At the heart of Christian Experience is the Person of Jesus. These early texts, all published in 1982, were then followed by two books on the Bible, one on Christmas and Easter and a fourth one on Christian Ethics. The final two books in the series published by Lutterworth were *The Eucharist* and a general introduction to *Christianity*.

CHARACTERISTICS OF TEACHING STRATEGIES USED IN CLASSROOM TEXTS

Each author of the classroom texts published by the Project developed their own style – a legitimate source of criticism of the books at the time. The philosophy behind the materials, however, remained consistent with the aims of the Project; it was the style of learning incorporated within each book which varied. This variety, however, was also a strength as the pupils did not have to suffer the same stylistic and task-driven approach in every book – a lesson for the authors of some multiple series of RE classroom text books today! That the Project has always sought to avoid reducing RE to a narrowly phenomenological and descriptive approach can be illustrated by reference to the innovative pedagogy adopted by Erricker in two of the Project's publications – *Christian Experience* (1982) and *Christian Ethics* (1984).

In *Christian Experience*, Erricker juxtaposed (i) the Story of the Garden of Eden, (ii) *American Gothic* by Grant Wood, and (iii) *The Snake Charmer* by Henri Rousseau. How, he asked, are they connected?

'What do you feel they and the passage are saying?

   a) about yourself?

   b) about man's [sic.] relationship to the world?

   c) about man's [sic.] relationship to God?'

In Christian Ethics he used a moral dilemma depicted in a story by P.C. Schumacher and encouraged pupils to rank the characters in the story in order of their moral acceptability and to give reasons for their ranking. He then asked them to consider which of the characters acted in a Christian way.

In both cases Erricker provided some information, but the essential ingredient of learning was seen as the student's response. The aim of the tasks was to use the student's insight and experience to develop a response to what was being studied. From its inception the Project has always tried very hard to place the student's experience, opinion and developing knowledge at the heart of each book. This has meant that a balance has been sought between, on the one hand, a didactic approach to informing students about Christianity and, on the other hand, involving them in active learning strategies intended to develop their own understanding and perspective.

The most popular book was *Jesus* by Trevor Shannon. This was one of the first classroom textbooks to look at the way the Person of Jesus has been represented by Christians in different parts of the world. Shannon tended to use the style of (a) check your reading, (b) use your imagination and (c) find out for yourself. In *Christmas and Easter* he used passages from literature and the device of individuals being present at one of the great Christian festivals and providing an eye-witness account. By using this approach Shannon , like Erricker, placed considerable emphasis on the importance of encouraging pupils to empathise with the feelings and emotions of Christians involved in the events, not just on acquiring factual information. This meant that he was able to produce two very readable and imaginative textbooks on topics which were already well worn in school religious education textbook history.

The author of *Christian Communities*, Alan Brown, wrote in the first person as if he had been present at all of the communities in the book ranging from the early Christian community to the Taizé Community of the mid 20th century. In *The Eucharist* John Rankin provided an almost perfect teaching model for confirmation candidates, with the most effective strategy being 'In remembrance of me' (page 5) which explored the very different ways in which past events are remembered. The activities set for the students tried to cultivate their understanding of the importance of eating together, sharing familiar stories, remembering past events and the social bonding such shared events and experiences can create.

The three books written by Peter Curtis – two on the Bible and one on Christianity – probably represent the most didactic approach of any of the textbooks published by the Project. That said, Curtis provided a masterly selection and exposition of the essential features of Christianity suitable for pupils at Key Stages 2 and 3 and a very sensitive treatment of the Bible appropriate to pupils at Key Stages 3 and 4. The title and perspective of *The Christian's Book* reflected the Project's phenomenological emphasis and was in sharp contrast to many previously published school texts on the Bible which failed to contextualise the study within either the Jewish or Christian faith community's use or understanding of the Bible as the source of their understanding of God and how they should respond to Him.

Sustaining the Project

It would be a story in itself if all the projected books and authors who were willing to contribute to the Chichester Project materials could be listed. Over twenty-five people joined the Project with seventeen leaving or having their work rejected.

It should be said that the rejection of a proposal was not always related to quality, though this was often the case. More significant was the diversity of educational philosophies represented among would be authors. Some believed the Project was essentially about Ethics, or about the Ultimate Truth of Christianity, or about whatever happened to be their own pet concern. This is why the location of the Project's work within the Shap Working Party was so important. It provided a focus, a rationale and an ideology from which the Project did not divert. The reasons for this were largely due to the rigour and tenacity of the then Project Director, John Rankin, but also to the creation of a small like-minded group who were prepared to criticise and be criticised.

There emerged nothing on Christian Belief, nothing on Rites of Passage, and nothing on Christianity and Inter-faith Dialogue. All texts fell short of the required standard, either because they were too didactic or too controversial or because they were felt to be potentially beyond the understanding of students. For example, students need to know more about a faith before they can understand how it may function when it rubs shoulders with another faith. The complexity of any religion is its essence and yet it can be so difficult to teach that complexity in an environment where complexity is regarded as beyond the reach of the learner and, more controversially, where complexity is ruled out in favour of the simplistic convenience model. To engage with the complexity and diversity of Christianity is to engage with its sense of mystery and the numinous. Successful learning and understanding follows when students can be encouraged to 'engage with' not just 'learn about' Christian experience and belief and when they can 'appreciate' *why* Christians (or members of any other religion) choose to believe or belong, not just 'know the facts' about what Christians do and what they believe.

CRITICISMS OF THE PROJECT

The main criticisms of the classroom textbooks produced by the Project have been directed towards their lack of colour (given the brilliance of their covers!), the diversity of their styles; the contents of some books being less accessible to students than others; the limited choice of topics, and the lack of books on Christian Belief and Rites of Passage in particular. The teacher's handbook and the two books written for primary school teachers were well received, though all three were written in a different style for a different audience.

Some of these criticisms can probably be gathered together and seen to be a consequence of the Project being too long in gestation, too self-critical and self-conscious about what it was attempting to achieve, and, too prone to misunderstanding on the part of the publisher about what this new style of approach required in terms of presentation. Colour photographs in such a series would, at the time (1982), have been a quantum leap forward in the style of RE books, full colour materials not becoming commonplace until the mid to late 1980s. Perhaps the marker for that style of production was *The Christian World* published by Macdonald in 1984. The issues of variation in written styles and accessibility are an inevitable consequence of a series of ten books being written by five different authors. As indicated earlier, there may be a strength in this weakness.

All projects must have a natural life. The current work of the Chichester Project is to work with The National Society and perhaps one or two other interested partners to produce a different style of resource material for teaching Christianity, or Christianities across Key Stage 1-3. Such material should be available in 2001 or 2002 and will draw a line under the 25 year history of the Chichester Project.

CONCLUSION

It would be too much to suggest that the Chichester Project changed the face of Religious Education. It did, however, ensure that the teaching of Christianity was placed firmly within the context of a world religions approach. Supporting a philosophy which was compatible with the thinking of the Shap Working Party on World Religions in Education, it applied criteria to the teaching of Christianity which were new, or relatively so, at the time. It also attempted to promote a style of teaching whereby students were invited to engage with the material and not simply be taught about it. If there are successes to be recognised, they are to be evaluated in terms of the progress that has subsequently been made in the development of materials for teaching Christianity in an educational manner, many of which still owe something to the style and concerns of the Chichester Project.

PUBLICATIONS BY THE CHICHESTER PROJECT

Brown, Alan (1982) *Christian Communities* (Lutterworth/Clarke) KS3/4.

Curtis, Peter (1984) *Exploring the Bible* (Lutterworth/Clarke) KS3/4.

Curtis, Peter (1984) *The Christians' Book* (Lutterworth/Clarke) KS3/4.

Curtis, Peter (1986) *Christianity* (Lutterworth/Clarke) KS2/3.

Doble, Peter and Hayward, Mary (1987, revised 1993) *A Bibliography for the Teaching of Christianity* (Chichester Project) KS3/4.

Erricker, Clive (1982) *Christian Experience* (Lutterworth/Clarke) KS3/4.

Erricker, Clive (1984) *Christian Ethics* (Lutterworth/Clarke) KS3/4.

Erricker, Clive (1987) *Teaching Christianity* (Lutterworth/Clarke) KS3/4.

Jones, Alan (1984) *Evaluation of extant material on teaching Christianity in Secondary Schools* (Chichester Project) KS3/4.

Rankin, John (1982) *Christian Worship* (Lutterworth/Clarke) KS3/4.

Rankin, John (1985) *The Eucharist* (Lutterworth/Clarke) KS3/4.

Rankin, John, Brown, Alan and Hayward, Mary (1989) *Religious Education: Topics for the Primary School* (Longmans) KS3/4.

Rankin, John, Brown, Alan and Hayward, Mary (1991) *Religious Education Across the Curriculum: Topics for the Primary School* (Longmans) KS3/4.

Shannon, Trevor (1982) *Jesus* (Lutterworth/Clarke) KS3/4.

Shannon, Trevor (1984) *Christmas and Easter* (Lutterworth/Clarke) KS3/4.

CHAPTER 4

THE RELIGIOUS EXPERIENCE AND EDUCATION PROJECT:
EXPERIENTIAL LEARNING IN RELIGIOUS EDUCATION

David Hay

BACKGROUND

The Religious Experience and Education Project was set up at the University of Nottingham in the second half of the 1980s. It grew out of work I had been doing for some years with Alister Hardy at the Religious Experience Research Unit in Oxford. To make clear my understanding of the pedagogy underlying experiential learning in religious education, I need to begin by summarising this theoretical and empirical background.

Like myself, Hardy was a zoologist and in the Gifford Lectures which he delivered at the University of Aberdeen (Hardy 1965, 1966) he offered an account of religion in terms of natural history. His central thesis was Darwinian: 'Religious experience' (by which he meant an awareness of a presence or a power which transcends the everyday self), has been selected for in the process of organic evolution because it has survival value. This seemed at the time, to put it mildly, a rather daring conjecture. At a historical moment when formal adherence to the mainstream religious institutions had been in decline in Western Europe for many years, Hardy was suggesting that religious experience is a human universal.

The results of the national and in-depth survey work during the thirty or so years since Hardy's lectures were both surprising and supportive of his thesis (Hay & Morisy 1978; Hay, 1979; Hay, 1982; Hay & Morisy 1985; Lewis, 1985; Hay, 1994). They made it clear that very large numbers of people in Britain understand at least some of their life experience in spiritual or religious terms. The great majority of these people do not belong formally to any religious institution, yet their interpretations are of considerable significance for an understanding of religion. This is because the experiential aspect of religion is highlighted in many academic accounts, perhaps most accessibly in the work of Ninian Smart (Smart, 1971, 1992). Smart judges experience to be the most important of the six constitutive dimensions of religion (the other five are ritual, mythological, doctrinal, ethical and social). From his point of view all of the other dimensions depend for their cogency on religious experience, though of course in turn these dimensions themselves shape that experience.

In contemporary Britain, religious experience expresses itself in many ways (Hay, 1990). Here are some examples:

(1)   A few people feel that they are permanently aware of a sacred dimension to their lives. Adherents of the theistic religions usually feel this as an awareness of the presence of God. Members of nontheistic religions like Theravadin Buddhism use other terms. Thus in Buddhist meditation, practice is directed to the development of a continuous awareness of what is conceived to be true rather than illusory reality.

(2)   Very large numbers of people (at least half and possibly two thirds of the adult population) report sporadic or spontaneous religious awareness. Though they describe it as if it was rather like a physical perception, these people almost always say that they don't perceive anything through the normal sense organs. Usually they say they have been surprised by an unexpected awareness of God; sometimes by another sacred presence such as an angel or a saint. On the other hand some people refuse to use orthodox religious language to describe their experience, perhaps because they have been alienated from the religious institutions. Whether religiously practising or not, statistically speaking, people reporting religious experience are usually better educated and in a better psychological state than people who say they have no such experience. There is thus a paradox running through society, since the popular stereotype is that people claiming such experience are most probably stupid or perhaps slightly mentally unbalanced. This is significant from an educational perspective because fear of stereotyping means that already by the age of ten most people have become embarrassed about sharing their experience with other people (Hay & Nye, 1998).

(3)   For religious believers spiritual awareness is most obviously awakened through the practical exercises of their religion. Here we see an indissoluble unity of the public and the personal which it is important for the religious educator to underline. Thus there are many rituals which enable the faithful to relive important moments in the history of their religion. In Judaism the celebration of the Passover is one such occasion, as is the celebration of Christmas and Easter in Christianity. Another way in which awareness of the sacred is heightened is through the reading of sacred texts. This is especially true of Islam, where the divine presence is made manifest in the words of the Qur'an itself. In the many different forms of prayer, meditation or contemplation we come to the heartland of religious practice where believers place themselves before God or ultimate reality. Finally, believers come across the experience of reality itself as a divine communication. In Christianity this is sometimes spoken of as 'finding God in all things' (Hebblethwaite, 1994). At times this may be through the noting of odd or extraordinary patternings of experience. Or people may experience their dreams as religiously meaningful. Most often though, it is the total untidy experience of life that people interpret as God's dialogue with them.

RELIGIOUS EXPERIENCE – SALIENT YET HIDDEN

For committed believers this experiential dimension is by far the most significant aspect of their religion. Here the most important religious impulses take their motivation – to worship, and to act justly and mercifully. Yet because of the taboo I mentioned, from the perspective of the outsider the experiential dimension is likely to seem remote and unreal. In contrast it is hard to miss the public phenomena of religion. Simply to walk the streets of any large town in Britain is to pass numerous churches as well as synagogues and, increasingly, mosques, Hindu temples and gurdwaras. The media report regularly on huge religious gatherings such as those stimulated by the travels of the Pope, whilst violent and bloodstained arguments between people of differing religious persuasions are making headline news as I write this chapter. Religious symbols (Cross, Crescent, Wheel, Yin and Yang etc.) are amongst the most familiar 'logos' that confront us on the streets, on television, or as stickers on cars. Whilst these aspects of religion are certainly of importance or concern to religious believers, they are subordinate to the experiential dimension.

I must emphasise that the distinction I am making between the experiential and the other dimensions of religion is not intended in a dualistic sense – as if personal experience were prior to and distinct from the culture which plays a part in its creation. But I do also want to insist that the possibility of religious or spiritual experience depends on the existence of the biologically determined predisposition which I discussed above. When the rituals and other publicly observable activities of religion, however vivid, politically significant or aesthetically moving are not an expression of or a response to this predisposition then they cease to be religious. At best they are well meaning make-believe, at worst they are corrupt. Hypocrisy, the concentration on a public performance which has become detached from its spiritual roots, is something the great religious leaders are constantly warning against. Thus, in his teaching Jesus reserves his fiercest criticism for people who do this. They are likened to 'whitewashed tombs that look handsome on the outside, but inside are full of dead men's bones and every kind of corruption' (Matt. Ch. 23, v. 27).

At the time that the Religious Experience and Education Project was set up I had the feeling that the experiential dimension of religion was being ignored by RE teachers, or at least treated with kid gloves. I suspected that this was partly because of a fear of being accused of indoctrination. But an educational approach to religion that avoids its practical life is rather like a scientific education which prohibits students from entering a laboratory for fear they should be coerced into becoming scientists. The experiential aspect of religion, seen as a human phenomenon, can be approached with the same educational integrity as any other school subject. The perspective taken is one of assisting students to have empathy with the personal world of believers, recognising the extent to which they are struggling like every other human being with the enigma of the human condition. This in no way requires students to accept any of the religious beliefs they study, nor on the other hand does it prohibit such acceptance.

SOME PRELIMINARY PEDAGOGICAL TASKS

How then is the teacher of Religious Education to approach this issue responsibly? Certainly not by abandoning a study of the publicly available phenomena of religion. Without a rootedness in the concrete realities of religion, reference to religious experience has no meaning. On the other hand all of these activities will themselves seem remote or incomprehensible unless an attempt is made to achieve some empathic insight into the personal perspective of the believer. In other words understanding depends on a grasp of the inseparability of 'culture' and 'biological predisposition' (Durham, 1991) in the creation of human experience, including religion.

The paradox facing the teacher of Religious Education is this. On the one hand no-one, whether they be religious believer or sceptic, can avoid the immense political and social impact of religion on people's lives in the contemporary world. On the other hand in a nation like Britain, where only a minority of people are religiously practising, religion is often seen as a marginal or alien phenomenon. In this circumstance the task of the teacher is to help pupils to escape from the narrowing effects of the culture to which they belong, in other words to broaden their minds. Religious educators are often accused of indoctrinating their students. In communities where secular interpretations of reality are very dominant, the task of religious education is the reverse of this. Properly conducted, it is more like deconstruction or de-indoctrination, helping to question hidden cultural assumptions that constrain our possibilities as human beings. All teachers have this responsibility, but in responding to the requirements of the 1988 Education Reform Act with regard to Spiritual Education, the RE teacher has a particularly important obligation because of the historical connection between religion and spirituality. There are three tasks the teacher must attend to. In one sense they are preliminary, laying the groundwork for an educationally responsible understanding of the religious person's perspective. In another sense these tasks must be undertaken throughout the course of the RE curriculum:

1. Helping students to keep an open mind

The power of a culture to construct our assumptions about reality is at its greatest when those assumptions are at their most self-evident. Ways of understanding reality that seem so obvious that other possibilities look ridiculous are in fact indoctrinatory in the strict sense, since they close the mind to alternatives. Many years ago the philosopher of science Karl Popper devised a clever exercise for use with his students in Vienna to demonstrate the falsity of assuming that there is only one perspective on reality (Popper, 1972). Without further explanation he requested the students to 'observe' for the next five minutes and write down what they observed. They were at first bewildered by Popper's instruction because it is without qualification. I know, because I have used this exercise many times myself. 'Observe what?' is the implicit question on people's faces, because of course there is an infinity of possibilities. When they do settle down to respond they produce lists of observations which are always unique. Some list objects in the room, but never a list identical to anyone else's; others list the sounds heard outside the room; others write poetry; still others review their personal mood changes; once, someone spent the whole five minutes describing the toe of his shoe.

Popper's exercise is quite similar to the observation exercises given to children in elementary science classes, usually with predetermined correct answers in the mind of the teacher. In general when teachers are inducting children into the norms of a culture there is a quite rigid set of guidelines to which they expect them to conform. Possibly a more important way children are pushed into conformity is the multitude of images that are purveyed in the commercial media, dictating with great power standards of dress code, what it is acceptable to take an interest in, and what it is acceptable to believe. Teachers can counter these narrowing influences and this is a particularly important aspect of the religious educator's emancipatory role.

2. Exploring different ways of seeing

It is not enough to demonstrate that there are different ways of seeing. When we have been trained by our culture into interpreting the world in a particular manner it becomes surprisingly difficult to see it in any other way.

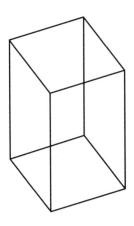

My favourite illustration of this is Don Ihde's beautiful demonstration of the nature of deconstruction, using the Necker cube (Ihde, 1979). I have invited literally hundreds of people, young and old in several different cultures, to tell me what this diagram represents (Figure 1). Not even once has anyone offered to interpret it as anything other than a cube. Yet as Ihde points out, it can be construed in many other ways: for example as a flat surface, as an oddly cut diamond, as a pyramidal structure with the tip cut off, or as a badly shaped workbasket. When these possibilities are pointed out to people they recognise them briefly, yet they return to the cube interpretation as by far the most obvious one. It seems that the salience of this way of seeing is related to the fact that most or all of us have lived inside cube-like rooms since the day we were born, and have seen endless drawings and photographs of such shapes. Therefore they dominate our perceptual interpretations. Some people even become angry about the alternatives, asserting that these suggestions are foolish. In an entirely passive and benign sense there has been a kind of cultural indoctrination simply because of the way the environment is. Here we see the potentially dangerous power of cultural construction to limit open vision and replace it with dogmatic certainty.

3. Encouraging immediacy of awareness

A third preliminary task is to encourage the raising or recovery of personal awareness. The Edinburgh psychologist Margaret Donaldson writes of the importance of the 'point mode' of consciousness, meaning the here-and-now of one's experience, as opposed to the 'line mode' where the mind ranges backwards and forwards in time (Donaldson, 1992). Donaldson notes that before about 18 months infants appear to spend almost the whole of their time in the point mode. On the other hand by the time we reach adult life most of our time is taken up with the line mode, remembering and sometimes regretting the past, or planning and speculating about the future. Consequently the point mode gets squeezed out.

Yet it is here that young children and religious people find common ground because the exercises of prayer, meditation and contemplation are based upon consciously choosing to remain in the point mode. Examples are *vipassana* or Buddhist awareness meditation where the central task is to remain aware of the breathing, or the processes of walking, as they happen in the here-and-now. In Christianity the practice of placing oneself in the presence of God requires the same attention to the immediacy of the situation, or as the French Jesuit Jean-Pierre de Caussade called it, 'the sacrament of the present moment' (Caussade, 1971).

THE PEDAGOGICAL STRUCTURE OF THE MAIN PROGRAMME

These preliminaries continue to need reinforcement throughout the main programme, to which I now turn. This was developed over a period of three years with the help of a group of Primary and Secondary School teachers in the East Midlands, (1) and is strongly practical in orientation. We decided that if religious education is to do its job properly it cannot be conducted at arms' length. As hinted at above, its subject matter unlike much of traditional education is very directly connected with the personal experience and existential concerns of the students themselves. This of course demands a high degree of maturity and self knowledge on the part of the teacher. None of us can expect to understand the subjectivity of another person without attempting first to become aware of and to understand our own subjectivity. That implies entering into something very like Personal and Social Education. Many of the strictures and safeguards that apply to PSE also apply to the use of the practical exercises advocated in the Project.

Some teachers of Religious Education see PSE as a threat to their subject, but from the perspective of the Project it is an excellent opportunity. Though the model of the person in PSE often seems to be drawn implicitly from a secular perspective, it does respect subjectivity and the nature of relationship. From the religious person's point of view, to take these things seriously is to take an interest in familiar territory. However the methodology does require a fairly radical change in perspective for someone who is used to teaching didactically. Whilst there is not space in a short chapter to deal with these adaptations they are treated in detail in *New Methods in RE Teaching: An Experiential Approach*, especially in Parts I and III (Hammond, Hay et al, 1990).

We decided to base the practical work on the notion of 'awareness' because of its centrality in the life of the religious believer. By inviting pupils to study their awareness we were asking them to make a careful investigation of an ordinary aspect of their own nature. But of course this dimension of human nature has been of particular interest to religious people and, in relation to it, the religions have developed a vast array of highly sophisticated practices and interpretations. These methods of prayer, and the associated rituals, narratives, doctrines, ethical and social practices provide the main factual input of religious education. The exercises are in no way meant to replace this normal RE syllabus, but to complement it. If they are used without relating them to the substantive content of religion they have lost their purpose.

The classroom activities are of six types:
1. Getting started
2. Raising awareness
3. Embodying awareness
4. Framing awareness
5. Extending awareness
6. Endings:

1. Getting started

Experiential RE asks pupils to explore personal aspects of themselves and they need a climate in which they can share their views comfortably and safely. New ways of learning can seem like a waste of time, making pupils anxious or confused, so some groundwork needs to be done which helps them to accept what is going on. Building effective working relationships in the group means getting to know everyone else, exchanging names with people who are strangers and chatting informally with acquaintances, in other words, the familiar ice-breaking exercises that are often used in PSE.

2. Raising awareness

> Be still and know that I am God.
>
> *Psalm 46, 10*

> Sitting quietly and doing nothing,
> Spring comes and the grass grows by itself.
>
> *Zenrin*

Awareness is like a spotlight, allowing details to emerge, sharpening and clarifying the image so that I can perceive more clearly. It is selective, directing attention to what I regard as relevant to me and excluding information which appears to be of no interest or value. My concentration span varies and so awareness is usually transient; there is a tendency to generalise, to wander from immediate experience so that whilst I think I am aware of what is going on around me, in fact my mind has strayed elsewhere.

So attending to the here-and-now is not easy. Yet the realisation that the present moment is all I have lies at the heart of religious practice. Thus the repetition of the Jesus Prayer as a mantra in the Eastern Orthodox Church is intended to concentrate the mind, still the thoughts and ultimately set the soul 'face to face with God' (French, 1972). Similarly the concept of mindfulness in Buddhism can be seen in the light of consciousness of the moment, just listening when listening, seeing when seeing. Consequently the exercises in this section are designed to give pupils practice in stilling and listening, so that they gain insight into the dimensions of ordinary human awareness attended to by religious believers in the practices of prayer and meditation.

3. Embodying awareness

> If you cannot find it in yourself, where will you go for it?
>
> *Chinese proverb*

> What can I do, Muslims? I do not know myself. I am no Christian, no Jew, no Magian, no Muslim. Not of the East, not of the West. Not of the land, not of the sea. Not of the mine of Nature, not of the circling heavens. Not of earth, not of water, not of air, not of fire My place the placeless, my trace the traceless. Neither body nor soul: all is the life of my Beloved...
>
> *Jal al-din Rumi*

When stilling and listening, pupils are invited to be mindful of their own bodies and to notice the use of body language. In the section entitled 'Embodying awareness' time is given to exploring the fact that each of us has a life history which gives us a unique personal identity. This life history is the product of the particular culture and era in which we live. Thus, my experience of the world differs according to whether I am male or female, rich or poor, my ethnic group, my physical appearance, the beliefs of those in charge of my upbringing, as well as the ups and downs of my life. If in the midst of this uniqueness I choose to focus for any length of time on the question 'Who am I?' the answers can go beyond these external details of my life history. 'Who is it that has this name, this nationality, this life-history?' To the devout individual, this is not only a secular question. It is a profoundly religious question, explored through meditation, prayer and theological and philosophical reflection. Here once more we find that a natural feature of human experience, the question of identity, is a central preoccupation of religion (Mol, 1976, Cumpsty, 1991). Paradoxically, this is so even in Buddhism where the existence of a 'self' is denied. The exercises in this section are therefore concerned with helping pupils to recognise the embodied nature of their own human awareness and to empathise with the self perceptions of others.

4. Framing awareness

> Krishna is: the soul in the heart of all things; the beginning, the middle and the end; the sun; the moon; consciousness; the destroyer; the lord of wealth; fire; a mountain; a priest; a vast lake; the word OM; silent prayer; the Himalayas; a tree; a seer; a musician; a horse; an elephant; a king; a thunderbolt; a creator; a serpent; a snake; the ruler of death; a demon; time; the king of beasts; a bird; the wind; a warrior; a fish; the Ganges; knowledge; reason; the sound A; fame; prosperity; speech; memory; intelligence; constancy; forgiveness; a song; a poem; a month; a season; the cleverness in the gambler's dice; beauty; victory; goodness; a poet; a king's sceptre; wise policy; silence; the seed of all things.
>
> *Bhagavad Gita*

> God is love.
>
> *1 John 4, 8*

Human experience is framed by what we learn from others: parents, teachers, friends, the media. It is in the process of adopting the symbols and metaphors dominant in the community in which we grow up that we try to make sense of our own experience. The example of the Necker cube shows that living in an environment full of cuboid shapes is enough to affect the way we see an arrangement of lines on a page. Similarly our images of other people are in part determined by our culture as well as our individual feelings at a particular moment. We make assumptions about people belonging to a different culture or religious group from ourselves because we see them in terms of the symbols and metaphors of our own religious (or non-religious) group.

In the present context, the main reason for looking more deeply at the metaphors and symbols that frame our awareness is because of the great importance of metaphor in religious language (Soskice, 1985). If we are to speak, however stumblingly, of what transcends language we are forced to do so obliquely. Metaphor never succeeds in trapping what it refers to, but it points to it in a way that has practical value for the religious believer. For example, a central idea in Buddhism is dharma, sometimes translated as the teachings of the Buddha, or the Path. However, dharma is not just an idea, it has a practical effect on the way a Buddhist experiences reality. Just as the Buddha advocates the 'Middle Path', so Jesus is described as 'the Way, the Truth and the Life', Hindus are on the 'Wheel' of the Dharma and Islam rests on five 'Pillars'. Religious metaphors are the vehicles used to articulate experience. Therefore the activities in this part of the programme are designed to encourage pupils to investigate how metaphors affect their own and other people's perceptions of reality. The exercises are preparatory to an examination of more explicitly religious metaphors and symbols in the next section.

5. Extending awareness

> When I see the heavens, the work of your hands, The moon and stars which you arranged, What is man that you should keep him in mind, Mortal man that you care for him?
>
> *Psalm 8*

> Many cultures throughout history have employed fantasy as the traditional place where man transcends himself, communicates with God, and where ultimate truths are revealed.
>
> *Anthony de Mello SJ*

It is no accident that amongst the first things we recognise about a religion are the stories and symbols that represent it. Within each religious group an extremely rich set of meanings and interpretations of reality has evolved around these central narratives and imagery. Whether in secular or religious life, when we let our minds wander imaginatively in fantasy, we continue to use the stories and symbols supplied to us by our upbringing to provide the materials for our creativity. In the case of the faith communities the imaginative use of narrative and symbol is often used as an exercise for deepening religious awareness, as in the vision quest of a number of primal religions, or in the Spiritual Exercises of St Ignatius in Roman Catholicism. Therefore in this section the practical activities include an investigation of the imaginative use of symbols and the use of story and guided fantasy.

6. Endings

Experiential learning always depends on trust and cooperation not only between teacher and pupils but also between pupil and pupil. In some activities pupils will have delved quite deeply into their feelings, relying on the support of their classmates. They may need time to reorientate themselves and adjust before moving on to other things, for example another class which is not operating on the same principles. There may also be a sense of regret that the session or the programme is over and a felt need to mark the ending. The exercises here assume that the group members know each other well and are able to show sensitivity to each others' feelings.

DEVELOPMENTS SINCE 1990

Relational Consciousness

When *New Methods* first came out in 1990 (2) there was relatively little research evidence available about the spiritual life of children (Hay, Nye & Murphy, 1996). Such work as existed almost always assumed that children would express their spirituality in the language and forms of Christianity. If Hardy's conjecture is correct, then in a secularised culture this is to ignore many, possibly most of the ways spirituality expresses itself. We know that in adult life most people learn to hide their spirituality; perhaps even to repress it. But if we have to be taught to be secular, because spiritual or religious awareness is natural to us, then the most obvious place to find spirituality ought to be amongst children before they have picked up the idea that it is unimportant.

Recently Rebecca Nye and I published the results of a study of the spiritual life of six year old and ten year old children in two primary schools in Nottingham and Birmingham (Hay with Nye, 1998). The principle which guided our research was the attempt to speak to the children about spirituality without the use of religious language (Nye & Hay, 1996). We invited the children to comment on a set of photographs of children of much the same age as themselves, in situations where spiritual matters might be expected to arise (for example, a girl gazing into the fire in the evening, a boy looking out of his bedroom at the stars, a girl crying because her pet hamster has died). The transcripts convinced us that every child, even the most secularised, had a spirituality and was able to be articulate about it, though very often it was not expressed using traditional religious language. In its absence the languages of fairy tale, science fiction, technology, dreams and many other forms of expression were appropriated.

We did a computer assisted analysis of the transcripts of the conversations in an attempt to discover some common ground linking together what the children had said. The common denominator which emerged was 'relational consciousness', which has two components:

1. In every case where children talked about spirituality there appeared to be an unusual level of awareness or perceptiveness compared with their conversation on other matters.

2. Without exception, all spiritual talk referred to how the children related to reality; either to God, other people, themselves, or the material world.

If this is correct, it becomes clear that nurturing relational consciousness in the classroom is itself the first step in creating the conditions for an insight into the roots of religion. All children know that when teachers are with them in the classroom the primary matter that they are communicating is a way of being human – how they as adults approach life. But in a highly individualistic culture and in an educational system geared to scores on academic league tables the temptation to forget about relationships and allow technical reason to take over is very strong. To some degree teachers can get away with this in subjects where the skills of accumulating and manipulating data are of central importance. But spiritual insight is not just another educational commodity. Of its essence it is relational and spiritual understanding can only develop if the relationship is right.

CRITICISMS

I have space to mention only two of the most substantial published criticisms of the experiential approach. Firstly it has been suggested that it represents a privatised understanding of the nature of spirituality, isolating it from its communal, linguistic and cultural context (Thatcher, 1991; Mott-Thornton, 1996, Wright, 1996). This was never my view (Hay & Hammond, 1992), but I am now sufficiently detached from the debate to see that some of what was written in this area could be interpreted that way. Our use of terms like 'inner experience' led some people to believe that we were adopting a dualistic, Cartesian stance. In the present chapter I have tried to avoid such language, and our finding of the importance of 'relational consciousness' should make it sufficiently clear that this is not our view.

The second important criticism has more to do with the praxis of the teacher (Grimmitt, 1987, Chapter 5). What do teachers who use this method believe they are doing? If the teacher is implicitly attempting to inculcate religious belief of some kind by the use of practical exercises, then this is an abuse of their position. My assumption is that the task the teacher is engaged in is a close examination of what I have come to call relational consciousness. Conceived in this manner, it is beginning to look very like the human predisposition that Alister Hardy discussed in his Gifford Lectures. Relational consciousness is often damaged or forgotten in the highly individualistic culture to which we belong (Macmurray, 1995). Yet it underlies the human desire for justice, care for other people, for future generations and for the planetary environment. It thus contributes to human survival, as Hardy conjectured. Historically and well-nigh universally, as far as we can see, it has also underlain religious behaviour in the human species. That is why it should be given close attention by the religious educator.

NOTES

1.Apart from my debt to the authors of *New Methods in RE Teaching* I am also grateful to the following people for other kinds of contribution to the Project: Alison Jones (now Leech) who was Research Fellow; Ginny Straugheir who followed Alison; the group of East Midland Primary and Secondary teachers who met regularly over two years in the University of Nottingham and who devised or tested many of the materials used in the book: Jenny Abram, Dai Bevan, Julia Bigger, Phil Doughty, Nancy Driver, Ruth Harris, Tom Limb, Alan McKenzie, Brian Netto, Vivien Peters, Kathy Raban (now Nettleton), Sister Margaret Mary Ryan, Charles Reilly, Roger Stevens, Mike Wallace, Alan Webster and Jonathan Yarnell.

2. *New Methods in RE Teaching* is currently out of print. My colleague John Hammond and I are engaged in planning a new edition which takes account of developments since 1990.

REFERENCES

Cumpsty, J.S. (1991) *Religion as Belonging: a General Theory of Religion* (New York: University Press of America).

Donaldson, M. (1992) *Human Minds* (London: Allen Lane).

Durham, W. (1991) *Coevolution: Genes, Culture and Human Diversity* (Stanford University Press).

French, R.M. (1972) *The Way of a Pilgrim* (London: SPCK).

Grimmitt, M. H. (1987) *Religious Education and Human Development* (Great Wakering: McCrimmons).

Hammond, J., Hay, D., Moxon, J., Netto, B., Raban, K., Straugheir, G. & Williams, C. (1990) *New Methods in RE Teaching: An Experiential Approach* (London: Oliver & Boyd/Longman).

Hardy, A.C. (1965) *The Living Stream: A Restatement of Evolution Theory and its Relation to the Spirit of Man* (London: Collins).

Hardy, A.C. (1966) *The Divine Flame: An Essay towards a Natural History of Religion* (London: Collins).

Hay, D. (1979) 'Religious experience amongst a group of postgraduate students: a qualitative study', *Journal for the Scientific Study of Religion*, 18 (2), pp.164-182.

Hay, D. (1982) *Exploring Inner Space: Scientists and Religious Experience* (London: Penguin Books).

Hay, D. (1990) *Religious Experience Today: Studying the Facts* (London: Cassell).

Hay, D. (1994). ' "The biology of God": What is the current status of Hardy's hypothesis?', *International Journal for the Psychology of Religion*, 4 (1), pp.1-23.

Hay, D. & Hammond, J. (1992) ' "When you pray, go to your private room": a reply to Adrian Thatcher', *British Journal of Religious Education*, 14(3), pp.146-149.

Hay, D. & Morisy, A. (1978) 'Reports of ecstatic, paranormal or religious experience in Great Britain and the United States: a comparison of trends', *Journal for the Scientific Study of Religion*, 17 (3), pp.255-68.

Hay, D. & Morisy, A. (1985) 'Secular society/Religious meanings: a contemporary paradox', *Review of Religious Research*, 26 (3), pp. 213-27.

Hay, D. & Nye, R. (1996) 'Investigating children's spirituality: the need for a fruitful hypothesis', *International Journal of Children's Spirituality*, 1(1), pp.6-16.

Hay, D., Nye, R. & Murphy, R. (1996) 'Thinking about childhood spirituality: review of research and current directions', in, Leslie Francis, William K. Kay & William S. Campbell (eds) *Research in Religious Education* (Leominster: Gracewing Press).

Hay, D. with Nye, R. (1998) *The Spirit of the Child* (London: HarperCollins).

Hebblethwaite, M. (1994) *Finding God in All Things: the Way of St Ignatius* (London: HarperCollins).

Ihde, D. (1979) *Experimental Phenomenology* (New York: Paragon Books).

Lewis, D. (1985) 'All in good faith', *Nursing Times*, 18/24 Mar., pp.40-43.

Macmurray, J. (1995) *The Self as Agent* (London: Faber & Faber) (originally published in1957).

Mol, H. (1976) *Identity and the Sacred: a sketch for a new social-scientific theory of religion* (Oxford: Basil Blackwell).

Mott-Thornton, K. (1996) 'Language, dualism and experiential religious education: a critical appraisal of the debate between Adrian Thatcher and the authors of New Methods in RE Teaching', *British Journal of Religious Education*, 18(3), pp.155-165

Nye, R. & Hay, D. (1996) 'Identifying Children's Spirituality: How do you start without a starting point?' *British Journal of Religious Education*, 18(3), pp.144-154.

Popper, K. (1972) *The Logic of Scientific Discovery* (London: Hutchinson).

Smart, N. (1971) *The Religious Experience of Mankind* (London: Fontana Books).

Smart, N. (1992) *The World's Religions* (Cambridge University Press).

Soskice, J. (1985) *Metaphor and Religious Language* (Oxford: Clarendon Press).

Thatcher, A. (1991) 'A critique of inwardness in religious education', *British Journal of Religious Education*, 14 (1), pp. 22-27.

Wright, A. (1996) 'Language and experience in the hermeneutics of religious understanding', *British Journal of Religious Education*, 18(3), 166-180.

CHAPTER 5

THE WESTHILL PROJECT:
RELIGIOUS EDUCATION AS MATURING PUPILS' PATTERNS OF BELIEF AND BEHAVIOUR

John Rudge

INTRODUCTION

The educational world of the early 1980s was, of course, very different from today. For one thing, the Department of Education and Science was willing to fund a religious education centre at Westhill College in Birmingham, to provide resources and in-service training for teachers. The centre had been established in 1973 by Michael Grimmitt, its first Director, under a scheme for promoting centres of excellence in various areas of the curriculum, and set up by the Secretary of State at that time, Margaret Thatcher. With Geoff Robson, Michael Grimmitt gathered a considerable collection of resources in a wide variety of media, and set up a programme of training for teachers of religious education, both primary and secondary, which received widespread recognition.

When both members of staff moved, one to Birmingham University and the other into the Inspectorate, a new team was formed which brought together Garth Read, an Australian curriculum development specialist, John Rudge, a teacher from a Manchester inner city comprehensive school, and Roger Howarth, a local teacher who had contributed extensively to the development of support materials for the Birmingham Agreed Syllabus. These three began working together on April Fool's Day, 1980, and out of their collaboration, and the insights and co-operation of teachers on in-service courses, the project known as the *Westhill Project RE 5 – 16* came into being.

THE PROJECT MATERIALS

From the beginning, Garth Read was instrumental in keeping the work of the centre focused on the principles of curriculum development and pedagogy, rather than on the more detached world of religious studies or theology. This gave rise to the main purpose of the project, to produce effective classroom resources linked directly to a conceptual grasp of the subject and a methodology for translating it into a programme for planning and teaching the subject.

Within that aim, the project set out to interpret the insights of academic discourse on philosophical, religious and educational issues about the subject in a way that would make sense to classroom teachers, and to balance this against the needs and concerns of teachers in devising useful and usable materials. Devising a new and radically original conceptual framework was not regarded as the most pressing or desirable factor. Rather, the project should try to draw together insights from a range of current thinking and weld them into a coherent programme. The project does not therefore start with a detailed rationale and argument for its approach; instead, it treats the stated aims of religious education as given, and develops its pedagogical principles and practice from that basis. The view was taken that there were, in any case, others who were much better qualified and more competent in their respective fields, and that the best use of the expertise of the Westhill team, and the needs of teachers, dictated that a curricular approach was more appropriate at that stage.

The thinking behind the project was therefore indebted on the one hand to an ongoing academic debate about religious education in state schools, and on the other hand to those teachers who participated in the RE Centre's courses.

During the 1960s and 1970s, religious education had undergone profound changes in terms of focus, outlook, philosophy and aims; and there had been a parallel proliferation of resources, particularly in the audio-visual field. But there seemed to be no adequate catalyst for drawing these disparate elements together into a coherent whole; no clear pedagogy which would help teachers translate an overview of the subject into schemes of work and lessons; no adequate guidelines on how religious education may develop coherently and programmatically from the early years to at least the age of 16.

The changes in focus and philosophy had been brought about by distinguished thinkers and researchers, both in the educational field in general and in the subject in particular. The project set out to draw on these important contributions, on the basis that all would be eventually superseded by new thinking – or already had been – but that important insights would remain as part of the structure of the subject. So, in the wider field, the educational theories of Piaget and Bruner, particularly in relation to conceptual development, were used as building blocks. In the field of religion, the frameworks of such writers as Cantwell Smith and John Hick in relation to the conceptualisation of religion, and of Ninian Smart in the area of phenomenology, also included important insights which contributed to the thinking behind the project; and the researches of Goldman and Loukes in the field of religious education, particularly in their concern to make the subject comprehensible and relevant to the lives of pupils, needed to be taken into account.

There were, however, more direct influences which need to be acknowledged. Much of the thinking which influenced the project also influenced the 1975 Birmingham Agreed Syllabus, a remarkably forward looking document which set out both a programme of study for religious education and, in its introduction, an outline of pedagogical principles, within the context of a fully multi-faith framework. In some respects the Westhill project may be seen as a development of the basic structure of that syllabus. More directly still, the three-circle model of the field of enquiry of religious education, which is fundamental to the project, had its genesis in work done in the centre by Michael Grimmitt and Garth Read in 1975. Garth Read then shared this model with the Religious Education Curriculum Project team of which he was a member, working in the Department of Education in Queensland, Australia.

The Westhill Project team also drew extensively on insights and practical strategies derived from teachers on in-service training, particularly those involved in the Diploma in Religious Education and the module on the principles and practice of religious education. One of the purposes of the materials produced by the project was to support teacher training on long and short courses, in order to give practical expression to its pedagogical structure. The teachers kept the project team's feet on the ground by discerning flaws in the materials, as well as by introducing many helpful suggestions and examples.

The synthesis of all these sources was the project manual *How do I teach RE?* first published in 1986. Although this was the first formal part of the project to be published, earlier formative work had resulted in an audio-visual pack *Festivals* which embodied the principles of the project, in some ways more accurately than some of the later materials. The conception of the project envisaged parallel resources of teachers' manuals, and pupils' books covering the main religious traditions and related to the early primary, junior, lower secondary and upper secondary phases (currently Key Stages 1 to 4), and supported by a photopack for each tradition comprising 20 large format pictures, each with explanatory notes. In the first phase of publication, the teachers' manuals on Christianity, Judaism and Islam were published, along with their parallel pupil books 1 to 4, and the respective photopacks. At a later stage, a *Hindus* photopack was produced, accompanied by a shorter teachers' handbook.

The next stage involved the generation of materials for the early years, in association with a group of teachers from the Walsall LEA. The outcome was *Life Themes in the Early Years*, three packs of artists' paintings and photographs, in large format, with teachers' notes.

During the production of these materials, Garth Read returned to Australia and Roger Howarth moved to a local authority advisory post, and Geoff Teece, who had worked on the early years materials, joined the team and added a strong primary perspective to the centre's work. He was instrumental in developing the next publication *Living Questions* (strictly speaking the last one in the original conception of the project), comprising a teachers' resource book and pupils' text book for Key Stage Three. This publication broke with the tradition of the earlier project materials by including activities for directly engaging the pupils, as opposed to simply providing resource material for teachers to use as they saw fit.

Following the 1988 Education Reform Act, the centre was increasingly drawn in to curriculum issues dictated by the need to respond to the new agenda affecting all subjects. From this agenda, the centre produced a range of publications which addressed particular issues, whilst keeping to the basic principles and pedagogy of the Westhill Project – *Attainment in RE; A Handbook for Teachers: Assessing, Recording and Reporting RE; A Handbook for Teachers: How to write your school policy for RE; How to write your scheme of work for RE*. There were also two publications produced as resources for understanding multi-faith British society – the Black Christians photopack and a video produced in collaboration with West

Mercia Police called the *Changing Face of Britain*. During this post 1988 period, a second edition of *How do I teach RE?* was published to take account of issues raised by the Education Reform Act.

PEDAGOGICAL PRINCIPLES

Aim of religious education

During the development of the project, it became clear that religious education was tending to follow three broad lines of development, one interpreting the subject in terms of the knowledge and understanding to be gained from the study of the major religions, another giving greater emphasis to the personal development of pupils through their engagement with issues which were fundamental to their own lives, and a third strand with a focus on helping pupils to become aware of and sensitive to the religious dimension of life through their own encounter with experiences such as awe and wonder, belonging and commitment, caring and compassion. It was evident that each of these approaches contained important insights into the potential of religious education, but none provided an adequate framework either on its own or by assuming dominance over the others. At the same time it was recognised that, from a practical point of view, many teachers were intuitively drawing on these three perceptions in devising their school teaching programmes. In spite of this cross-fertilisation of ideas, there was nonetheless a tendency for religious education in practice to become an uncritical process of transmitting information about the major religions, with little concern for discriminating between the more and less valuable aspects of this body of information, and with no recognisable pedagogical framework beyond the transmission model. It was a religious education of facts, founders, festivals and frilly bits, which did justice neither to the great religious traditions it purported to represent, nor to the needs of pupils growing up in a rapidly changing world dominated by secularist, materialist and pluralist norms.

As a starting point, there seemed to be a need to define the subject in a way which could embrace a meaningful pedagogy, and a structure for dealing with the content of religious education in the classroom. Framing a statement of aims in a succinct way has never been easy, but from the beginning the project worked with the following definition of the aim of religious education, as being

92

to help children mature in relation to their own patterns of belief and behaviour through exploring religious beliefs and practices and related human experiences. **(1)**

This statement encompasses a number of pedagogical principles. Firstly, it gives priority to the pupils' personal development. This identifies the project with that strand of thinking which emphasises the subject's potential impact upon the pupils' own lives, rather than seeing them as simply recipients of a body of knowledge. Such a view is in harmony with wider views of the educational process as being concerned with *realms* of meaning or with *forms of knowledge.* **(2)** Secondly, in relating the aims of religious education to the process of the pupils' own maturing patterns of belief and behaviour, the statement takes seriously the pupils' own context in the world in which they are growing up, the requirement to be seen to be relevant to the needs and aspirations of the pupils, and the necessity for structuring a programme of teaching and learning which takes account of their developing awareness and abilities.

Thirdly, religious education, according to this aim, involves pupils in an encounter with two related areas of knowledge, those understood by 'religious beliefs and practices' and those referred to as 'human experiences'. The aim therefore encompasses the field of enquiry of the subject. Knowledge and understanding of the field of enquiry is not an end in itself, but a means to an end. The content of field of enquiry is *instrumental* in the process of personal development.

Fourthly, the statement suggests that the process of religious education involves an *encounter* with the field of enquiry. Religious education is therefore to be seen as a process whereby the pupils' engagement with the content of the subject is designed to contribute to their personal development.

The case for a child-centred approach, rather than a content-centred approach, has been well made by others. It is, of course, open to challenge, not least by those who see education as having a utilitarian or institutional purpose. The argument for seeing religious education within a developmental context stems from the assumption that the formation and maturation of beliefs and values is an exercise in which every human being, including the child, is inevitably involved. It stems from the conviction that the educational process has a valid and worthwhile contribution to make to pupils' developing beliefs and values in their formative years. The outcome of such an education is not conformity to a social or institutional norm, but an autonomy based on an ability to reflect on one's own beliefs and values and to subject them to the scrutiny of the beliefs and values of others. The outcome is not an anarchical libertarian, but a mature person committed to recognising and affirming the rights, needs, worth and dignity of others. It is right, therefore, that religious education should be seen as making a major contribution to the spiritual, moral, social and cultural development of pupils.**(3)**

Field of Enquiry

A major feature of the Westhill Project was the attempt to map out the field of enquiry of religious education, to define the areas of content or information from which the subject matter for exploration and reflection in the classroom is to be drawn. This map is represented in the model reproduced on page 95 **(4)**.

This model shows that content may be drawn from three broad areas. 'Traditional Belief Systems' is a generic term for referring to the major religions of the world. Whilst the term is not wholly adequate, it does highlight certain features of the major religions for educational purposes. There is a focus on tradition, handed down over a long period of time and continuing to influence peoples' lives in a variety of ways. There is an emphasis on belief, not in an external or propositional form (though some religious beliefs are expressed and function in this way), but because beliefs and values are the focal points of educational exploration. They are systematic, not in the monolithic sense of clearly and separately definable entities, or static world views but certainly in the communitarian sense of providing a point of identity for those who follow their beliefs and belong to their groups.

The point of defining the great religions in this way is to draw attention to their *function* in religious education. It is impossible to represent the wholeness of the traditions in all their colour, diversity, history, culture and expression. The educational enterprise does, however, require the teacher to select those areas of exploration which focus on their *educational value*. In this case, for example, 'belief' is an important focal point because pupils in religious education are encouraged to explore, think about and reflect on the beliefs, values and world-views of others as a catalyst for their own development.

Interrelationships within the field of enquiry

Traditional belief systems   Shared human experience

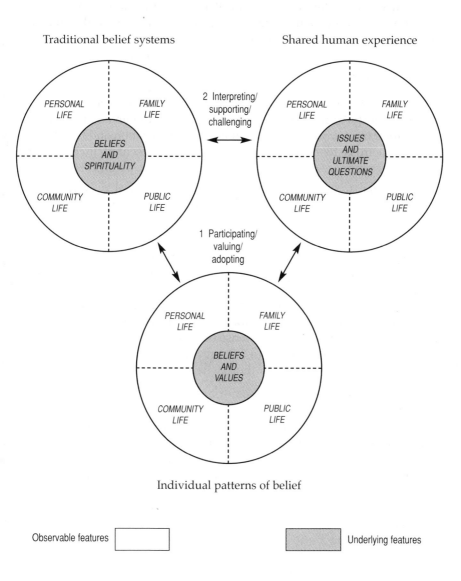

Individual patterns of belief

Observable features [ ]   Underlying features

A second element of the field of enquiry is referred to as 'shared human experience'. As the name implies, it refers to experiences of life which are common to all, or most, human beings simply because of their shared humanity. The value of these experiences for Religious Education is to be found in the issues and ultimate questions they raise. This element of the field of enquiry is not simply to do with any, common human experience, but with those experiences which have significance for people because they raise profound issues and questions about the human condition. Such experiences as the awareness of human limitations and the finite nature of life raise questions which can only be answered from the perspectives of believing and valuing. Such questions concern the purpose of life, its meaning and value, people's sense of identity, issues about personal and cosmic origins and destiny, and about the authority for belief. They may be summarised in the question, 'what does it mean to be human?' In practice the developers of the project concluded that there are a number of areas of human experience which have always tended to prompt ultimate questions, and which therefore provide appropriate areas of exploration for religious education. They are classified in the project as the natural world, relationships, rules and issues, stages of life, celebrations, lifestyles and suffering.

A third element of the field of enquiry is referred to as 'individual patterns of belief.' It refers to the experiences, beliefs and values that pupils (and teachers) bring with them into the classroom. These will, of course, tend to be as varied as the individuals who make up the class, whatever features and homogeneity they share in common.

There has been some debate about whether this third element really does constitute a different area of content from the other two. Those who support the view that individual patterns of belief are a distinctive part of the field of enquiry will argue that no individual is, or should be seen as, simply a microcosm of the sum of common shared human experience, since experience is so infinitely variable. Due weight must be given to individuality. Likewise, no child or teacher is ever going to be a clone of the traditions into which they are born or of the family customs with which they have been raised. Therefore, due emphasis should be given to content derived from the experiences, beliefs and values which the individuals bring to their learning. These are a focus of exploration and dialogue in the classroom, and constitute one of the elements with which all may engage as a vehicle for personal development. Others will take the view that such matters should be excluded from the classroom, because they constitute an infringement of privacy, or because 'individual patterns of belief' are either a teaching device for introducing the more esoteric experiences associated with the religions, or are simply part of the process of religious education, rather than a separate area of content. The project team's conclusion has tended to favour the first view, but to maintain that 'individual patterns of belief' are part of both the content and the process of religious education.

In the model, the outer circles represent the observable phenomena associated with each of the areas of exploration. In the case of the traditional belief systems, the outer circle represents the actions, words, symbols, stories and observances associated with the followers of that tradition. In shared human experience it represents the experiences associated with dramatic moments in life, the practical lens through which ultimate questions and issues are focused. In the case of individual patterns of belief, it represents the actions and observable behaviour of individuals, which provide a window into their world of beliefs and values. For the purposes of religious education, the model also suggests that teachers need to take account of four contexts for observing and defining appropriate content, namely the contexts of individual, family, community and public behaviour.

A further refinement represented in the model concerns the dynamic relationship that may be observed between the three areas. This dynamic relationship is itself an important part of the field of enquiry. There is firstly a dialogical relationship between the beliefs and spirituality associated with the traditions and the issues and ultimate questions which arise from shared human experience. It is not, as has often been suggested, that religious beliefs are simply the answers of particular communities to ultimate questions. Religious beliefs also have a function of raising questions about life. In this sense they often provide a heightened awareness and sharper focus for defining what the important questions about life really are. Likewise, ultimate questions themselves raise issues about religions, not least about the views which support conflicting claims to truth.

The inter-relationship of these two areas is therefore described in terms of interpretation, support and challenge. Interpretation is concerned with the way in which religious traditions and human experiences may be mutually illuminating and refining. Support refers to the psychological dimension of the relationship in confronting and dealing with critical experiences of life. Challenge describes the way in which everyday pragmatic solutions to life issues are confronted by the more holistic world views associated with the traditions, and in which such world views are themselves confronted by the realities of experience and the perceptions of non-religious outlooks.

At the same time there is a symbiotic relationship between individuals, in their own patterns of belief and behaviour, and the patterns of believing and valuing represented by the systems. There are varying degrees of relationship between the two. At one level the relationship may be purely participatory, in the sense that a person may participate in a general way in a particular culture without any conscious sense of commitment to it or to its values. At another level, people may value the cultural and religious norms within which they have been brought up, but still have only a rudimentary understanding of the traditions which underlie them. There will also be those whose commitment to and understanding of a tradition to which they belong provide the principal motivating force in their lives. In this case, the word 'adopting' indicates that they have made the tradition their own and are glad to demonstrate their commitment in overt ways. It still remains the case, however, that individuals continue to have their own perceptions and interpretations of their traditions and manifest these in their own lifestyles.

At the same time, individuals inevitably participate in shared human experience, though their perceptions of the questions and issues that are raised by their own experiences may be suppressed or sublimated by other experiences which enable them to put such questions to one side. Others are more aware that their own experience of life raises issues for them and for others, but they articulate their questions only at a pragmatic level. For many, however, profound, disturbing and far reaching questions are raised by involvement in the turmoil and uncertainty of life, and they feel a need both to ask and to find answers to these questions.

At this point, it is important to bear in mind that the concern is simply to describe and delineate the field of enquiry from which the content of religious education may be drawn. It is an attempt to describe what is, in terms of three sources of information and in terms of the dynamic relationship between them. The next stage of the project's rationale is concerned with the criteria for selecting content for religious education, and the process involved in teaching it.

Criteria for the selection of content

There are already within the aim of Religious Education and its field of enquiry some hints about criteria for the selection of content for exploration in the classroom. For example, the aim implies that there will be some balance between an exploration of traditional belief systems and an engagement with shared human experience. The mapping of the field of enquiry suggests that the study of the outward phenomena of both religious observance and human experience will be used as a means of exploring the beliefs, values, spirituality and questions and issues to which they relate. In other words the mapping of beliefs and questions, and the emphasis placed on them, provides a criterion for selecting those aspects of the observable phenomena which best exemplify or illustrate the beliefs and questions. Teachers are encouraged to identify and select for study those phenomena which will enable pupils to focus most clearly on their meaning, both for themselves and for those who give them meaning. In other words, this criterion for the selection of content is based on the perceived educational value of the material to the pupils, rather than on anything intrinsic to the material or to the place it occupies within the perceptions of particular religious communities.

A further criterion is suggested by the mapping of the dynamic relationships of the three areas of content set out in the model. The relationship itself is part of the content. Therefore, religious education should also help pupils to explore these relationships, and the process of religious education should provide them with opportunities to do so.

The second part of the teachers' manual *How do I teach RE?* (1992) sets out the next stage of the criteria for selecting content for religious education. This selection is based on defining the concepts, attitudes, skills and knowledge pupils will be encouraged to explore. The order of these four elements is important. The conceptual framework is first. Since the key concepts of religious education have an existential and empirical dimension, and are not merely attempts to delineate the world objectively and descriptively, they are closely linked with a range of attitudes which are regarded as a formative part of the educational process. Certain skills are needed, some generic to the educational process as a whole and others more particular, but not exclusive, to religious education, in order to facilitate the development of concepts and attitudes. Lastly, and arising out of the first three, appropriate content or information ('knowledge') for the classroom is chosen to provide a vehicle and means for learning.

Key concepts are listed in the manual under two categories, those relating to shared human experience and those relating to traditional belief systems. Under shared human experience, the concepts are divided into three categories, those relating respectively to ultimate questions, to particular examples of shared human experiences, and to generic aspects of the study of religion. So, for example, authority and identity fall in the first category, devotion and suffering in the second, and deity and symbolism in the third. With the traditional belief systems, the concepts are listed separately under each religion and set out the key ideas, beliefs and values associated with them.

General educational attitudes include such goals as having a sense of curiosity and respect for evidence; attitudes emphasised in religious education include developing a sense of mystery and fascination about the world, confidence in one's own sense of identity and willingness to value diversity of religion and culture in others. Skills, set out under the same educational headings, include the more general skills such as the ability to communicate clearly in writing and speech, and those skills more directly relevant to religious education, such as the ability to use periods of stillness or silence for reflection.

The reason for placing knowledge last in these four educational categories is to draw attention to the point that content or information or facts are selected from the field of enquiry in order to support the other three educational goals. Knowledge must be contextualised and its selection for teaching must be guided by its value in educational terms for exploring the field of enquiry.

Planning and process in religious education

The project sets out two sets of planning principles. The first principle deals with the issue of *progression* in religious education. This recognises that the way pupils learn is related to their ages, abilities and stages of development, even if the latter cannot be defined in quite the neat and tidy way sometimes envisaged by interpreters of Piagetian principles. The Brunerian model, with its focus on conceptual development helps the teacher to recognise that concepts may be taught to pupils at any age, provided that the structure of learning appropriate to that age has been understood, and that pupils are introduced to the concepts through appropriate examples and illustrations. The project therefore describes the kind of learning that is best suited to pupils at the different stages of their schooling and identifies the contexts within the field of enquiry which are best suited to the different age groups.

The second group of planning principles essentially draws together two approaches to teaching religious education. These are referred to as the 'systems approach' and the 'life themes approach'. The purpose of the systems approach is to help pupils to develop their understanding of what it means to be a follower of a particular religious tradition. The life themes approach gives pupils the opportunity to explore a particular issue or question about life. The two approaches are different only in the emphasis they give to the selection of content. The systems approach draws material from *one tradition only*, in order to build up a conceptual awareness of the key beliefs, values and world-views found within that tradition. The exploration will, however, also be contextualised within a framework of questions, issues and experiences which arise from the study of the material.

In the life themes approach, the emphasis shifts to the exploration of an aspect of shared human experience, but this exploration will also in turn be contextualised by reference to the teachings and practices of *at least two* different religious traditions (whether or not these are found within the same religious community). The traditions serve to illuminate the life theme by showing how people with different outlooks and world-views have understood the theme and addressed the questions and issues it raises. In one approach the emphasis is on building a framework of concepts related to beliefs and values, and in the other the focus is on developing an awareness of issues about life and the ultimate questions they raise. Thus it is possible for the same material from one aspect of the field of enquiry to be used in either approach, but the approach will determine how the material is used to aid learning.

The distinction between the two approaches serves other purposes as well as that of defining the process of religious education. On the one hand it provides a means of establishing *balance* within the religious education programme. It may be expected that a well-balanced programme across the ages and phases of schooling will show how the two approaches are given emphasis at different stages. In the project, the life themes approach is given more emphasis at Key Stages 1 and 4, and the systems approach at Key Stages 2 and 3. On the other hand, the two approaches enable the teacher to avoid some of the pitfalls of teaching the subject in a way which does not do justice to its inner dynamic and purpose, and which can lead to confusion on the part of the pupils. For example, teaching religious education through themes which purport to transcend different traditions, such as festivals, founders and holy books, *is representative of neither the life themes nor the systems approach, as defined above*. This kind of thematic planning and teaching tends to distort any possible understanding of what it means to be a believer in any one tradition, and it does nothing to illustrate how the theme may be related to issues about life and ultimate questions.

As part of the planning process, the project offers guidance on the identification of suitable topics for units of work across the age and ability range, as a way of exemplifying the pedagogical principles described above. It illustrates how material selected from the field of enquiry can be deployed at different stages for both the life themes and systems approaches. This is followed by a section on designing units of work, incorporating some of the project materials and examining the kind of objectives which are appropriate for religious education.

Attainments, learning outcomes and assessment

It was in the later stages of the development of the project that attention was given to a discussion of these issues, largely as a result of the Education Reform Act 1988, with its emphasis on attainment targets, programmes of study and assessment arrangements. These elements have all undergone profound changes in interpretation since they were first introduced, with the result that today the use and application of these terms is some way removed from the original intentions. Nonetheless it is entirely in keeping with the principles outlined in the project that religious education teachers should be clear about the key learning outcomes towards which they are working, the programme of study (content and process) which will contribute to those outcomes, incorporating the further principles of progression and continuity, and the means they will use to establish how far the outcomes have been achieved. These matters were dealt with in the second edition of the project manual, and in other publications related directly to these issues.**(5)**

The three attainment targets for religious education were defined as the acquisition of knowledge and understanding of religions, the development of awareness about experiences of life and the questions they raise, and the capacity to reflect on, respond to and express their own beliefs and values in relation to the knowledge, understanding and awareness they had developed. These targets were then related to the content and process of religious education described in the project as the basis of setting out programmes of study. The attainment targets also serve to describe the desired learning outcomes which can then be assessed in a variety of ways appropriate to the ages and abilities of the pupils.

The attainment targets are directly related to the three main areas of exploration set out in the model of the field of enquiry. The field of enquiry model, describing the content of religious education, then started to take on a more process oriented dimension, so that the three circles were related to the desired outcomes of the subject and were used to set out, in diagrammatic form, the interaction of content and process, as suggested in this later development of the model;

The RE Process

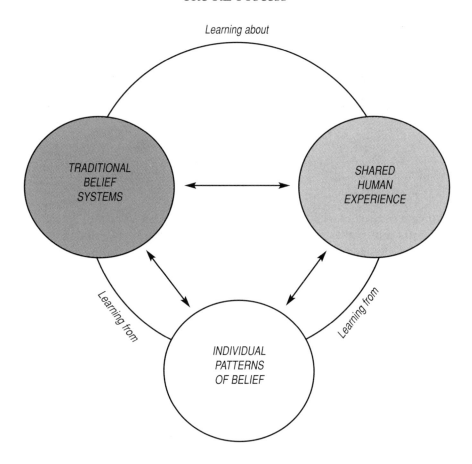

CRITICISMS

Like all projects of this kind, it is always best to see them as another contribution to the ongoing debate about religious education in the state sector, rather than as a definitive and final solution. In any case, one of the basic principles of curriculum development is that it moves on, and the contributors to the Westhill Project would be only to glad to think that they had made a modest contribution to that process.

Self evaluation and evaluation by others is an important factor in the developing process. This third section examines six areas of debate about the project and its methodology.

The first and over-riding criticism arises from the identification of the project with a human development model of religious education. The critique comes mainly from those who take the view that the aim of religious education is for pupils to acquire a knowledge and understanding of religions, in other words those who equate religious education with religious studies. The argument is that any attempt to define or to incorporate into a pedagogy the responses which pupils might make to the study of religion is fraught with difficulties and leads to indoctrination. Pupils will respond to religion however they see fit. It is not for the religious educator to attempt to structure those responses. The intention of the project has been to show how such a structure may be used in an open and critical way without infringing the autonomy of the child or the concerns of parents about indoctrination.

The critique of the developmental model also comes from some religious communities who are suspicious of the intentions of the religious educator in treating religion in an instrumental way, and in according parity of esteem to the different traditions, by implication undermining the authority of the community over children's lives, or at least the authority of the community's gatekeepers and guardians. This however is part of the price to be paid for any participation in an open and plural system of education. Moreover, communities have no reason to fear a form of education which is concerned to encourage pupils to clarify, value and own their family traditions, rather than simply to conform unreflectively with the community's norms.

A further development of this critique concerns the inclusion of ultimate questions within the framework of religious education, on the basis that shared human experience is not a separate area of content for the subject, but simply represents a pedagogical device for providing an entry into religious subject matter, which is seen as the real focus of study. This view is a direct challenge to the thinking behind the project, which views the interaction between issues and questions as a universal focus, and beliefs and values as a particular focus, as central to the rationale.(6) Ultimate questions, moreover, help pupils to focus on those matters which are relevant to any view of spirituality and spiritual development which has a universal framework, and which is therefore applicable to a concept of education for all. It is recognised that the form of the questions, the way they are phrased in each generation, even the priority which is given to some questions rather than others in particular environments, are all subject to variation, change and revision. The urge to ask the questions, and to suggest possible answers, is one of the great motivating forces for humanisation, and lies at the heart of the civilising arts such as music and literature.

A second area of debate concerns the usefulness of some of the terminology used in the project. On the whole, the project has sought terminology which will not carry with it some of the inferences from past debates. Thus references to categories such as 'implicit' and 'explicit' have been omitted, so as to avoid confusion with other conceptions of the subject. (7) The term 'life themes' has been used, and this has led to some confusion on the part of those who are familiar with the work of Ronald Goldman. On reflection, a term such as 'life issues' might have served the purpose of identifying one approach to teaching more clearly.

A further issue, which has exercised the project team throughout its development is whether the classroom materials and resources really do exemplify the pedagogical principles. The answer to this would appear to be, on the whole, positive. The best examples would be the early years life themes materials and the living questions materials for key stage 3. The photopacks, on the other hand, whilst providing good source material, were wholly focused in the accompanying descriptions on systematic understanding of religions. The same applies to a lesser degree to the pupil and teacher books relating to the traditional belief systems, which only offered token reference to links with shared human experience. A more profound question, along these lines, would be whether the project provides an adequate conceptual synthesis between shared human experience and traditional belief systems.

There is also an issue about whether the project's theory gives too structured an approach to the subject, when many teachers might prefer a more experiential and less cognitively dominated model. This is a fair challenge. At the same time the point needs to be made that, within an educational framework, it is essential to have clear structures for planning and teaching so that the subject stands up to professional educational scrutiny, and is not dismissed as academically invalid.

The issue of structure raises a further question about the accessibility of the structure for teachers under pressure in schools. The project team's experience is that where the materials have been used in in-service training and have been placed firmly within the project's theoretical and pedagogical framework, teachers have been able to see the potential for approaching religious education in the way suggested. On the other hand, anecdotal evidence clearly suggests that many teachers purchase the materials, particularly for example the photopacks, without any recourse to the educational framework.

Some teachers have questioned the wisdom of a project which provides only a methodology and resources, albeit with copious examples of how the materials can be incorporated into a valid and interesting programme of study, without linking the materials to particular classroom activities. It must be remembered that the project was generated at a time when much published material consisted of books with two-page spreads, information to read on one side, and questions and tasks, often limited to comprehension exercises, on the other, on the basis that this sort of material was best for non-specialist teachers who could simply give the books out and tell the pupils to get on with the work. The project was an attempt to cultivate an atmosphere of engagement and reflection on the part of the teacher as well as the pupil and, although sales were undoubtedly diminished by this approach, it is nonetheless still felt to be a worthwhile attempt. Most teachers who are committed to their subject would not approach it in any other way.

A final critique offered by some teachers is that the project – and, for that matter, religious education in general – does not give sufficient place to non-religious stances for living, because of the narrow way in which religions are perceived to be the object of exploration. What about those who wish to express their beliefs and values in non-systematic, non-traditional, non-religious ways? How does religious education cater for them, particularly when they constitute the overwhelming majority of the school population? The answer from the project's point of view lies with the 'shared human experience' and 'individual patterns of belief' areas in the field of enquiry and the life themes approach in the pedagogical process. Both enable those who in some way are not directly adherents of religions to explore issues, raise questions and express their own ideas and values. There cannot be, in religious education, a hidden agenda which is attempting to draw pupils into a religious net. It has to be a process of education, through religion, for all pupils, whatever their background.

CONCLUSION

It may be helpful to conclude this review of the Westhill Project, not by simply summarising what has already been said, or by arguing the case for its pedagogical excellence, but rather by suggesting a few of the questions which are still perceived by the project team to require answering, or at least debating, in any future developments.

The first is the question of who 'owns' religious education, and who is it for. We have recently gone through a period when ownership of the curriculum has passed from teachers to the religious communities. The focus has moved to the needs of those pupils from families directly linked to religious communities, and therefore to the avoidance of critical thinking about religion, and of controversial matters which might cause offence. How can we address the needs of the great majority of pupils for whom the religious world represents a different planet from the one they inhabit? An interesting way forward might be provided by the religious communities themselves, if they were prepared to divert their attention from those matters which separate them from others, requiring them to guard their separate and exclusive identity. They might then turn their attention to the question of what there is, in all their traditions, that might contribute to the spiritual and moral education of all pupils in school, whether or not they have a religious family background.

A further question that needs re-addressing is, what do we mean by religion? Not by 'religions' because that has been defined out of existence. Ninian Smart posed the question in an essay in 1977. He answered it partly, of course, by reference to his dimensional approach to the phenomenology of religions. But the other part of his answer indicated that we can only understand religion if we are clear about the distinction between a question about a religion and a religious question. Why do pilgrims go on a pilgrimage to Mecca? is a question about a religion. Why do people have to suffer? or What lies beyond death? are religious questions. **(8)** There is a tendency at present to use the terms interchangeably. What kind of questions is religious education really about? What we need to answer that question is a fresh and shared understanding of religion.

Finally, a question for teachers, and especially for training teachers. How can we avoid allowing our teaching to fall into mere factualism, the process by which religious education degenerates into the transmission of information about religions, because it is the easiest thing to do, it does not require us to think about why we are giving out this information, and it avoids controversy? It is the basis of a curriculum for no-one, with no educational purpose, going nowhere. On the other hand, to keep constantly before us the question of how our teaching might enrich pupils' lives and point them towards spiritual possibilities, suggests a worthwhile, relevant and vibrant pedagogy.

NOTES

1. Read, G., Rudge, J., Teece, G. & Howarth, R . (1992) *How do I teach RE?* (Cheltenham, Stanley Thornes) Second Edition, p. 2.

2. See, for example, Hirst, PH, (1974) *Knowledge and the Curriculum* (Routledge & Kegan Paul), and Phenix, P. (1964) Realms of meaning. (McGraw Hill)

3. This necessarily brief summary broadly reflects the thinking expressed in much greater detail and clarity in Grimmitt, MH, (1987) *Religious Education and Human Development* (McCrimmons), especially Chapters 3, 4 and 6.

4. Read, G. et al, op cit p. 24

5. Ibid, Part 5 pp 69-79 and Rudge, J. (1991) *Assessing, Recording and Reporting RE – A Handbook for Teachers* (Birmingham, Westhill RE Centre).

6. See, for example, the discussion in Bates, D. 'Developing RE in Topic Based Approaches to Learning' in Bastide, D (ed) (1992) *Good Practice in Primary RE* 4-11. (London, Falmer Press). He views the inclusion of ultimate questions as 'Already formulated religious 'answers'...going in search of questions...' (p. 116)

7. The avoidance of these terms is elaborated in Attfield, D., 'Implicit Religion' in *British Journal of Religious Education* (Autumn 1984) pp. 8-13

8. Smart, N. 'What is Religion?' in Smart, N. & Horder, D. (eds) (1975) *New Movements in Religious Education*, (Temple Smith).

The Westhill Project Publications

All publications listed are available only from Westhill RE Centre, University of Birmingham, Westhill, Selly Oak, Birmingham B29 6LL.

Publications marked † are currently out of print

Publications marked • are also available from Stanley Thornes Ltd., Publishers, Ellenborough House, Wellington Street, Cheltenham, Glos., GL50 1YW

Westhill Project Teacher's Manual

How do I Teach RE?, 3rd edition 1998

Materials on Christianity

Christianity Teacher's Manual, second edition 1995
Christians Photopack, second edition 1995
Black Churches, Black Traditions Photopack and booklet, first edition 1995

Christians pupil books

 † Book 1 (yrs 3-4)
 † Book 2 (yrs 5-6)
   Book 3 (yrs 7-9)
 † Book 4 (yrs 10-11)

Materials on Islam

Islam Teacher's Manual, second edition 1995
Muslims Photopack, second edition 1996

Muslims pupil books

Book 1 (yrs 3-4)
 Book 2 (yrs 5-6)
 † Book 3 (yrs 7-9)
 † Book 4 (yrs 10-11)

Materials on Judaism

Judaism Teacher's Manual, second edition 1999
Jews Photopack, second edition 1995

Jews pupil books

    † Book 1 (yrs 3-4)
    † Book 2 (yrs 5-6)
    † Book 3 (yrs 7-9)
    Book 4 (yrs 10-11)

Materials on Hinduism

Hindus Photopack and Teacher's booklet, first edition 1992

Materials on Sikhism

Sikhs Photopack and Teacher's booklet, yet to be published

Materials on Buddhism

Buddhists Photopack and Teacher's booklet, yet to be published

Materials on Life Themes

Life Themes in the Early Years 1990

    Three large format photopacks with Teacher's booklet
    †   Pack 1: The Natural world and Celebrations
       Pack 2: Relationships and Rules and Issues
       Pack 3: Stages of Life and Life Styles

Living Questions (Key Stage 3) 1993

    • *Living Questions*: Pupil book
    • *Living Questions*: Teachers book with photocopiable worksheets

Video

The Changing Face of Britain: A Guide to the customs, traditions and lifestyles of Britain's minority ethnic communities. Video and booklet: first edition 1993

Other curriculum materials

† *Attainment in RE: A Handbook for Teachers,* first edition 1989
Assessing, Recording and Reporting RE: A Handbook for Teachers,
first edition 1991

*How to Write your School Policy for RE: Religious Education and
Collective Worship in the Primary School,* first edition 1994

*How to Write your Scheme of Work for RE: Religious Education in the
Primary School,* first edition 1996

OTHER PUBLICATIONS

Rudge, J (1993) *RE and Spiritual Development,* Westhill Occasional
Paper 2, Westhill College.

Teece, G (1993) *In Defence of Theme Teaching in Religious Education,*
Westhill Occasional Paper 3, Westhill College.

Teece, G (1997) *'Why John Hick's Theory of Religions is Important for
RE'* in *Resource, The Journal of The Professional Council for RE,* Vol 20:1
Autumn

Teece, G (2000) *A Handbook for Primary RE,* Nash Pollock.

CHAPTER 6

RELIGION IN THE SERVICE OF THE CHILD PROJECT: THE GIFT APPROACH TO RELIGIOUS EDUCATION

John M. Hull

BACKGROUND

In the mid nineteen – eighties the religious education research group in the University of Birmingham School of Education became increasingly dissatisfied with the way religion was being taught to young children. The experiential method, so brilliantly introduced and advocated by Ronald Goldman twenty years earlier, had proposed teaching religious education through a series of life themes in which the daily experience of the child would be used to prepare children's understanding for more explicit religious material. (1) However, Goldman's concept of readiness for religion and his description of very young children as being pre-religious or sub-religious had discouraged teachers from presenting explicit religion. The result was that the first part of the life-themes was being presented without explicit religious content. (2) Themes such as the wonder of growing things, the five senses and families were taking the place of explicit religious education. Although such themes were valuable in sensitising children to spiritual values such as respect for life and wonder in the presence of the natural world, the team came to believe that this kind of teaching was in danger of becoming a flight from religion. It was felt that the view that young children were not capable of understanding religion was based very largely upon a misunderstanding of the nature of religion, which was more concrete than was often realised. (3) Moreover, children who thought in a concrete manner might nevertheless be capable of a great deal of worthwhile learning whilst still remaining in the concrete level. (4)

The main alternative to implicit religion or life-theme teaching in the primary school seemed to lie in the phenomenological approach. This also had a history of about twenty years, having been brilliantly promoted by Ninian Smart, and was perceived as being to some extent a reaction towards the teaching of explicit religion away from the implicit approach. **(5)** However, this approach was tending to become stereotyped in a series of methods which either taught religions more or less systematically one by one, or concentrated upon cross-religious topics such as festivals or places of worship. **(6)** The team was beginning to think that the systems approach, while being very necessary for secondary students, was too general and abstract for many younger children. When taught as a series of cross-religious topics, the phenomenological method often seemed to fail to engage the interest of children, and it was not always clear how the study of festivals or sacred books would contribute to the human and educational development of the child. **(7)**

These deficiencies were felt to be particularly acute in the training of primary teachers in religious education. When the religious studies or phenomenological approach was being used by the teacher-trainers, the emphasis was too frequently on the religious content and students were often left with little guidance about teaching method. Indeed, the team felt that religious education as a whole was suffering from a preponderance of curriculum over method. The agreed syllabuses, for example, were required by law to prescribe content not method. Faced with large classes of primary student teachers, many of whom knew little or nothing about religion, lecturers often felt that imparting knowledge about the content of religion together with lists of resources and teaching aids was sufficient. On the other hand, when the life-theme approach was recommended, students were often left feeling that the religious element was lacking.

Too often teachers in primary schools seemed to be caught between the approach which advised them to plant bulbs or keep guinea-pigs and the approach that told them to visit a mosque and teach their children the four noble truths, the five Ks, the six days of creation, the seven sacraments and the eight-fold path. It was time to re-image primary school religious education.

FIRST STEPS

In 1984 a seminar on teaching religion to young children was commenced. This consisted of approximately thirty lecturers, local and national inspectors, and primary heads and classroom teachers. The approach was exploratory. Visiting specialists in teaching mathematics, art and English to young children explained their views, and the seminar discussed the possibility of adapting the concepts and approaches to the teaching of religion. New approaches to the teaching of religious education in secondary schools were explored for their relevance to younger children. An example was the new work on core values and human development being developed by Michael Grimmitt. **(8)**

After about eighteen months of such work, we decided that we were ready to launch a more intensive enquiry. A number of charitable trusts showed an interest **(9)** and in September of 1987 two experienced primary school teachers were appointed to the staff of the University of Birmingham School of Education. **(10)** The project was given the title Religious Education in the Early Years. Primary school teachers from seven local education authorities in the West Midlands were invited to join the project team, and there were nearly two years of detailed classroom experimentation. By the end of this period the main outlines of a new approach had been created. The relationship between the learner and the subject was reversed. Whereas most approaches to religious education suggested that the purpose of religious education was to enhance the children's understanding of religion, the team now felt that the purpose of religious education was to make a contribution to the human and educational development of the child. **(11)** Of course, this could not take place without knowledge and understanding of religion, but this was now conceived of as an end to a means. The end was the development of the child; the means was the study of religion. Religion was instrumentalised to religious education, and religious education was instrumentalised in the interests of children.

This was the thinking which lay behind the change in the title of the project when its second stage was launched in September 1989. It was now called the Religion in the Service of the Child Project and this occupied three years. The main task of the team during these three years was to turn the strategy which had been formulated into a publication. This involved the testing and the evaluation of the materials in the classroom. Another purpose of the Religion in the Service of the Child Project was to develop a process of teacher-training based upon the new method. (12) In addition, it was proposed to study the impact of the method upon specific children, whose progress and development were to be monitored by their classroom teachers over a two year period. (13) The project materials were published in July 1991 by Simon & Schuster Education under the title *A Gift to the Child: Religious Education in the Primary School*. The package consists of a teachers' book, fourteen pupil books and an audio cassette. (14)

THE MAIN FEATURES OF THE GIFT TO THE CHILD APPROACH TO RE

A specific religious item is selected for study by the children. This may be a picture, artefact, selection from a sacred text, a sound (such as the sound of the Shofar or the ringing of cathedral bells), a story, a picture or a person and so on. The item selected must have an authentic and semi-independent life within a religious community, and must indicate something of the beauty of holiness within that religion. We distinguish between such authentic religious items and teaching aids. It would not be appropriate to select a video, a transparency, a photograph or a poster, since these are educational aids which provide information about the religion but do not constitute religious items in themselves. The item must obviously be small enough to be taken out of its original religious context and presented in the classroom. Thus a religious picture, a stained-glass window or a ten foot statue could not be studied by this method. In saying that the item must have an independent life within the devotional life of the religion, we might take the 23rd Psalm which begins "The Lord is my Shepherd". It would be the Psalm as a whole which would be chosen, rather than, let us say, the first verse. The first verse contains a metaphor about God, who is described as being like a shepherd, but that single metaphor does not function independently within Christian communities. The Psalm as a whole, however, is the subject of many hymns, meditation and anecdotes, and is treasured and loved in its own right.

The chosen item must appeal to one or more of the senses of the children. It must be concrete in the sense that it must provide something to look at or to listen to or to touch and so on.

At first these were described as pieces of 'religious stuff' since we were unable to think of a better term. Later in the project, we began to describe the religious items as *numena*, a term which we derived from the work of Rudolph Otto. Originally a numen was a spirit or sacred presence characteristic of a dedicated place or shrine, and in the vocabulary of the project it came to mean a religious element charged with the sacred beauty of faith and thus offering to the child something of the numinous. **(15)** This indicates the desire of the project team to emphasise the specific religious content of religious education and to present religious material directly and immediately to the children. These considerations might be called the *phenomenological criteria* for the selection of the material to be used.

A second criterion in the selection of the material – the *experiential criteria* – had to do with the *response* of the children. This brings us to the concept of *the gift*. Religion offers itself through religious education as a gift to the child. When a numen has been selected for possible classroom use, the next stage in the preparation by the teacher is to ask of the numen what its gift to the children might be. The team found that this was not always easy to predict. Sometimes a numen, although charged with beauty and significance for the members of the team, did not provoke a response from the children. At other times, following the rather tentative selection of a numen, the team were taken aback at the enthusiasm of the children's response.

Early in our work we selected the famous devotional painting by Holman Hunt (1827-1910) entitled "The Light of the World". This picture is frequently found in Sunday school classrooms, or in the children's devotional corner of a church. In the form of a post-card, or a bookmark, many Protestant adults have treasured this picture, which shows Jesus carrying a lighted lantern standing before a door which is tightly closed, has no latch and over which weeds and creepers have grown. The scene is depicted at night, and one can see the dark mysterious orchard or forest through which the Christ has come, and the lantern-light reveals his pale, intense face and his hair, with the crown of thorns. The idea of the allegory is that the door of the human heart can only be opened from the inside.

The children failed to respond to this picture, partly because the younger ones found it rather frightening, but mainly because all the children had been told by their parents not to open the door at night to strangers. There was thus no cultural rapport between the children and the picture. This particular item had passed the *phenomenological* test but failed the *experiential* test.

The two-fold criteria for the selection of numena led to a situation which we began to describe as *boot-strapping*. The teaching process was unpredictable, and preparation could never be more than experimental. The selection of the material by the teacher had to be verified by the responses of the children, and through repeated trial and error the phenomenological and experiential would gradually converge.

The need to ask about the nature of the gift which a numen might offer to children created an educational discipline for the team. Somebody might suggest what appeared to be an excellent numen, but what exactly was the nature of its gift? In the case of Ganesha, the four-armed, elephant-headed deity of South-Asian, Hindu devotion presented a fairly straightforward answer. Ganesha was his own gift; he himself was the gift. **(16)** However, in the case of the cross, the answer seemed to be less clear. Was the crucifix itself the gift? Or would it be better to select an empty cross rather than a crucifix? Would this change the nature of the gift? Was the gift the doctrine of the atonement, or was it simply the story of the crucifixion?

The demand to predict the gift or gifts which the material might offer placed members of the team under a theological demand. Would the gift be presented only to the children, or was there a gift for us teachers as well? We learned to sit before the numen, often quietly, seeking to open our hearts to the significance of the material. Our Lady of Lourdes seemed to assure us through the visions offered to Bernadette that there would always be hope in this dark world. The story of Jonah, chosen on phenomenological grounds because it appeared in the sacred literature of all three of the Abrahamic religions, seemed to tell us as adults that our calling to be teachers would not be taken away even in spite of our disobedience and our distractions. However, the gift which the numen might offer to us as adults might not necessarily be the same as that offered to the children, and indeed there often seemed to be developmental factors at work. Bernadette of Lourdes (1844-1879), herself a young teenager when she had her visions, seemed particularly moving for girls and sometimes for boys aged eleven plus, but often seemed less appealing to younger children.

THE GRID OF GIFTS

A gift was conceived of as an *expectation*, a possible benefit which children might derive from encounter with this material. The expectation was based upon the experience of the teachers and children who had worked with the material. It was at this point that our approach to religious education as contributing to the development of the children rather than as being mainly concerned with teaching for an understanding of religion became crucial. The gifts which religion itself offers to both young and old are gifts of meaning and purpose, of blessedness, of faith and salvation. However, these blessings might be conceived differently in various religions. We in the team were not priests, ministers or evangelists, not even catechists or instructors in the religious sense, but educators working in multi-faith classrooms within the context of secular education, offering our teaching as a compulsory part of the curriculum. The question for us was thus not only what gifts religion might offer, but what gifts religious education might offer.

Working with the project helped all of us to be more open to the myths and symbols of religion. It was at this point that Thoth, the ibis-headed deity of ancient Egypt, offered us a gift. This was the realisation that the gifts which Thoth offered to the ancient Egyptians were not confined to religion. Thoth was the giver of writing, of astronomy and medicine. So it was that we came to realise that the gifts of religious education were not necessarily of a religious nature. The numen might offer gifts of vocabulary, an arousal of curiosity, a stimulation to the asking of questions, an enrichment or a challenge to identity, a more critical sense of values, and an ability to empathise with others.

Gathering in the experience of the team in the classroom, we listed the kinds of questions and reactions of the children to each of the numena, and presented them in a chart entitled "The Grid of Gifts". **(17)** It was around the expectation of such educational outcomes that the strategy of the teacher would be directed. Of course, the items in the grid were always open to revision as the boot-strapping experience continued week by week with different children and with different material.

There still remained the question of religion. Even when mediated through a secular religious education, the numen might offer gifts to children which were of a religious nature. It would be strange, we thought, if the gifts of religion were all secular, and we remembered that Thoth also gave the Egyptians worship and sacrifice, mythology and ritual. How could this be done, however, in a multi-faith classroom?

The numen might give a gift of *belief*. Faith itself or the strengthening of faith might be the gift. At this point, and only at this point, the grid of gifts distinguishes between the gift of belief or faith offered to the believing child, and that offered to the unbelieving child. The believing child is the child who is identified with the religion from which the numen is taken. The unbelieving children are the other children, regardless of whether they may have some other religious faith or not.

Thus, it would be strange indeed when the Song of Guru Nanak was being studied if a very special gift of encouragement and affirmation were not given to the Sikh child. Early in our work, we had a vivid experience of this when a group of Hindu children from Bangladesh reacted with beautiful smiles and cries of joy when the covering was taken off Ganesha. "Gumpity-Dada!" they cried, "That's our God!" We discovered that Ganesha was known as Gumpity-Dada in the villages of Bangladesh from which these children came. Was this not a teaching which conveyed a real sense of faith being affirmed for these children?

However, every child, whether from a religious family or not, could receive some gift of faith or belief from the numen. The Sikh child would be strengthened in faith through approaching the Song of Guru Nanak but the other children could come to believe that they also had a calling to sing their own songs to the world, and a confidence in believing that although, like Nanak, they might find times in their lives when they appeared to sink in a deep river, they would return with their lives refreshed and made stronger. (18) So we distinguished between *religious gifts* for the specifically religious, and *secular gifts* for the others.

It must be emphasised that even in this strong form of religious education in which children are confronted directly by a religious item of content, there are gifts to be gained by secular children. After all, the great majority of our children come from families where there is little or no religious affiliation. Thus if a numen offered a gift of identity to the believing children, the identities of all the children would be clarified and strengthened. A Muslim child would learn that he or she belonged to Allah while a Christian child would learn that he or she belonged to God through Jesus Christ. We were delighted and encouraged by the children from secular families who announced in response to the question "Who do you belong to?" that they belonged to their parents or to the school, or to their country. We accepted with good humour the responses of children who told us that they belonged to the local football team, and we were delighted with the child who proudly announced, "I belong to me".

CLOSENESS AND DISTANCE

The problem of teaching children from many religious traditions and from none, and doing this in a secular classroom, in such a way as to be genuinely educational, had to be tackled head-on. We could not evade this challenge by allowing the religious material to more or less disappear, as had happened so often in the life-themes approach, nor could we allow the religious material to become distant, abstract and merely anthropological,

119

as sometimes seemed to happen in the systems approach. How could religion be presented directly, appealing powerfully to the imagination and the emotions, and yet remain truly educational, and offering educational benefits to all?

In our exploration of this problem, we began to conceive of religious education as operating under two requirements. These were conceived of as being children's rights. First, children had a right to be drawn close to the mystery and beauty of religion. Secondly, children had a right not to be drawn too close. **(19)** When translated into the dynamics of the teaching process, this seemed to require two stages in the lesson, or series of lessons. First, the children would be brought near. Next, the children would be placed at a distance.

In order to highlight the shift in consciousness, or the different attitude implied by closeness followed by distance, the team created a number of simple techniques, called respectively 'entering devices' and 'distancing devices'. After an entering device, the typical method would include the telling of a story, listening to music, participating in a guided fantasy, all of which invited the child to identify imaginatively and emotionally with the numen. The entering device itself might consist of the holding of a story-ring. This was a simple bamboo ring or hoop covered with silver paper, which half a dozen children sitting around a table would be asked to hold. The teacher would also hold the story-ring, and the story itself would come up, as it were, out of the ring. With a larger group of children, the same effect could be obtained by inviting the children to sit on a round story-carpet. Entering devices might also be the lighting of a candle, the sounding of a single bell, the dramatic striking of a hammer several times upon a piece of wood, or simply the children closing their eyes and resting on their desks. At the end of the period of closeness, the entering device would again be used, indicating to the children that the period of fantasy, or heightened involvement, had come to an end. In these concepts, we were influenced by the ideas of Alfred Schutz about the finite zones of consciousness **(20)**.

However, having brought the children in, we now must thrust them out, in order to ensure that the educational requirements of the multi-faith classroom in the state school are fully met. This was where the distancing devices were used, and the methods which followed them were more descriptive, objective or phenomenological. When Ganesha had been introduced to children through his statue, the story-ring would be held in order to help the children listen to stories about Ganesha. The next time the children come into the classroom, however, they do not find an intimate, approachable Ganesha sitting in the middle of the classroom. Instead, they stop abruptly, because now Ganesha is on a table in a far corner of the room. He is under a beautiful canopy which is lit with fairy lights. On either side are lamps, and in front of him are dishes containing rose petals and pieces of apple. Today, Ganesha is very special. The children run towards the shrine, but are stopped by the teacher who says "Stop! You must not come too close!" About three metres from the shrine are two rows of chairs. The children are told to sit on these chairs, or to stand behind them. They are not to take off their shoes because they are not on holy ground. Ganesha is holy but they are not sitting with Ganesha today.

At this point, the teacher produces a second distancing device, of which the project has made considerable use. This consists of a little book of coloured photographs, in which the devotion of a believing child towards Ganesha is depicted. The child is called Kedar. This is what Kedar does, because he belongs to Ganesha. With his parents, he lights the lamps, and sprinkles the rose petals over Ganesha. "No", the teacher would say to the children. "You cannot sprinkle the rose petals because you do not belong to Ganesha. You must stay in your seat". Then Kedar does this and that, and so the teacher takes the children through the steps of the Ganesha Puja. When this is finished, the fairy lights are turned out, a cloth is placed over the shrine, and the children return to their normal seats.

Some teachers felt that this contrast between intimacy and distance was rather abrupt, and might place the children under some kind of strain. The overwhelming impression of the team, however, was that the children responded with sympathy and understanding to the different kinds of situation. There is a holiness about religion which everyone can experience, but there is a deeper holiness which only the faithful know. Moreover, there is no doubt that this method secures the identity of the children. Although the critics of inter-faith education are fond of claiming that multi-faith means no faith, and that the teaching of several religions simply confuses children, our team has found exactly the opposite. We have found that children that pass through the gift approach are clearer about their religious identity, and more understanding and even loving towards the religious identity or the secular lives of others.

After a lesson about Ganesha, a little Muslim boy of four years old asked us if he could have a Ganesha to take home. Somewhat at a loss for an appropriate reply, one of our team suggested that the child should first go home and ask his parents to whom he belonged. If the parents said that he belonged to Ganesha, well and good. The next day the child returned beaming with pleasure "My dad and mum say that I belong to Allah and to the mosque". "So you don't belong to Ganesha?" "No, but I still love him". Love for others combined with a strengthening of family religious identity: are these not precious gifts which religious education can bestow upon secular and multi-faith communities?

THE PEDAGOGICAL STRATEGIES OF THE GIFT APPROACH

Gradually, the procedures and experiments which the team passed through resulted in a specific teaching strategy. **(21)** This consists of four steps in the lesson. Sometimes all four steps might be present in one short lesson, lasting no longer than twenty minutes. At other times, a lesson might consist of the first two steps, while steps three and four might take place in a subsequent lesson. Other teachers found that the four steps could be thought of as four perspectives which might be adopted at different points in the dynamic of teaching, but might not necessarily be sharply distinguished, following one after the other. Nevertheless, most of the team found that the steps suggested a natural process of learning. The steps are: (1) Engagement, (2) Exploration, (3) Contextualisation and (4) Reflection.

1. Engagement

By now the team had abandoned the idea that a long, experiential introduction was necessary before religious content could be presented. We had discovered that religious material spoke for itself directly to the children. Nevertheless, it was necessary to start somewhere. The engagement period refers to the opening moments when the attention of the children is attracted to the numen. This might consist of asking children to guess what was under a beautiful black velvet cloth as it was slowly lifted. Nursery children, about to be offered the story of Jonah, might play with a plastic bath with toy fish for a few minutes. The length and character of the engagement period usually depended upon the degree to which the numen might be unfamiliar to the children, or might come out of a very different cultural context.

2. Exploration

This is the time when the children are encouraged to approach the numen, to observe it, to listen to it or whatever. It is during this period that the children come close to the material through the entering device.

3. Contextualisation

The children pass through the first two stages without necessarily realising that the material comes from a religious tradition. They study Ganesha but are not told a word about Hinduism. They learn about Bernadette of Lourdes without hearing a word about Christianity, let alone Roman Catholicism. In the contextualisation stage, the numen is placed back into the context of the community or tradition which venerates it. Now we learn about Aideen, who worships in the Church of our Lady of Lourdes, lights a candle before her, and still in her wheelchair travels on pilgrimage to Lourdes. (22)

4. Reflection

This is the time when the gifts are made articulate. Bilal was the first Muslim to shout out aloud, calling people to prayer. (23) What would you shout out to everyone if you could get up on a high place with a microphone? Jonah was called to Nineveh. What do you think you might be called to do one day? What are you being called to do today?

ANSWERING SOME QUESTIONS

Finally, I will indicate some of the questions or objections which are sometimes put to the team.

What place does the religious community have in selecting the material?

Although the project had an advisory panel, consisting of representatives from various religions, they were not asked to participate in the selection of the material. Their role was to verify and, if necessary, to correct. The material was chosen by the teachers and the children through exploration and experiment.

Is it not a distortion of the religious material to take it out of its natural habitat and isolate it in the classroom?

It is true that there is a distance between the educational context and the religious context. This is an enduring tension in all forms of public or state religious education. We believe, however, that there are considerable educational benefits to be gained when educational requirements take precedence over the preferences and self-understanding of the religious communities. **(24)**

How can a piece of religious material, what you call a numen, convey the beauty and holiness of religion in itself? Surely the meaning of the material is always conveyed by the believers in context, and to take it out of the context is to turn it into a kind of fetish.

This is certainly a danger, but we do insist that teachers using this method should study the background and meaning of the numen. This is why in the Teachers' Book, each chapter opens with the question "What is …?" or "Who is …?" and the next section is called "Why teach so and so?" The teacher must be equipped with a full and confident knowledge of the material. Moreover, in the contextualisation stage the material is quite firmly put back into its religious context.

Would not the handful of items which your project cover make a rather strange kind of curriculum? **(25)**

This question reveals a misunderstanding of our project. We are not a curriculum project and have almost nothing to say about a religious education syllabus. We are a methodological project. We suggest how to teach, and the material on what to teach is only provided by way of necessary illustration. We believe that a good deal of what most syllabuses suggest, but certainly not everything, could benefit by being taught through our method.

You have been critical of teaching through life-themes and through religious systems. Do you believe that these other methods should be used?

The criticisms which we offer of these other methods merely indicate that every method has its strengths and weaknesses. We do not believe that it would be appropriate to teach religious education using nothing but the Gift to the Child approach. Our view is that the good teacher should have a repertoire of methods, and here our approach has something to offer.

Is the Gift to the Child approach appropriate in the Secondary School?

The approach has been used in Years Seven and Eight, but older pupils need the wider perspective which the systems approach or the cross-religious topics approach offers.

You admit then that the Gift to the Child approach lacks cognitive perspective?

This is one of the weaknesses of our method. You can study an ocean by examining charts of the oceans of the world, or you can go sailing. Our method is to take a bucket of water from the ocean and begin by plunging the hands of the child in the bucket, before throwing the water back into the sea. It is impossible to gain this immediacy without some lack of perspective, but to restore perspective is the task of the curriculum, and cannot be required of this method.

Is not the Gift approach very demanding upon the teacher?

Yes and no. It is necessary for the teacher to study both the method and the selected numen very closely indeed, but, on the other hand, the Teachers' Book offers a whole series of carefully scripted lessons, which the teacher can follow like a manual. Moreover, by studying one or two numen, it is possible for any teacher to start giving religious education lessons almost immediately, without having to know a great deal about several world religions.

Is the method appropriate for the training of RE teachers?

It is particularly appropriate in the training of the primary school teacher, who is ordinarily not a religious education specialist.

Instead of devoting the limited time available to questions such as the nature of religion, the philosophy of religious education and so on, it is possible by means of this method to launch Primary school student teachers immediately into the task. A student teacher who has gained confidence with six or eight numen has sufficient material to teach religious education for a whole term, if not for a whole year. Moreover, teachers can be trained to make their own selections of new material.

What is the greatest strength of the Gift approach?

The strength of the approach **(26)** is its transforming impact upon teachers. Often baffled by the complexities of religion, and nervous about the inadequacies of their knowledge, primary school teachers find in this approach a practical way of making religious education come alive for themselves and for their children. In this way, the Gift approach is not only a gift to the child; it is also a gift to the teacher.

NOTES

1. Goldman, R. (1965) *Readiness For Religion* (London, Routledge and Kegan Paul).

2. See Hull, J.M. (1984) 'The Theology of Themes', 'Theme Teaching as a Method of Religious Education' and 'History, Experience and Theme in Religious Education' in *Studies in Religion and Education* (London, Falmer Press) pp. 135-162. Also Bates, D. (1992) 'Developing RE in Topic-based Approaches to Learning' in Bastide, D (Ed.) (1992) *Good Practice in Primary Religious Education* 4-11 (London, Falmer Press), pp. 101-130.

3. Hull, J.M. (1998) 'The Religious Education of the Young Child' in *Utopian Whispers, Religious and Spiritual Values in Schools* (Norwich, Religious and Moral Education Press), pp. 70-73. For an alternative view see Bastide, D (1980) 'Religious Education and the Trainee First School Teacher', *British Journal of Religious Education*, vol.3, no.1, Autumn 1980, pp. 5-8.

4. Hull, J.M. (1991) *God-Talk with Young Children: Notes for Parents and Teachers* (CEM, Derby 1991 ISBN 1-85100-024-0) and American edition, Philadelphia, Trinity Press International 1991 ISBN 1-56338-028-5.

5. Smart, N. (1968) *Secular Education and the Logic of Religion* (London, Faber and

Faber) and Schools Council Working Paper 36, (1971) *Religious Education in Secondary Schools* (London, Methuen).

6. Robert Jackson offers a searching critique of the phenomenological method in Jackson, R (1997) *Religious Education: an Interpretative Approach* (London, Hodder and Stoughton).

7. Grimmitt, M.H. (1987) *Religious Education and Human Development* (Great Wakering, McCrimmons 1987) pp. 40-46.

8. Grimmitt, M.H. (1987) Ibid.

9. The principal grants were provided by the Saint Peter's College Saltley Trust, the British and Foreign School Society and the All Saints Education Trust.

10. Julie Grove, who remained with the REEY Project and its successor, the RISC Project, for the whole of their duration, and Kathryn Raban, (now Nettleton) who remained with the Project for one year. In the Summer Term of 1988 Louise Spencer (now Tellam) joined the Project as a teacher seconded by the East Sussex LEA and remained until the end of the second project. In September 1988, Sandra Walton joined the Project team for one year, on secondment from the City of Birmingham LEA , Both projects were jointly directed by Dr Michael Grimmitt and myself.

11. J. Grove, 'Religious Education: A Reformation for the 1990's' *Education 3-13* vol.19, no.3, Oct. 1991, pp. 20-25.

12. Tall, G and Grove, J. 1993. 'A Study of the Effectiveness of the Religious Education in Early Years Project In-Service course' *Panorama: International Journal of Comparative Religious Education and Values* vol.5, no.1, 1993, pp.101-115.

13. Comments from many of the children were included in *A Gift to the Child: Teachers' Source Book* under the section headings "Why teach..."

14. Michael Grimmitt, Julie Grove, John Hull and Louise Spencer, *A Gift to the Child: Religious Education in the Primary School*

Teachers' Source Book	£20.50	ISBN 0-7487-5794-5
Set of 14 Pupils' Books	£39.00	ISBN 0-7501-0129-6
Cassette Tape	£12.34 inc.VAT	ISBN 0-7487-2394-3
Complete Set	£71.84 inc.VAT	ISBN 0-7487-2699-3

Details of Pupils' Book (in pairs):

The Story of Bernadette
Aideen's Book

A Story of Ganesha
Kedar's Book

The Story of Nanak's Song
Sabjit's Book

The Story of Bilal
Yaseen's Book

The Story of God's Words to Muhammad
The Angels' Book

The Story of Jonah
Rebecca's Book

A Story of Hallelujah
Natalie's Book

All the Project's materials are available from: Customer Services, Stanley Thornes Ltd., Ellenborough House, Wellington Street, Cheltenham, Glos., GL50 1YW, Tel: 01242 267280, Fax: 01242 267695.

The above documents represent the final report of the project. See also *Religion in the Service of the Child Interim Report September 1989-July 1991* (Birmingham, School of Education, University of Birmingham) 1991.

15. We were influenced by the work of Rudolph Otto who introduced the concept of the numinous in his *The Idea of the Holy* (1923) (London, O.U.P).

16. The point is that in Christian devotion the cross is a symbol whereas in Hindu devotion Ganesha is a deity. Of course, he is not without ambiguity, and in a more detailed specification of this gifts it would be necessary to distinguish his various aspects.

17. Grimmitt, M.H. et al (1991) *A Gift to the Child* pp. 124-5.

18. Grimmitt, M.H. et al, Ibid., pp. 44ff.

19. The United Nations Convention on the Rights of the Child refers both to the child's right to freedom of thought and to familiarisation with his or her religious heritage. See, Hull, J.M. (1998) *Utopian Whispers* p.59.

20. Schutz, A. & Luckmann, T. (1973) *The Structures of the Life-World* (Evanston, ILL., North Western University Press) pp. 21ff.

21. Grove, J. (1991) 'Religion in the Service of the Child: A New Strategy for Primary Religious Education', in *Planning RE in Schools* (Derby Christian Education Movement) pp. 32-34.

22. Grimmitt, M.H. et al (1991) *A Gift to the Child*, pp. 24f.

23. Grimmitt, M.H et al (1991) Ibid., p.68.

24. Grimmitt, M.H. (1991) 'The Use of Religious Phenomena in I have briefly discussed the similarities and differences between the Birmingham approach Schools: Some theoretical and practical considerations' *British Journal of Religious Education*, vol.13(2), Spring 1991, pp. 77-88.

25. The items dealt with are Our Lady of Lourdes, Ganesha, Nanak's Song, the Call to Prayer, Angels, Jonah and Hallelujah.

26. and that of the University of Warwick in my review of Robert Jackson (1997) *Religious Education: An Interpretive Approach* in *British Journal of Religious Education* vol.20, no.2, Spring 1998, pp. 125-128.

CHAPTER 7

THE WARWICK RELIGIOUS EDUCATION PROJECT:
THE INTERPRETIVE APPROACH TO RELIGIOUS EDUCATION

Robert Jackson

INTRODUCTION

The approach to religious education outlined in this chapter arose from three related strands of work. The first was a series of studies of individuals from a range of religious groups in Britain, with a concentration on studies of children and processes of transmitting religious culture. The second was a concern with issues of method in relation to practice and theory, which related both to the research studies in the field and to religious education. These studies opened up a critique of some of the ways in which religions have been portrayed and interpreted conventionally in the history of religions and in religious education. Questions derived from fieldwork, especially questions relating to the inner plurality of religions, to the personal yet group-tied nature of religious expression and to the relationship between the researcher and the object of study, led to a synthesis of experience based on ethnographic studies and theoretical perspectives from a number of disciplines and fields in the social sciences and humanities. Recent debates in social anthropological theory, religious studies and cultural theory, for example, were reviewed in relation to methodological and disciplinary issues both in ethnographic fieldwork and in religious education. Finally, an approach to religious education was developed (and continues to be developed) in the light of all this, partly through an experimental curriculum development project (the Warwick RE Project) and partly through on-going work in RE that draws on further field studies of various kinds and relevant theory. Work up to 1997 is reported in the book *Religious Education: An Interpretive Approach* (Jackson 1997a). Some further developments are mentioned in Jackson (1999b).

ORIGINS AND DEVELOPMENT

Ethnographic research on religions in Britain has been carried out at the University of Warwick since the 1970s (Jackson 1976). Research specifically on children began in the 1980s (e.g. Jackson and Nesbitt 1986; 1993) as part of the Religious Education and Community Project, based in the Department of Arts Education. This programme was incorporated into the Warwick Religions and Education Research Unit (WRERU) in 1994 and based in the newly formed Warwick Institute of Education.

The Warwick RE Project was the curriculum branch of a research project entitled 'Ethnography and Religious Education' funded by the Economic and Social Research Council. (1) This work itself grew out of earlier research studies at Warwick on the religious upbringing of children and young people (e.g. Jackson and Nesbitt 1993) and earlier curriculum studies (Jackson 1989; Jackson and Nesbitt 1990). In retrospect, it is important to point out at the outset that the main pedagogical methods and principles associated with the project are not inextricably bound up with ethnography; they are associated with theory from an eclectic range of sources in the humanities (e.g. philosophy and cultural history) and social sciences (e.g. anthropology and psychology), and with methodology from the social sciences that is influenced by hermeneutics. In a sense, the hermeneutical method is the most important element, and it could be applied pedagogically without doing ethnographic fieldwork.

As stated in the research proposal to the ESRC, the aims of 'Ethnography and Religious Education' were as follows:

1. To increase knowledge and understanding of the transmission of religious culture to children and young people within selected families of four religious traditions in Britain by use of ethnographic research methods.

2. To develop this research material for publication in article and book form and for use on an MA course for teachers of religious education.

3. To develop a theoretical framework for translating ethnographic source material from the project into material for use in religious education.

4. To develop and publish material for use by pupils studying religious education and by teachers of religious education, drawing on the project's theoretical work in religious education.

The first and second aims were fulfilled through a series of ethnographic studies of children from different religious backgrounds (see publications list) and through the design and implementation of an MA course in religious education. The MA, which draws on much of the Warwick research material and includes a training in community and school-related research relevant to religious education, was introduced in 1994. A distance learning variant of the MA and a related masters level postgraduate certificate course in religious education took their first students in 1998. Some MA students (Margaret Barratt, Dave Bennett, Simon Bennett, Sarah Davies, Sarah Edwards, Julia Ipgrave, Ursula McKenna, Jo Price and Elisabeth Wayne) became part of the project team or of WRERU in a wider context, and contributed to curriculum writing or to ethnographic research or both. Some visiting Fellows, allocated to Warwick as part of the Farmington Fellowship programmes, have also made contributions to WRERU's research and development work. The theoretical background to the project plus an account of wider possibilities for the approach (aim 3) were published as *Religious Education: An Interpretive Approach* (Jackson 1997a), while the fourth aim was achieved through the publication of the Warwick RE Project. Thus the curriculum project was only part of the wider work being done by the research and development team in the Warwick Religions and Education Research Unit. The curriculum project does not reflect the totality of the pedagogical thinking that can be derived from the team's work. More of this is to be found in various publications (e.g. Jackson 1997a), and the ideas are still being developed (e.g. Edwards 1999; Ipgrave 1999; Jackson 1999b).

KEY PEDAGOGICAL PRINCIPLES

The theoretical work developed during the ESRC study raises three key sets of issues (Jackson 1997a):

- issues of representation,

- issues of interpretation and

- issues of reflexivity

Representation

Using scholarly material from the history of the portrayal of religion and religions in the West, the approach deconstructs Western, post-

Enlightenment models of representing 'world religions' as schematic belief systems, whose essence can be expressed through a series of propositions or doctrinal statements (Said 1978, 1993; Smith 1978).

The approach is equally critical of simplistic representations of cultures and of the relationship between religion and culture. Recent debates in social anthropology and other social sciences are employed to advance more sophisticated models of the representation of cultures, cultural change and ethnicity (e.g. Barth 1981; Clifford 1988; Baumann 1996; Geertz 1973; Hylland Eriksen 1993; Said 1978). Cultures are seen as dynamic, internally contested and fuzzy edged, while individuals are seen as capable of contributing to the reshaping of culture through making personal syntheses which might draw from a range of cultural resources, including their own ancestral traditions.

The project develops a model for representing religious material which encourages an exploration of the relationship between individuals in the context of their religio-cultural groups (Tajfel 1981) and the wider religious tradition to which they relate. The tradition is seen as a tentative 'whole', but the contested nature of that whole is recognised: for example, different insiders (as well as different outsiders) might have varying understandings of the nature and scope of, say, the Christian or Hindu traditions. The model encourages a view of religions which acknowledges their complexity, internal diversity, and their varying interactions with culture. It especially emphasises the personal element in religions, seeing religion as part of lived human experience. However, the approach is not relativistic with regard to truth, acknowledging varying and often competing truth claims (Jackson 1997a, 122-6).

Interpretation

In developing a methodology for interpretation, the project rejected some of the assumptions of 'classical' phenomenology of religion as interpreted by some writers on religious education (see Sharpe 1975, for example), especially the view that it is possible to lay aside one's presuppositions and that the use of skills of empathy is unproblematic. The project's interpretive methodology has some features in common with Jacques Waardenburg's 'new style' phenomenology (Waardenburg 1978), but most closely relates to work in recent interpretive anthropology. Rather than asking learners to leave their presuppositions to one side, the method requires a comparison and contrast between the learner's concepts and conceptual schemes and those of the insider. The approach requires an oscillating movement between the learner's and the insider's concepts and experiences. Sensitivity on the part of the student is regarded as a prerequisite, with genuine empathy only being possible once the 'grammar' of the other's discourse has been assimilated.

The other aspect of this hermeneutical approach lies in *applying* the model of representation outlined above - moving backwards and forwards between individuals in the context of their groups and the wider religious tradition. The two elements overlap in practice.

There is a strong influence from the work of the American anthropologist Clifford Geertz (e.g. 1973, 1983), but there is criticism of some aspects of his work, especially his lack of involvement of insiders in the construction of texts and his sparing use of direct quotation from insiders. These points are seen as a manifestation of a more general lack of attention to issues of power in Geertz's ethnographic writing (Clifford 1988; Crapanzano 1986).

The interpretive methodology of the project was not just influenced by discussions of theory and methodology, but was informed by the project team's own experience of ethnographic fieldwork. Studies of children from a range of different religious backgrounds in Britain were used as a basis for methodological reflection and as a direct source of data for curriculum development (see publications list).

Reflexivity

There are a number of issues concerning reflexivity - the relationship between the experience of students and the experience of insiders whose way of life they are attempting to interpret. Here three aspects of reflexivity should be encouraged:

- the learner re-assessing her or his understanding of her or his own way of life (edification);

- making a constructive critique of the material studied at a distance;

- developing a running critique of the interpretive process.

All of these have implications for pedagogy. There needs to be an approach to teaching that encourages reflection and constructive criticism. Clearly, the more the teacher is aware of the religious and ideological backgrounds of students, the more sensitive and focused the teaching can be, whether it be through discussion or the setting of activities. The pedagogy for this approach to RE also requires methods that allow students to gain insight from their peers and to be able to examine different ideas of truth held within the classroom. The 'content' of RE is not simply data provided by the teacher, but includes the knowledge and experience of the participants and an interactive relationship between the two. The specialist religious education teacher working with children from diverse backgrounds needs the professional skill to manage learning that is dialectical. If teachers can have the right degree of sensitivity towards their students' own positions, as well as to the material studied, and can develop appropriate pedagogies, then a genuinely conversational form of RE can take place which can handle diversity.

Edification

One of the key aims of RE is concerned with helping pupils to reflect on their studies of ways of life that are different in some respects from their own. With regard to this, there are many examples in the anthropological literature in which ethnographers write about how their studies of others have prompted some form of re-assessment of their understanding of their *own* ways of life, or some insight into the human condition in general (e.g. Leach 1982, 127). Following the terminology of the American philosopher Richard Rorty, who also discusses how one's self-understanding might be deepened by studying other worldviews, I have called this form of learning 'edification' (Rorty 1980). This concept probably shows more similarities to than differences from Michael Grimmitt's idea of 'learning from' religion (Grimmitt 1987, 225; Jackson 1997a, 131-2).

This kind of reflective activity is not separable from the process of interpretation. The interpretive process might start from the insider's language and experience, then move to that of the student, and then oscillate between the two. Thus the activity of grasping another's way of life is inseparable in practice from that of pondering on the issues and questions raised by it. Such reflective activity is personal to the student. Teachers cannot delay the process of reflection to a later date, just as they cannot guarantee that it will happen. They can, however, enable it by providing structured opportunities for reflection. It also happens to be the case that making this type of connection often helps to motivate students to participate more fully in RE. As Harold Loukes found in the 1960s (Loukes 1961), and as Keijo Eriksson's recent research in Sweden has shown (Eriksson 2000), a religious education disconnected from pupils' own questions and concerns is very likely to fail to engage them. We need to encourage young people to articulate these concerns.

Whatever differences there might appear to be culturally or religiously between the student's way of life and the way of life being studied, there may also be points of contact, points of overlap and points in common. What might appear to be entirely different and 'other' at first glance can end up linking with one's own experience in such a way that new perspectives are created or unquestioned presuppositions are challenged. This seems to be an inevitable product of the interpretive process.

Edification need not only result from studying religions or cultures other than one's own. The study of *one's own* ancestral religion or culture can also give new insights in re-examining one's sense of religious identity, as the Jewish anthropologist Barbara Myerhoff has indicated in her study of elderly people in a Jewish community in the USA (Myerhoff 1978). These insights can be applied to religious education and there is the possibility for young people to study a number of religions, including the one of their own ancestry, examined at some stage through a new lens. Ethnographic source material, plus data from locally conducted studies, could provide a basis for this. Christianity, for example, might be seen from different personal and community perspectives and understood in new ways (e.g. Ashenden 1995; Jackson and Nesbitt 1992; Nesbitt 1993c).

Constructive Criticism

Part of the reflexive process is to be able to engage critically with that which is studied. The management of such critical work is an important pedagogical issue, especially in teaching situations that are strongly pluralistic. There is another role for criticism as an element of reflexivity. Just as researchers should spend time reflecting on the effectiveness and the ethics of the methods they have used, so a critique of the interpretive process used in RE should be part of its content. This methodological self-awareness can reveal issues of representation and can also generate creative ideas for improvement, in the presentation of material studied to others, for example (Jackson 1990).**(2)**

Pupils might change through taking part in the interpretive process. If this seems threatening to some parents, perhaps it is worth considering that children from any religious background have to face the juxtaposition of their 'home' way of life and those which constitute the pluralistic, predominantly secular and increasingly globalised society around them. Religious education can, at least, be a site for a structured exploration of some of the issues.

THE WARWICK RE PROJECT

This curriculum development project arose from our 1990-93 ESRC study, but grew from earlier work. Members of the team had already contributed to educational broadcasts or published books using the life experiences of children in Britain. Jackson had been using ethnographic sources for schools broadcasts on religions in Britain since 1975, and both Jackson and Nesbitt had been involved in using ethnographic material in curriculum texts (Jackson 1989; Jackson and Nesbitt 1990). The ESRC Project provided further structured ethnographic research, a new theoretical framework and a set of methods. **(3)**

Project team members had various roles, with some members taking on more than one (e.g. Margaret Barratt was both a curriculum developer, and contributed an ethnographic study). The Director's role consisted in supervising ethnographic research and curriculum development; contributing theoretical and methodological ideas; arranging meetings to provide an on-going review of progress; and contributing to the project's writing programme. The main role of the ethnographers was to conduct field studies and disseminate findings. Their additional role was to liaise with the Curriculum Development Co-ordinator (Judith Everington) and the curriculum developers; to provide them with fieldnotes, audio-taped interviews and slides; to introduce them to selected families in order to extend their involvement with the project; and to provide background briefing material for use by curriculum developers in writing books for pupils or teachers' resource books.

The Director introduced the curriculum developers to the project's methods and theory and dealt with relevant ethical areas such as confidentiality. The Curriculum Development Co-ordinator supervised curriculum development work, including liaising with all participants (Everington 1996a), being responsible for organising trials of material in schools (Everington 1996b), and contributing to the project's writing programme (Everington 1993a and b; Jackson, Barratt and Everington 1994).

The project team aimed to find ways to connect the experience of children in communities with the practice of RE in schools. Our ideas and materials *could* have been developed for in-service training of teachers or for use in initial training. However, we eventually settled for a curriculum project. It was never intended to cover all the main religious traditions in Britain, but only those on which members of the team were doing research. Nor did we have the resources to cover all key stages. Sadly, the publisher set too tight a deadline for the KS2 publications on Sikh and Jewish children to appear. The key goal was to *experiment* with applying some of the theoretical ideas and some of the ethnographic data from our studies in books for children and young people. The following account gives a brief summary of the content and pedagogical approach of the texts written for pupils at key stages 1-3.

Key Stage One

At key stage one, each children's book focuses on a single child from one religious group. The portrayals of two Christian girls, a Jewish boy, a Muslim girl and a Buddhist boy are based on studies conducted by members of WRERU. Each tells a story illustrating how children learn through participation in religious activities within the family (Barratt 1994a, b, c, d, e). There are two versions of each pupil text, one printed in the *Teacher's Resource Book* to be read by the teacher and used as a basis for discussion (Jackson, Barratt and Everington 1994), and a simpler text for pupils reproduced in the children's books. The interpretive process is also introduced in the materials in the *Teacher's Resource Book* which help children to relate concepts, feelings and attitudes encountered in the stories to their own language and experience. Actions, objects and technical terms identified from the pages of the story books are grouped together under general headings as 'key ideas'. These general concepts suggest areas where bridges can be made from pupils' experience of life to the experience of the children introduced in the story.

Reflexivity (at least the 'edification' element) at key stages one and two is introduced as follows:

> Bridging to and from pupils' concepts, feelings and attitudes and those of the characters in the stories not only helps children to

interpret an unfamiliar way of life. It also raises questions in relation to the pupils' own experience. The exploration of these is just as important a part of RE as learning about different faiths.

These explorations and discussions are not meant to question the child's home traditions, but are intended to broaden their horizons and to stimulate thought and reflection. The bridging discussions include some ideas for encouraging children to be more reflective and to make their own contributions spontaneously.

This reflective activity can contribute to children's spiritual, moral and cultural development as they explore their own ideas, emotions and attitudes, and recognise similarities and differences between their own experience and that of people in the stories. (Jackson, Barratt and Everington 1994, 6-7; Barratt and Price 1996b, 5)

Key Stage Two

At key stages two and three the focus is on several young people associated with various membership groups, and the emphasis changes to a portrayal of learning and reflection in groups associated with the family's religious practice. The subject matter relates mainly to 'formal nurture' (children being instructed in their tradition within the community and religious school).

Meeting Christians: Book One, aimed primarily at the lower end of KS2, introduces a girl with a United Reformed background, and a boy whose family belongs to the Salvation Army. The reader follows the girl through her activities in the Junior Church, the youth club and Brownies, while the boy is seen as a Junior Soldier, a member of the choir and a youth club member. Quotations from children and adults are interwoven with a descriptive narrative and original photographs (Barratt and Price 1996a). *The Teacher's Resource Book* provides background material, advice on planning and teaching, and charts showing ideas, feelings and attitudes related to the topics covered in the children's book. Ideas for using the experience of pupils as a starting point for interpreting the symbols and actions of the children portrayed in the texts are also suggested. Photocopiable activity sheets offer children supplementary information as well as setting interpretive tasks. Ideas for 'bridging discussion', linking ideas, feelings and attitudes of the young people in the children's book with those of pupils in class are also suggested. The discussions cover topics from the ethnographic source material for the books and include 'joining', 'learning', 'believing and worshipping', 'prayer and praise', 'the Bible', 'living as a Christian', 'sharing' and 'caring for others' (Barratt and Price 1996b).

In the book for older juniors, three young British Christians with different ethnic histories are introduced, from Roman Catholic, Baptist and Pentecostal family backgrounds (Everington 1996c). Readers encounter each young person taking part in activities within the family and in different parts of their church communities. The material is arranged under the headings 'learning', 'preparing', 'responsibilities' and 'traditions'. Again, extracts from interviews are combined with an author-narrated text, illustrated with photographs taken during fieldwork or supplied by the families. Links are made to other parts of the Christian tradition and the Teacher's Resource Book gives advice on method. It also provides information for pupils and activities using the project's interpretive methodology, moving between the language and experience of the children in the text and of the pupils in class (Everington 1996d).

Key Stage Three

The emphasis at key stage three, is on engaging with the comments and reflections of young people linked to various groups within the traditions. Each book features four British teenagers, two girls and two boys. *Christians* introduces young people with Church of England, Greek Orthodox, Quaker (Religious Society of Friends) and 'New' Church backgrounds (Robson 1995). *Muslims* focuses on young Muslims with a Pakistani family ancestry (Mercier 1996). *Hindus* introduces young people whose lives relate to various aspects of Hindu tradition and whose family background is Gujarati (Wayne *et al* 1996). Each book gives general information about the young people and their interests, but concentrates on aspects of their religious life. Extracts from interviews with them and photographs taken during fieldwork are included. The books cover wide-ranging topics related to religious practice in contemporary Britain, all suggested by the material collected during fieldwork.

Students are given various activities related to each unit of work. '*Making it clear*' tasks check that students are familiar with the basic facts and ideas featured in the unit. '*Working it out*' activities help students to relate material from one of the three 'levels' - individual, membership group or tradition - to material drawn from another 'level'. The intention is to bring two pieces of material together so that each sheds light upon the other. *'Building bridges'* activities ask students to draw from their own experiences or ideas in order to interpret material featured in the unit. Students are asked to focus on personal knowledge and experience for comparison and contrast with material from the religious tradition. The familiar is used to make sense of or to gain insights into the unfamiliar.

'Edification' activities are headed *'Thinking it through'*, and encourage students to use material from a religious tradition as a stimulus to reflect upon matters of personal concern. As the teachers' notes state, the aim is 'to encourage students to examine or re-examine aspects of their own understanding in the light of questions, issues or experiences which are encountered in particular religious traditions, but which also have universal significance'. Of course, whether a person feels edified through reflecting on issues and questions raised through interpreting another's way of life is a personal matter, and it is impossible to guarantee it through activities provided in curriculum materials.

Constraints

In retrospect, it is possible to identify some of the constraints experienced by the project team:

1. We found it very difficult to explain the method to the publisher. The publisher was primarily interested in sales and was not keen on the team using time to develop material. Fairly rigid deadlines and various other constraints (on format, illustrations, length, size, use of work sheets etc) were imposed. In effect the books were not allowed to look too different from some other texts.

2. The textbook medium has its own inherent weaknesses. We were trying to set up a communication between living individuals who had to be represented through picture and word, and students in class who we would never meet. There was sometimes a feeling of distance from both parties.

3. We could not guarantee that teachers would use the books as intended. Many hours were spent trying to write straightforward and non-technical material for non-specialist teachers (see Jackson, Barratt and Everington 1994, for example), but there could be no guarantee that the ideas would be digested and applied. When we have managed to offer some in-service training in relation to the books, they have usually been used effectively. Unfortunately, we do not have as much time to do this as we would like.

4. Portraying real people, especially people who had participated in the editorial process of producing the books, raised various ethical issues we had to deal with. One consequence was that it was not possible to include the kind of critical element referred to above, even though this is integral to the interpretive approach more widely understood (Jackson 1997a, 129-30).

All of us who were involved in the Warwick RE Project probably had mixed feelings about the books and about the experience of producing them. However, a great deal was learned through the exercise, and the materials have been widely used and seem to be making a useful contribution.

WIDER APPLICATIONS OF AN INTERPRETIVE APPROACH

Whereas the pedagogy of the Warwick RE Project started from a consideration of the young people portrayed in the curriculum texts, the interpretive approach considered more generally can start at any point on the hermeneutic circle. The approach could start with an overview of a tradition, followed by a consideration of specific examples. This is the approach taken in the introductory text for students and teachers entitled *Approaches to Hinduism* (Jackson and Killingley 1988). The book starts with an overview of the Hindu tradition, but its limitations are pointed out to readers. There follows a treatment of some specific elements from the tradition through a series of case studies of individual Hindus. The source material for these was either ethnographic or biographical. The intention was that the introduction should make the case studies intelligible, while the case studies provided details of religious life, some of which were not generalisable, to point up the limitations of the overview and to extend an understanding of the Hindu tradition. Denise Cush has taken an analogous approach in introducing the Jain tradition through some of its key ideas, and taking care to include the experience of the learner as part of the hermeneutic circle (Cush 1999).

Recent Developments

The approach can also start from the questions and concerns of students, move to individuals or groups within a tradition or to general ideas from a tradition, and then back again to the student. Thus members of WRERU have considered it important to continue to take a research interest in the life-worlds of children and young people, partly in order to find potential starting points for pedagogic practice (e.g. Bennett, D 1999; Østberg 1999; 2000). One piece of ethnographic research on the mainly Muslim students of her junior school, especially relevant to pedagogy, has been conducted by Julia Ipgrave (Ipgrave 1998, 1999).

There is also work being done in WRERU on extending the critical aspects of the interpretive approach. For example, at secondary level, Sarah Edwards has attempted a synthesis of the approach with further ideas from critical theory (Edwards 1999). Simon Bennett has worked on the approach at key stage three using flexible learning methods (Bennett, S 1999). As developed in the Warwick RE Project, the interpretive approach concentrated on written and spoken communication. Joyce Miller is currently doing research for an EdD degree, developing the approach through using art in religious education. Anne Krisman has used her time as Farmington Fellow at Warwick to apply ideas from the interpretive approach to her work with young people with special educational needs (Krisman 1999). **(4)**

Julia Ipgrave's school-based research has led to doctoral studies on the religio-cultural and theological influence of the children upon one another, and their formation of new ideas through personal encounter. This recent development concentrates on the non-Muslim children in her school and has been informed by small discussion groups in which children have been free to explore and share their own ideas. The children themselves devised a series of questions to provide starting points for discussions. Although most of the children claimed to follow their family religion, some revealed attitudes different from those of their parents. Sometimes they showed a greater openness to the beliefs and religious backgrounds of their peers than the adults in their community would have done, bringing their religious identity into dialogue with other ways of believing and, drawing on both, and negotiating new meanings.

Ipgrave highlights three aspects of children's thinking evident in their dialogue. One is the experience-led nature of their understanding. Children drew on their own experience of religious plurality, including their relationships with their peers, in exploring religion. A second aspect is the integrative nature of their theology. Ipgrave's pupils provided many examples of bringing together ideas in an attempt to make them into a coherent whole. A third feature of much of the discussion was its realism. Rather than adopting a relativist stance in the face of a variety of religious stances, many of the children took the view that what is true is true for everyone (Ipgrave 1999b).

This extension of the interpretive approach, in which part of the source material for RE is the children themselves, has been complemented by preliminary work in using the intranet resource 'First Class' as a means to generate conversation between junior pupils from different religious and non-religious backgrounds in different parts of England. This was co-ordinated by Andrew Raine as part of a Farmington Millennial Fellowship, and drew on the expertise and co-operation of colleagues in WRERU and at St Martin's University College, Lancaster (Raine 1999).

CONCLUSION

This chapter has outlined an interpretive approach to religious education, illustrating it specifically through the example of the Warwick RE Project, but also indicating wider applications of the approach and some recent developments. The approach sees religions as dynamic and changing. Understanding is increased through studying the cases of individuals, in the context of their religio-cultural groups, in relation to various constructions of the wider religious tradition. The approach also requires the student to use familiar or analogous concepts and experiences in a process of comparison and contrast between one's own worldview and that of the people being studied. The source material for such studies can be of various kinds, but ethnographic studies that point up the complexity of religious and cultural interactions and challenge stereotypes are one particularly useful source.

An interpretive approach includes the possibility that students might have their own views deepened through the study of other positions, whether outside or related to their own traditions. It also offers an opportunity for students to apply their critical faculties skilfully and sensitively to material studied, as well as the chance to engage in methodological self-criticism and creative approaches to presentation. The approach also recognises that students' own religio-cultural experience can and should be part of the subject matter of religious education, and that there is the possibility of developing new ideas through pupils from different backgrounds interacting with one another.

Pedagogically, the more aware teachers are of beliefs and values embedded in the religio-cultural experience of students, the more they can take account of pupils' concerns and can provide teaching and learning situations which are designed to foster communication between students from different backgrounds.

The interpretive approach is conceived as standing outside any particular system of religious beliefs, being inclusive of people of different religious and non-religious positions as participants, and providing the opportunity for different religious and cultural positions to be understood in a methodologically sound and self-critical way. It also acknowledges the potentially transformative character of such studies, while equally recognising the limited and partial effect of schooling in the overall experience of the young.

Finally, there is scope for developing the interpretive approach in different ways. There is no reason why the approach should not start at any point on the hermeneutic circle - whether with a critical overview of a 'whole' religious tradition, with a study of an individual person or case study, with a concern or question from students or with a classroom-based interaction between pupils. There are also possibilities for developing the approach in relation to the interface between religion and other areas of knowledge and experience.

NOTES

1. ESRC Project Reference number R000232489

2. Methodological reflection can also help students to become more aware of bias in the techniques used in other forms of presentation. Once they have engaged in some methodological self-criticism they might better undertake a critique of the representation of Islam in popular newspapers, for example.

3. In the same way, when the Schools Council Secondary RE Project appeared in the early 1970s (Schools Council, 1971), it confirmed what many were beginning to do already, but gave them some theory and method to back their hunches and to use in developing their work.

4. As a complement to school-based studies of the life worlds of pupils, Judith Everington and Pat Sikes are conducting research on the life histories of RE students and teachers (Everington and Sikes, 1998).

References

Ashenden, C. (1995) *Christianity and the Primary School: The Contribution of Anthropology to Teaching about Christianity,* Unpublished thesis, University of Brighton.

Barth, F. (1981) 'Ethnic Groups and Boundaries' in *Process and Forms in Social Life: Selected Essays,* (London: Routledge and Kegan Paul).

Baumann, G. (1996) *Contesting Culture: Discourses of Identity in Multi-Ethnic London,* (Cambridge, Cambridge University Press).

Clifford, J. (1988) *The Predicament of Culture,* (Cambridge (Mass), Harvard University Press).

Crapanzano, V. (1986) 'Hermes' Dilemma: the Masking of Subversion in Ethnographic Description' in Clifford, J. &Marcus, G. (eds) *Writing Culture: The Poetics and Politics of Ethnography* (Berkeley, University of California Press) pp. 51-76.

Cush, D. (1999) '"Learning From" the Concept and Concepts of a Religious Tradition: Jainism in the RE Curriculum', *Journal of Beliefs and Values,* 20 (1), pp. 60-74.

Durham. (1970) *The Fourth R: The Durham Report on Religious Education* (London: National Society and SPCK).

Eriksson, K. (2000) 'In Search of the Meaning of Life: A Study of the Ideas of Senior Compulsory School Pupils on Life and its Meaning, in an Experiential Learning Context', *British Journal of Religious Education,* 22 (2), 115-27.

Geertz, C. (1973) *The Interpretation of Cultures* (New York, Basic Books).

Geertz, C. (1983) *Local Knowledge* (New York, Basic Books).

Grimmitt, M.H. (1987) *Religious Education and Human Development: The Relationship Between Studying Religions and Personal, Social and Moral Education* (Great Wakering, McCrimmons).

Habermas, J. (1972) *Knowledge and Human Interests* (London, Heinemann).

Hylland Eriksen, T. (1993) 'In Which Sense Do Cultural Islands Exist?' *Social Anthropology* 1, pp. 133-47.

Leach, E. (1982) *Social Anthropology* (Glasgow, Collins Fontana).

Loukes, H. (1961) *Teenage Religion* (London, SCM Press).

Myerhoff, B. (1978) *Number Our Days* (New York, Simon and Shuster).

Raine, A (1999) *Using Information Communications Technology in the Teaching of Primary RE,* unpublished report, Oxford, Farmington Institute for Christian Studies.

Ricoeur, P. (1971) 'The Model of the Text: Meaningful Action Considered as a Text', *Social Research*, 38, pp. 529-62.

Rorty, R. (1980) *Philosophy and the Mirror of Nature* (Oxford, Blackwell).

Said, E. (1978) *Orientalism* (London, Routledge and Kegan Paul).

Said, E. (1993) *Culture and Imperialism* (London, Chatto and Windus).

Schools Council (1971) *Religious Education in Secondary Schools, Schools Council Working Paper 36*, (London, Evans/Methuen).

Sharpe, E. (1975) 'The Phenomenology of Religion', *Learning for Living*, 15 (1), pp. 4-9.

Smith, W. C. (1978) *The Meaning and End of Religion* (London, SPCK).

Tajfel, H. (1981) *Human Groups and Social Categories* (Cambridge, Cambridge University Press).

Waardenburg, J. (1978) *Reflections on the Study of Religion* (The Hague, Mouton).

Warren, M. (1993) 'Religious Education and the Task of Cultural Critique', *Religious Education*, 88 (1), pp. 68-79.

PUBLICATIONS

Pupil texts and Teachers' Resource Books

Key Stage 1 and Key Stage 2 pupil texts and Teachers' Resource Books (Bridges to Religions) are available from Warwick Religions and Education Research Unit, Institute of Education, University of Warwick, Coventry CV4 7AL. Key Stage 3 books (Interpreting Religions) are still available from the publisher.

Barratt, M. (1994a) *An Egg for Babcha*, 'Bridges to Religions' series, *The Warwick RE Project*, (Oxford, Heinemann).

Barratt, M. (1994b), *Lucy's Sunday*, 'Bridges to Religions' series, *The Warwick RE Project*, (Oxford, Heinemann).

Barratt, M. (1994c), *Something to Share*, 'Bridges to Religions' series, *The Warwick RE Project*, (Oxford, Heinemann).

Barratt, M. (1994d), *The Buddha's Birthday*, 'Bridges to Religions' series, *The Warwick RE Project*, (Oxford, Heinemann).

Barratt, M. (1994e), *The Seventh Day is Shabbat*, 'Bridges to Religions' series, *The Warwick RE Project*, (Oxford, Heinemann).

Barratt, M. and Price, J. (1996a), *Meeting Christians: Book One*, 'Bridges to Religions' series, *The Warwick RE Project*, (Oxford, Heinemann).

Barratt, M. and Price, J. (1996b), *Teacher's Resource Book: Meeting Christians: Book One*, 'Bridges to Religions' series, *The Warwick RE Project*, (Oxford, Heinemann).

Everington, J. (1996c) *Meeting Christians: Book Two*, 'Bridges to Religions' series, *The Warwick RE Project*, (Oxford, Heinemann).

Everington, J. (1996d) *Teacher's Resource Book: Meeting Christians: Book Two*, 'Bridges to Religions' series, *The Warwick RE Project*, (Oxford, Heinemann).

Jackson, R. (1989) *Religions Through Festivals: Hinduism* (London, Longman).

Jackson, R. and Nesbitt, E. (1990) *Listening to Hindus* (London, Unwin Hyman).

Jackson, R, and Nesbitt, E. (2000) *Hindus Today* (Watford, Goloka Books).

Jackson, R., Barratt, M. and Everington, J. (1994) *Bridges to Religions: Teacher's Resource Book*, *The Warwick RE Project*, (Oxford, Heinemann).

Mercier, C. (1996) *Muslims*, 'Interpreting Religions' series, *The Warwick RE Project*, (Oxford, Heinemann).

Robson, G. (1995) *Christians*, 'Interpreting Religions' series, *The Warwick RE Project*, (Oxford, Heinemann).

Wayne, E., Everington, J., Kadodwala, D. and Nesbitt, E. (1996) *Hindus*, 'Interpreting Religions' series, *The Warwick RE Project*, (Oxford, Heinemann).

Scholarly and Professional Publications Relating to the Interpretive Approach

Bennett, S. (1999) *Can the Interpretive Approach to Religious Education be Delivered by Flexible Methods in Secondary Schools?*, unpublished MA dissertation, Institute of Education, University of Warwick.

Edwards, S. (1999) *RE and Emancipation: A Critical Approach to Cultural Development in the Comprehensive School*, unpublished MA dissertation, Institute of Education, University of Warwick.

Everington, J. (1993a) 'Bridging Fieldwork and Classwork: The Development of Curriculum Materials within the Religious Education and Community Project', *Resource*, 16 (1), pp. 7-10.

Everington, J. (1993b) 'The Relationship Between Research and Teaching within Teacher Education: An Account of Recent Work within the Religious Education and Community Project', *Journal of Beliefs and Values*, 14 (2), pp. 6-8.

Everington, J. (1996a) 'A Question of Authenticity: The Relationship Between Educators and Practitioners in the Representation of Religious Traditions', *British Journal of Religious Education*, 18 (2), pp. 69-77.

Everington, J. (1996b) 'Trial by Teachers: The Warwick RE Project's Experiences of Trialling Key Stage One Curriculum Materials', *Resource*, 18 (3), pp.13-17.

Everington, J. (1998) 'Evolution not Revolution: An examination of the Contribution of a Curriculum Development Project to the Implementation of New Agreed Syllabuses', *British Journal of Religious Education*, 20 (3), 144-54.

Everington, J. and Sikes, P. (1998) 'Becoming an RE Teacher: A Biographical Approach', Unpublished Paper, International Seminar on Religious Education and Values, Trinity College, Carmarthen.

Ipgrave, J. (1998) *'The Religious Education of Muslim Students'* (London, Teacher Training Agency).

Ipgrave, J. (1999a) 'Issues in the Delivery of Religious Education to Muslim Pupils: Perspectives from the Classroom', *British Journal of Religious Education*, 21 (3), pp. 147-58.

Ipgrave, J. (1999b) 'Thoughts on Religion and God: Children's Responses to their Experience as a Religious Minority in a Predominantly Muslim Inner-city Junior School', Unpublished Paper, Warwick Religions and Education Research Unit Seminar, June.

Jackson, R. (1990) 'Children as Ethnographers' in Jackson, R and Starkings, D (eds) *The Junior RE Handbook*, (Cheltenham, Stanley Thornes) pp. 202-7.

Jackson, R. (1993) 'Religious Education and the Arts of Interpretation' in Starkings, D. (ed) *Religion and the Arts in Education: Dimensions of Spirituality*, (London, Hodder and Stoughton) pp. 157-66.

Jackson, R. (1995) 'Religious Education's Representation of Religions and Cultures', *British Journal of Educational Studies*, 43 (3), pp. 272-89.

Jackson, R. (1996a) 'Ethnographic Research and Curriculum Development' in Francis, L.J., Kay, W.K. & Campbell, W.S. (eds) *Research in Religious Education*, (Leominster, Gracewing) pp. 145-62.

Jackson, R. (1996b) 'The Construction of "Hinduism" and its Impact on Religious Education in England and Wales', *Panorama: International Journal of Comparative Religious Education and Values*, 8 (1), pp. 86-104.

Jackson, R. (1996c) '"Hinduismus" im Religionsunterricht in England und Wales -Ergebnisse eines Forschungprojecktes', in M. Kwiran, P. Schreiner and H. Schultze (eds) *Dialog der Religionen im Unterricht, Münster, Comenius-Institut*, pp. 211-21.

149

Jackson, R. (1997a) *Religious Education: An Interpretive Approach* (London, Hodder and Stoughton).

Jackson, R. (1997b) 'La Nouvelle Éducation Religieuse en Grande-Bretagne: Bilan Partiel de Trente Années de Recherche' in Milot, M. & Ouellet, F. (eds) *Religion, Education et Démocratie: Un Enseignement Culturel de la Religion est-il Possible?* (Montreal, L'Harmattan) pp. 183-217.

Jackson, R. (1997c) 'Ethnographic Studies of Children and Interpretive Methods for Religious Education' in Trees Andree, Cok Bakker and Peter Schreiner (eds) *Crossing Boundaries: Contributions to Interreligious and Intercultural Education* (Münster, Comenius Institut) pp. 65-73.

Jackson, R. (1998a) 'Problems and Possibilities for Phenomenological Approaches to Religious Education' in Hans-Günter Heimbrock (ed) *Religionspädagogik und Phänomenologie: Von der Empirischen Wendung zur Lebenswelt, Weinheim* (Germany),(Deutscher Studien Verlag) pp. 47-74.

Jackson, R. (1998b) '"Hinduismus" im Religionsunterricht in England and Wales', *Braunschweiger Beiträge für Theorie und Praxis von Ru und Ku*, 83 (1) pp. 41-6.

Jackson, R. (1999a) 'The Warwick RE Project: An Interpretive Approach to Religious Education', *Religious Education* (USA), 94 (2), pp. 201-16.

Jackson, R. (1999b) 'The Inter-relatedness of Subject, Pedagogy and Research Approaches: Theology, Religious Studies and Religious Education in England and Wales' in Chidester, D., Stonier, J. & Tobler, J., *Diversity as Ethos: Challenges for Interreligious and Intercultural Education* (Cape Town, Institute for Comparative Religion in Southern Africa) pp. 84-101.

Jackson, R. (2000) 'Empirical Research in Religious Education', Editorial, *British Journal of Religious Education*, 22 (2), 66-70.

Jackson, R. and Killingley, D. (1988) *Approaches to Hinduism* (London, John Murray).

Jackson, R. and Nesbitt, E. (1997) 'Studying British Hindu Children and Representing Them in School Texts', in Holm, NAG (ed) *The Familiar and the Unfamiliar in the World Religions: Challenges for Religious Education Today*, Bo (Finland), (Bo Academia University) pp. 26-45.

Krisman, A. (1999) 'Building up to the Sky', *Resource*, 21 (2), 6-9.

Ethnographic Research by Members of WRERU

Bennett, D. (1999) *Laying the Foundations: a Field Study of Religious Nurture in a Pentecostal Church*, unpublished MA dissertation, Institute of Education, University of Warwick.

Davies, S. (1997) 'Sikh Children's Perceptions of the Transmission of Sikh Culture', *Sikh Bulletin*, 14, 1-8.

Jackson, R. (1976) 'Holi in North India and in an English City: Some Adaptations and Anomalies', *New Community*, 5 (3), pp. 203-10.

Jackson, R. and Nesbitt, E. M. (1986) 'Sketches of Formal Hindu Nurture: Hindu Supplementary Schools in England', *World Religions in Education*, pp. 25-9.

Jackson, R. and Nesbitt, E. M. (1992) 'The Diversity of Experience in the Religious Upbringing of Children from Christian Families in Britain', *British Journal of Religious Education*, 15 (1), pp. 19-28.

Jackson, R. and Nesbitt, EM (1993) *Hindu Children in Britain* (Stoke on Trent, Trentham Books).

Jackson, R. and Nesbitt, E. M. (1996), 'Orthodoxy and Openness: The Experience of Hindu Children' in Gates, B.E. (ed) *Freedom and Authority in Religions and Religious Education* (London, Cassell) pp. 138-48.

Nesbitt, E. M. (1990) 'Religion and Identity: The Valmiki Community in Coventry', *New Community*, 16 (2), pp. 261-74.

Nesbitt, E. M. (1991) *'My Dad's Hindu, My Mum's Side are Sikhs': Issues in Religious Identity*, Arts, Culture, Education Research Papers (Coventry, National Foundation for Arts Education).

Nesbitt, E. M. (1992) 'Photographing Worship: Issues Raised by Ethnographic Study of Children's Participation in Acts of Worship', *Visual Anthropology* 5 (3), pp. 285-306.

Nesbitt, E. (1993a) 'Drawing on the Ethnic Diversity of Christian Tradition in Britain', *Multicultural Teaching*, 11 (2), pp. 9-12.

Nesbitt, E. M. (1993b) 'Children and the World to Come: The Views of Children Aged Eight to Fourteen on Life After Death', *Religion Today*, 8 (3), pp. 10-13.

Nesbitt, E. M. (1993c) 'The Transmission of Christian Tradition in an Ethnically Diverse Society', in Barot, R. (ed), *Religion and Ethnicity: Minorities and Social Change in the Metropolis*, Kampen (The Netherlands), Kok Pharos, pp. 156-69.

Nesbitt, E. M. (1994) 'Valmikis in Coventry: The Revival and Reconstruction of a Community' in Ballard, R. (ed), *Desh Pardesh: The South Asian Presence in*

Britain (London, Hurst and Co) pp. 117-41

Nesbitt, E. M. (1995a) 'Celebrating and Learning: The Perpetuation of Values and Practices among Hindu Punjabi Children in Coventry, UK', *Indo-British Review, 20* (2), pp. 119-31.

Nesbitt, E. M. (1995b) *The Religious Lives of Sikh Children in Coventry*, Unpublished PhD thesis, University of Warwick. (revised version to be published by the Community Religions Project, University of Leeds in 2000).

Nesbitt, E. M. (1995c) 'Panjabis in Britain: Cultural History and Cultural Choices', *South Asia Research*, 15 (2), pp. 221-40.

Nesbitt, E. M. (1995d) 'Many Happy Returns: Some British South Asian Children's Birthday Parties', *Multicultural Teaching*, 4 (1), pp. 34-5, 40.

Nesbitt, E M (1997a) '"Splashed with Goodness": The Many Meanings of Amrit for Young British Sikhs', *Journal of Contemporary Religion*, 12 (1), pp. 17-33.

Nesbitt, E. M. (1997b) '"Sikhs and Proper Sikhs": Young British Sikhs' Perceptions of Their Identity', in Singh, P. & Barrier, N.G. (eds), *Sikh Identity: Continuity and Change* (Delhi, Manohar).

Nesbitt, E. M. and Jackson, R. (1992) 'Christian and Hindu Children: Their Perceptions of Each Other's Religious Traditions', *Journal of Empirical Theology*, 5 (2), pp. 39-62.

Nesbitt, E. M. and Jackson, R. (1993) 'Aspects of Cultural Transmission in a Diaspora Sikh Community', *Journal of Sikh Studies*, 18 (1), pp. 52-66.

Nesbitt, E. M. and Jackson, R. (1995) 'Sikh Children's Use of "God": Ethnographic Fieldwork and Religious Education', *British Journal of Religious Education*, 17 (2), pp. 108-20.

Østberg, S. (1999) *Pakistani Children in Oslo: Islamic Nurture in a Secular Setting*, Unpublished PhD Thesis, Institute of Education, University of Warwick. (to be published by the Community Religions Project, University of Leeds in 2000).

Østberg, S. (2000) 'Islamic Nurture and Identity Management: The Lifeworld of Pakistani Children in Norway', *British Journal of Religious Education*, 22 (2), 9-103.

Woodward, P. (1992) 'Jewish Children Under the Camera: An Ethnographic Study of Jewish Children in Britain', *Visual Anthropology*, 5 (3), pp.307-30.

For an upto date of WRERU publications visit:

http://www.warwick.ac.uk/wie/WRERU/wrerup1.htm

CHAPTER 8

THE STAPLEFORD PROJECT:
THEOLOGY AS THE BASIS FOR RELIGIOUS EDUCATION

Trevor Cooling

BACKGROUND

The Stapleford Project was set up in 1986 by the Association of Christian Teachers in England with the purpose of producing a range of materials to support teaching about Christianity in school religious education. The Project was designed to provide an alternative approach to the widespread perception that to teach Christianity was only to instil in pupils *knowledge* of Bible stories. In contrast the Project's aim was to emphasise the importance of exploring *meaning* in Bible texts and the way in which this meaning infused the life and thinking of Christians in the modern world. A major objective was to marry a distinctive theoretical rationale with classroom materials which were accessible to the non-specialist classroom teacher, be they themselves Christians or not.

The chief premise of the Project is that the key to understanding information about Christianity is to understand the ideas that make the faith meaningful and significant for Christians. For example, the language used in the Eucharist about the body and blood of Christ is unintelligible without some understanding of the doctrine of the Atonement and of concepts like sacrifice and reconciliation which lie behind the Good Friday and Easter stories. The Project therefore shares the concern of the phenomenological approach that pupils come to understand the meaning of Christianity for believers. It differs from this approach in that it suggests that this will only be achieved if more attention is given to exploring the theological concepts which are the source of meaningfulness and significance for Christians.

Since its inception, the Project has produced forty different books and resource packs and has sold in the region of 200,000 copies of its various titles. The most systematic representation of the Project's approach appears in the pupil textbook for secondary schools- called *Key Christian Beliefs* (1995). In June 1996, a new termly magazine for primary schools called *Cracking RE* was launched. This provides a regular source of ideas for teaching Christianity based on the Project's rationale and attracts around 2,500 subscribers a year. In addition, a number of articles dealing with the rationale of the Project have been published (e.g. Cooling, 1987, 1992, 1993, 1996a, 1997).

The Project team has also worked with other organisations, contributing to the production of materials which draw on the Stapleford approach. Two of particular significance are:

1. In 1994, the School Curriculum and Assessment Authority (SCAA) produced two Model Syllabuses of RE which were designed as guidance for English Local Education Authorities who are required, by law, to publish an Agreed Syllabus of RE for use in their schools. One of these syllabuses, known as Model 2 (SCAA, 1994a), drew heavily on the ideas of the Stapleford Project.

2. In 1996, the BBC broadcast a series of five programmes on Christianity called *Pathways of Belief* for seven to nine year olds. Together with the accompanying notes for teachers, these drew inspiration from the Stapleford Project's Concept Cracking methodology.

THE PROJECT'S PEDAGOGICAL PRINCIPLES AND PROCEDURES

The Basic Principles

The roots of RE lie in the post-war confessional vision that schools should be building the Christian character of the nation. Confidence in this vision collapsed in the 1970s as a result of growing awareness of religious pluralism and a growing concern to eschew anything that might smack of indoctrination. World religions became the new focus. The legacy of these changes was twofold. Either schools continued unreformed, teaching Bible based courses, but often without the enthusiasm engendered by the confessional vision (Crossman, 1993), or they adopted a descriptive, world religions approach. The frequent result in both cases was a didactic and uninspiring curriculum. The Stapleford Project grew out of a concern that

RE teaching had lost its way. It shared this concern with a number of other projects that also had their origins in the 1980s (Grimmitt, 1987, Hammond et al., 1990, Jackson, 1997).

Issues of particular concern to the Stapleford Project were:

- *The evidence that students were developing negative attitudes to institutional religion and, in particular, to Christianity.*

  The work of Kay & Francis over many years has demonstrated this (e.g. 1996). This change in attitude was partly a result of the increasing secularisation of society, but was also attributable to the way in which approaches to RE failed to make connections between the explicit study of religion and the concerns and experience of the students. Its effect was to increase resistance to learning about religion.

- *The influential notion that children were not able to handle abstract religious ideas until their teens.*

  This idea was derived from the work of Ronald Goldman (1964 & 1965) and led to many teachers, especially in the primary sector, being unwilling to tackle anything other than descriptive work with children when explicitly religious material was covered.

- *The evidence that work in RE was relatively undemanding as compared with other subjects.*

  The research of Trevor Kerry in 1984 was particularly important. More recent reports (e.g. Crossman, 1993, OFSTED 1997) show that this is a continuing problem. In particular there is a lack of progression in the way religious content is introduced to pupils as they move through the school (OFSTED, 1997, p29). A subject which does not make intellectual, personal and emotional demands (Day, 1986) is unlikely either to hold students' interest or to contribute to their educational growth.

In responding to these concerns, the Stapleford Project drew on the work of Jerome Bruner (e.g. 1977) and Margaret Donaldson (1978). In particular, two principles were gleaned from their writings which came to underpin the curriculum development work (see Cooling & Cooling, 1987 for further information):

- They argued that an effective curriculum was best constructed around the structural ideas of a subject as these were essential to understanding it. Going to the heart of a subject, rather than continually scratching at the surface, was the way to promote excellence in learning. Drawing on this insight, the Project emphasised the importance of identifying the key concepts that are central to religious education, rather than planning a curriculum solely around the information that was to be learnt (see also Rudge, 1991 & Kincaid, 1991).

- They also argued against Goldman's idea of readiness, which proposed that learning of abstract concepts could not be attempted before formal operational thinking was achieved. Instead, they suggested that any concept could be taught to any child as long as it was appropriately translated. In other words, it is the teacher's responsibility to ensure that any concept tackled is presented in a way that is age or stage appropriate so that it will make sense in that child's world of experience. The point is that it is not the abstract concepts that are the problem, but dumping abstract concepts on children using methods that are appropriate to adults. It therefore became a guiding principle for the Project that translation of concepts into stage appropriate forms is a key task in curriculum planning.

Drawing on these ideas, the Stapleford Project has developed an approach which is conceptually based with an emphasis on designing learning activities which help to translate these concepts into stage-appropriate forms. The focus is on communicating ideas rather than information. As the Project is concerned with the teaching of Christianity, the focus has been on theological concepts since Christianity is underpinned by doctrinal teaching.

THE PEDAGOGICAL STRATEGY DEVELOPED BY THE PROJECT

The methodology of the Project has become known by the catch phrase *Concept Cracking*. This has been described in detail elsewhere (Cooling. T, 1994a & Cooling. M, 1996), but can be summarised as a two stage process.

1. Stage 1 focuses on the importance of teachers understanding their subject matter and being clear as to exactly which concepts will be the focus of their teaching when covering any particular topic. The key tasks in this stage are, firstly, to unpack the range of concepts that are

embedded in the chosen topic and might be the focus of teaching and, secondly, to select one or two of these to be the focus of attention in this particular unit of work. Selection will be on the basis of a number of criteria including the appropriateness for the pupils, the balance in a scheme of work and, of course, the importance of particular concepts within Christianity.

2. Stage 2 entails planning teaching activities which translate the selected concept into a form that makes sense in the pupils' world of experience. This stage entails making links or bridges with the pupils' world and then designing learning activities which help the student both to understand the religious concept and its significance for the believer and to re-apply the concept in a way that helps the student in their own understanding of the world. There are parallels here with the work of other projects and in particular the ideas of 'bridges' and 'edification' in the Warwick RE Project (Jackson 1997) and the idea of the study of a religion making 'a gift to the child' in the Birmingham University Project (Grimmitt et al. 1991 & Hull, 1996).

As a practical classroom tool, the *Concept Cracking* approach has been broken down into four specific steps, which can be remembered using the acronym USER. Steps 1 and 2 constitute stage 1 and steps 3 and 4 constitute stage 2 above. I will illustrate this using the story from the New Testament where Jesus turns out the traders from the Temple in Jerusalem.

1. Unpack the Concepts

Before teaching any topic it is important to be aware of the different theological concepts that underpin it and are important to understanding its meaning and significance. If teachers are not clear about the ideas being covered, the pupils certainly will not be. In this case, the key concepts include anger, injustice, holiness, Jesus as God's son and judgement.

2. Select One or Two Concepts as the Focus for the Lesson

If a lesson is not focussed on one or two key concepts that are being taught, the pupils will become confused. In this example the concept of righteous anger could be a suitable focus.

3. Engage with the Pupils' World of Experience

This is perhaps the hardest and yet the most important stage in the process. The key is to find parallels in the pupils' world which relate to the concept of righteous anger. One possibility would be to ask pupils to give examples of instances when they have been angry and to divide these into occasions when they were right to be angry and occasions when they were wrong to be angry. The purpose of the activity is not so much to make a judgement on the particular instances, but to establish the idea in pupils' minds that there are right and wrong forms of anger and to begin the process of searching for criteria to distinguish between them. This will build the bridge between the pupils' world and the religious concept.

4. Relate to the Religious Concept

This is the point at which to introduce the story from the New Testament. An effective way of doing this is to use the painting called *Christ driving the traders from the Temple* by El Greco (see Cooling, M, 1998 for full details of how to do this) and to ask the pupils to comment on how Jesus' behaviour is being portrayed in the painting. In particular they will notice there are two groups of people, those who are the object of his anger and those who are being affirmed. A role play could then be used in which pupils take on the roles of members of the two groups and debate Jesus' behaviour. Finally there will need to be a whole class discussion in which the question of why the Gospel writer thought Jesus' anger was justified is explored. This should draw out themes like the importance of resisting injustice and exploitation, the holiness of the Temple and Jesus' special relationship with God which made his anger uniquely justifiable as far as the Gospel writer is concerned. Then pupils should be encouraged to express their own views, perhaps though the medium of a diary entry from someone who was present in the Temple, as to whether or not Jesus' anger was justified. This can then lead into an activity where pupils reflect on justified and unjustified anger in their own lives and its management.

Steps one and two represent important preliminary work which must be done by as teachers to clarify their own understanding of the topic. This is very important as a way of giving a lesson a clear focus. However, the actual teaching will often begin with step three in order to ensure that the lesson is relevant for the pupils. Many lessons will have to begin with an activity that is designed to build the bridge between the pupils' world and the religious topic.

ISSUES ARISING FROM THE PRINCIPLES AND STRATEGIES ADOPTED BY THE PROJECT

In developing its rationale and materials, the Project has had to take a particular position on a number of issues that are the subject of debate. Some of the more important are discussed below.

1. The Role of Doctrine

A basic premise of the Project is that the primary purpose of school RE, as with any other academic discipline, is to ensure that students gain an accurate knowledge and understanding of the subject material. When it comes to teaching Christianity, this is understood to mean that students are introduced to a systematic coverage of the key elements of Christian doctrine. So, if a teacher says that they do not like or feel comfortable covering a particular topic, as may be said, for example, about Easter, the reply would be that a teacher cannot pick and choose what to cover. It is the nature of the subject itself which determines what is important to teach. Few people would have a problem accepting this with science, we do not leave out gravity because it does not interest the teacher. The point is more debated when it comes to RE. In the Project the position taken is that doctrine defines the nature of Christianity and should therefore provide the fundamental framework within which to set the teaching of Christian texts and practices (see Cooling. T, 1996a).

2. The Challenge of Diversity

One objection to this suggestion is that it is simply not possible to identify a doctrinal essence to Christianity in the way required by the Project methodology (see Jackson 1997). It is said that Christianity is so diverse that it is misleading to present it as a uniform phenomenon in this way. There are in fact Christianities, not Christianity (Astley, 1992a). Of course, it is true that Christianity is a very diverse phenomenon, but this does not mean that it is not possible to identify a core of beliefs which the vast majority of Christians would recognise and identify with. The fact that this is possible was clearly demonstrated when SCAA carried out a national consultation in 1993 which led to an agreed statement amongst Christians from many different denominations as to what Christians believe and think should be taught in schools (SCAA, 1994b). This is not to suggest that Christianity is a clone, but it is to suggest that there are recognisable family resemblances between the many different versions which means it makes sense to teach it as one religion. In order to give students a feel for this 'unity amidst diversity' which characterises Christianity, the Project seeks to draw on examples from around the world and across denominations when dealing with any given belief.

3. RE is non-confessional

The focus on Christianity may give the impression that the Project is confessional in its approach, having the purpose of urging acceptance of Christian belief. That is not the case. It is important to distinguish between transmitting an accurate understanding of what it is Christians believe and how these beliefs influence the lives of Christians, and seeking to gain acceptance of these beliefs on the part of pupils. Although both these aims would be appropriate in a church educational context, the second would not be appropriate in a common school (see Cooling, 1994b).

What distinguishes confessional from non-confessional teaching is a hotly debated topic (Cooling, 1994b). The Project's position is that the difference lies in non-confessional teaching being governed by a code of conduct that requires teachers to avoid language and behaviour which seeks to induct students into belief. So we endorse the use of techniques such as 'owning and grounding language' (Read et al, 1992, p 67f) and 'distancing devices' (Grimmitt et al, 1991, Hull, 1996) which enable students to encounter the authentic faith without belief being assumed or actively sought on their part.

4. Catechesis or not?

The assumption often made is that doctrinal teaching is catechetical, concerned with transmitting a static tradition (Astley 1992b, Doble, 1993). This usually has two connotations. The first is that the approach is confessional, a point which I have just covered. The second is of a rote form of learning, where the mere repeating of phrases, often in obscure religious language, is considered to be evidence of educational attainment. The

Project however, in its emphasis on the importance of the effective translation of ideas, would be averse to using any approach which smacked of a 'password' mentality, simply requiring pupils to utter key words rather than explore the ideas behind them. There are three features in particular which distance the Project from the type of poor catechetical approach I have described.

First, the Project emphasises the importance of intuitive or tacit knowing (e.g. Polanyi 1967). Two phrases capture this idea. The first, *we know more than we can tell*, expresses the idea that we may have more of a grasp of a concept than we can actually express in words. Understanding transcends explanation. The second, *the feels that make the tolds fall into place*, captures the notion that to know a concept requires more than a cognitive experience, it involves the emotions as well (Rudge, 1991, p24). So, using a biological analogy, the Project distinguishes, on the one hand, between learning activities which encourage pupils to *regurgitate* information and, on the other hand, learning activities which encourage them to *reprocess* that information so that it is expressed in a way that makes sense to them by engaging with it *both* cognitively and effectively (Cooling, 1994a). The design of effective learning activities is therefore central to *Concept Cracking* and is the main means of creating a concept rich-environment in which pupils will learn best. This is much harder in religious education, because pupils' everyday world of experience is so secular, whereas with other subjects the concepts are more generally 'in the air'. The Project particularly emphasises the use of the creative arts as a way of addressing this challenge (Cooling, M, 1996 & 1998).

Secondly, the Project encourages teachers to draw on hermeneutical insights which emphasise the importance of the interaction between the horizon of the student and the horizon of the text. Clearly working with metaphor and narrative are central to this when reading the Bible. So often it has been assumed that the primary purpose of teaching the Bible text to students has been for them to gather information, in other words the emphasis is on knowing statements from the text. This is obviously important, but an overemphasis on this can mask the primary purpose of encountering Christian story, namely to encourage the reader or hearer to reflect on their own way of understanding the world in the light of that being expressed by the writer. This requires an ability to work with metaphor and narrative. Living in the light of a story is a creative process and demands the development of interpretative skills (Cooling. T, 1996a). Repeating statements is not enough. The importance of this has sparked off a major research project at The Stapleford Centre, looking at how the Bible can provide models or approaches for relating the Bible to education.

Thirdly, the Project embraces the idea that it is through exploratory conversation that children develop and expand their own religious ideas and vocabulary (Hull, 1991). This is very different to a password approach because, although it may entail a child using vocabulary that they do not fully understand, it requires them to explore that vocabulary using their own similes and metaphors rather than simply repeating religious jargon. So, many of the teaching activities employed encourage children to talk about their ideas.

5. The Personal Development of Pupils

Perhaps the most important question to have occupied religious educators in recent years is the relationship between the *learning about* and the *learning from* aspects of their subject This two dimensional approach to the subject, first introduced by Michael Grimmitt (1987), is now widely accepted (e.g. SCAA 1994). Robert Jackson helpfully summarises the effect learning about someone else's religion can have when he writes: 'What might appear to be entirely different and "other" at first glance can end up linking with one's own experience in such a way that new perspectives are created or unquestioned presuppositions are challenged' (1997, 130). The point is this: religious content in RE should be taught in such a way that it makes a contribution to the pupils' own personal development irrespective of whether or not the pupils accept the particular faith in question.

The Stapleford Project approach is particularly suited to promoting *learning from* since it focuses the pupils' attention on theological concepts rather than religious information. Theology is the way human beings come to understand their own experience of the world in the light of their understanding of God. So it is hardly surprising that studying Christian theology facilitates reflection on themes that are common to human experience generally. Our example of teaching the concept of righteous anger illustrates this.

A point of debate, however, is whether the nature of the religious content should or should not control the type of *learning from* that might be planned (see Cooling 1996a for a fuller treatment of this issue). Some would argue that the religions simply act as a quarry for helpful material for promoting personal development. Developing a systematic understanding of a religion is not a primary goal on this view. It is studied insofar as it offers helpful insights on personal development. Such an approach could be described as *pupil-structured*. Others would say, however, that the systematic understanding of the religion being studied is the controlling factor and that any learning from should arise out of this. Such an approach could be described as *content-structured* and reflects the position of the Stapleford Project. However, for the latter to be effective in promoting *learning from*, it must also be *pupil-related*. Hence the Project's emphasis on the hermeneutical process of translating the Christian concepts into forms that make sense in the pupils' world of experience.

This debate usually reflects a deep seated difference of opinion on the nature of religion. In the *pupil-structured* approach, religion is usually viewed as constituting the human activities of seeking to understand oneself and of trying to lead a more fully human existence. It is essentially functional. With the *content-structured* approach, religion is seen as the means by which humans seek to discover the truth about God and to reflect on the implications this has for their own lives. It is essentially a matter of revelation. The Stapleford Project takes the second position and therefore considers that the personal development outcomes of teaching Christianity should result from the development of a systematic understanding of Christianity.

CRITICISMS

No curriculum project can achieve everything. Each will have its strengths, which Project Directors will inevitably advertise! And each will have its weaknesses and critics will be quick to point them out. This final section is a brief discussion of those criticisms which have been levelled against the Stapleford Project.

1. The Project has developed materials exclusively for teaching Christianity. This should not be a surprise, since the Association of Christian Teachers, which sponsored the Project, is a faith-based group. As one only finds materials on teaching Buddhism in the ClearVision catalogue, a Buddhist educational charity, so one only finds Christianity featuring in the Stapleford Project's listings. So are the educational needs of schools being ignored in concentrating on one religion?

The response to this is to make two observations. First, it should be pointed out that there was a dearth of materials which equipped teachers for a theological approach to Christianity when the Project was set up. Meeting this need was the specific task the Project set out to tackle. Secondly, the approach can be applied to other religions, as was done in the case of the SCAA Model 2 syllabus (1994a). But, if Bruner is right, it requires those who really understand the subject matter to do justice to the individual religions. Superficiality is too evident in RE already. It also needs adding that not every religion is conceptually structured in the way Christianity is. The approach may not therefore be equally appropriate for all religions.

More seriously, the Stapleford approach may seem to ignore the fact that there are other concepts that are integral to RE (Rudge, 199,1 p25). These include those relating to human experience, such as commitment, and those relating to cross-religious, thematic studies, such as worship. But the particular contribution of the Project has been to focus on those concepts which have been under-represented in RE up to now, namely the theological concepts specific to a religion. The task, therefore, has been to redress a balance, which is *not* to suggest that the other types of concept are unimportant, but is to recognise the focus of this particular Project. The Project did not set out to produce an RE scheme of work, only to offer the resources for teaching Christianity in a conceptual way for use within the different schemes that exist in schools.

There is currently a debate as to whether a religion-by-religion (systematic) approach or a cross-religious themes (thematic) approach is the best way to teach. Certainly the Stapleford Project would be seen as a systematic approach and would attract the criticisms made of that (e.g. Hull 1995). This is a complex debate which cannot be embraced here. (For a fuller treatment see Cooling. T, 1996b). Suffice it to make two brief points. First, both approaches have something to contribute, it is not a case of either/or but of fitness for purpose. Second, the theological, conceptual approach has something to offer to a thematic approach by encouraging the formation of legitimate themes through links between religions which are theological in nature. The major criticism of the thematic approach as traditionally practised in religious education is that it forced links where there were none and thereby distorted the religions.

2. A point that we have already touched on is that the approach does emphasise the unity of Christianity at the expense of representing its diversity. It therefore needs balancing with other materials which offer a different perspective as, for example, is done in the Warwick RE Project (e.g. Robson, 1995, Everington, 1996)

3. A difficulty with any Project which adopts a step by step approach to teaching, is that there will be times when it breaks down. In other words the approach is too rigid if followed slavishly. This is particularly true when making links with pupil experience. Sometimes religious material has its own inherent ability to communicate (Grimmitt et al, 1991). The assumption that there is a comprehension gap between the world of Christianity and the world of the pupil may not always be correct (Wright, A, 1997). It is, therefore, a weakness if the approach is treated as a recipe which must be followed, rather than as an inspiration to good teaching. In the Project's secondary school materials (Wright, C, 1995), the author departed from strict adherence to the *Concept Cracking formula* on a number of occasions.

4. Finally, in a comprehensive critique, Andrew Wright (1997) argued that, in its emphasis on students comprehending Christianity, the Project does not confront the lack of authority and legitimacy that this religion may hold for the student. It assumes that because Christianity is there, it ought to be studied. It does not address the issue of student rejection of Christianity, except insofar as it makes the study of it more relevant and interesting. As Wright puts it, the Project 'must then be developed to embrace a critical appropriation that moves beyond comprehension to tackle questions of legitimacy, coherence and authority' (p 151). It can hardly be disputed that developing critical skills (or 'religious/theological literacy' as Wright calls it) is a central task for religious education. In defence, it can be said that the Project has also published materials which promote such a critical encounter with Christianity (e.g. Brown et al. 1997). It might also be argued that criticism is dependent on comprehension.

CONCLUSION

The Stapleford Project is misunderstood if it is seen to be offering a total package for teaching RE. Rather it is a contribution to a bigger task. Its specific concern has been to focus attention on the importance of the effective teaching of theological concepts using Christianity as the case study. In this we hope it has made a significant contribution. Others, it is hoped, will apply this to other religions as appropriate. However, like any curriculum project, it is not a panacea. It needs balancing with other approaches. Every Project is a product of a particular time, place and age. Some make a lasting contribution. Whether the Stapleford Project will is for time to judge.

REFERENCES

Astley, J. (1988) 'Theology and Curriculum Selection', *British Journal of Religious Education*, 10 (2), pp. 86-91.

Astley, J. (1992a) 'Will the Real Christianity Please Stand Up?', *British Journal of Religious Education*, 15 (1), pp. 4-12.

Astley, J. (1992b), 'Tradition and experience: conservative and liberal models for Christian education' in Astley, J & Day, D. (eds), *The Contours of Christian Education* (Great Wakering, McCrimmons).

Brown, A. et al. (1997) *God talk: Science talk – a teacher's guide to science and belief*, (Oxford, Lion)

Bruner, J. (1977) *The Process of Education* (Harvard, Harvard University Press).

Cooling, M. (1996) *Toolkit: three volume pack* (Swindon, Bible Society)

Cooling, M. (1998), *Jesus through Art* (Norwich, Religious and Moral Education Press).

Cooling, T. & M. (1987) 'Christian Doctrine in Religious Education', *British Journal of Religious Education*, 9 (3), pp. 152-159.

Cooling, T. (1992) 'Christianity in the Primary School', *Resource*, 14 (3), pp.1-3.

Cooling, T. (1993) 'The Use of Christianity in the Primary School Curriculum', *British Journal of Religious Education*, 15 (3), pp. 14-22.

Cooling, T. (1994a) *Concept Cracking: Exploring Christian Beliefs in School* (Stapleford, Stapleford Project Books).
Now available on www.stapleford-centre.org

Cooling, T. (1994b) *A Christian Vision for State Education* (London, SPCK)

Cooling, T. (1996a) 'Education is the Point of RE – not Religion?: theological reflections on the SCAA Model Syllabuses' in Astley, J. & Francis, L. (eds), *Christianity Theology and RE* (London, SPCK).

Cooling, T. (1996b) *Mishmash with Integrity: Resolving the tensions between systematic and thematic approaches to RE* (Cheltenham, Cheltenham and Gloucester College of Higher Education, RE Unit).

Crossman, L. (1993) *Salvation Through Schools: A Report and Reflection on Trainee-Teacher Attitudes to RE* (Lancaster, S. Martin's University College).

Day, D. (1985) 'Religious Education Forty Years On: A Permanent Identity Crisis?', *British Journal of Religious Education*, 7 (2), pp. 55-63.

Day, D. (1986) 'How Demanding is RE?' *Religious Studies* Today, 11 (2).

Donaldson, M. (1978) *Children's Minds* (London, Fontana)

Doble, P. (1993) 'Belonging before believing: some doxological reflections on teaching Christianity', *British Journal of Religious Education*, 15 (3), pp. 23-30.

Everington, J. (1996) *Meeting Christians: Book 2* (Oxford, Heinemann)

Goldman, R. (1964) *Religious Thinking from Childhood to Adolescence* (London, Routledge, Kegan & Paul).

Goldman, R. (1965) *Readiness for Religion* (London, Routledge, Kegan & Paul).

Grimmitt, M.H. (1987) *Religious Education and Human Development*, (Great Wakering, McCrimmons).

Grimmitt, M.H. (1991) 'The Use of Religious Phenomena in Schools', *British Journal of Religious Education*, 13 (2), pp. 77-88.

Grimmitt, M.H. et al. (1991) *A Gift to the Child: Religious Education in the Primary School* (London, Simon & Schuster) (now available from Stanley Thornes Ltd, Cheltenham, Glos. GL50 1YW).

Hammond, J, Hay, D. et al. (1990) *New Methods in RE Teaching: An Experiential Approach* (Harlow, Oliver & Boyd/Longman).

Hull, J.M. (1991) *God-Talk with Young Children: Notes for Parents and Teachers* (Derby, Christian Education Movement).

Hull, J. (1995), 'Religion As A Series of Religions' in *World Religions in Education*, (London, Shap Working Party).

Hull, J. (1996) 'A Gift to the Child: A New Pedagogy for Teaching Religion to Young Children' *Religious Education*, 91 (2), pp. 172-188

Jackson, R. (1997) *Religious Education: an interpretative approach* (London, Hodder & Stoughton).

Kay, W. & Francis, L. (1996) *Drift from the Churches* (Cardiff, University of Wales Press).

Kerry, T. (1984), *Teaching Religious Education* (London, Macmillan).

Kincaid, M. (1991) *How to Improve Learning in RE* (London, Hodder & Stoughton).

Office for Standards in Education (OFSTED), (1997) *The impact of new agreed syllabuses on the teaching and learning of religious education*, (London, HMSO).

Polanyi, M. (1967) *The Tacit Dimension* (London, Routledge, Kegan & Paul).

Read, G.T. et al. (1992), *How Do I Teach RE? 2nd Edition* (Cheltenham, Stanley Thornes).

Robson, G. (1995), *Interpreting Religions: Christians* (Oxford, Heinemann).

Rudge, J. (1991) *Assessing, Recording and Reporting RE* (Birmingham, Westhill College).

School Curriculum and Assessment Authority (1994a) *Model Syllabuses, Model 2: Questions and Teachings* (London, SCAA).

School Curriculum and Assessment Authority (1994b) *Model Syllabuses: Faith Communities' Working Group Reports* (London, SCAA).

Wright, A. (1993) *Religious Education in the Secondary School: Prospects for Religious Literacy*, (London, David Fulton Publishers).

Wright, A. (1997), 'Mishmash, Religionism and Theological literacy. An Appreciation and Critique of Trevor Cooling's Hermeneutical Programme', *British Journal of Religious Education*, 19 (3), pp. 143-156.

Wright, A. (1998) 'Hermeneutics and Religious Understanding, Part Two: towards a critical theory for religious education', *Journal of Beliefs and Values*, 19 (1), pp. 59-70.

Wright, C. (1995) *Key Christian Beliefs* (Oxford, Lion)

Other publications connected with the Stapleford Project

Cooling, T. (1994c) 'The Bible in the Secondary School' in King, Janet (ed.), *Teaching RE in Secondary Schools* (Crowborough, Monarch).

Cooling, T. (1997) 'Theology Goes to School: The Story of the Stapleford Project', *Journal of Christian Education*, 40 (1), 47-60.

Cooling, T. (2000) 'Pupil Learning' in Brandom, A-M. & Wright, A. (Eds) *Learning to Teach Religious Education in the Secondary School* (London, Routledge)

Hartland, Ian (1995), 'A Christian Vision for State Education', *Resource*, 17 (3), pp. 7-9.

Mead, J. (1990) *The Educational Rationale Underlying Early Years RE with Special Reference to Some Brunerian-based Developments*, Unpublished MA thesis, King's College, University of London.

Wright, C. (1992) *A Conceptual Approach to Teaching Christianity in the Secondary School*, Unpublished MA thesis, King's College, University of London.

CHAPTER 9

THE SPIRITUAL EDUCATION PROJECT:
CULTIVATING SPIRITUAL AND RELIGIOUS LITERACY
THROUGH A CRITICAL PEDAGOGY OF RELIGIOUS EDUCATION

Andrew Wright

INTRODUCTION AND CONTEXT

The Spiritual Education Project in outline

The *Spiritual Education Project* was based at King's College, London, and operated during a five year period between 1996-2000. The initial two phases of the project were made possible by the generous financial support of All Saints Educational Trust. The project's aim was three-fold:

- to analyse and evaluate the nature of contemporary spiritual education in England and Wales;

- to develop an alternative critical rationale;

- to present proposals for a new critical pedagogy.

The approach of the project was theoretical, concerned with the conceptualisation of spiritual education rather than with generating fresh empirical evidence of classroom practice. It proceeded via a critical review of the nature and rationale for spiritual education as this was presented in academic literature.

Phase one of the project, which ran from 1996-1998, set out to survey, critique and reconstruct the conceptualisation of contemporary spiritual education. The initial report was published as *Spiritual Pedagogy* (Wright 1998a). Phase two ran from 1998-1999 and sought to apply the theoretical aspects of phase one to the practical teaching context. The report of this phase was published as *Discerning the Spirit. Teaching Spirituality in the Religious Education Classroom* (Wright 1999). It combines a teacher-friendly

170

summary of the original research with an exploration of the implications of the research findings for classroom teaching. Phase three ran from 1999-2000. Its concern was to relate the findings of the initial two phases beyond the boundaries of religious education and explore their implications for cross-curricular issues and whole school policies. The report of this third phase was published as *Spirituality and Education* (Wright, 2000c).

The *Spiritual Education Project* does not stand alone. It forms part of a broader attempt to develop a critical rationale for religious education, an embryonic version of which was first outlined in *Religious Education in the Secondary School: Prospects for Religious Literacy* (Wright, 1993). This wider agenda proceeds on the basis of two overlapping research trajectories:

- the deconstruction of the mind-set of contemporary liberal religious education;

- the construction of a critical theory for religious education.

The Critique of Liberal Religious Education

A recurring theme within liberal religious education is its adoption of an anthropology rooted in the modern ideal of the autonomous individual. Here our identity is seen to be dependent on our self-understanding. It is through introspection and self-reflection that we come to develop our sense of identity. This image of the autonomous individual has had a profound effect on the way the relationship between language and experience is perceived. As our identity is rooted in introspection, so our language operates as the secondary expression of primary experience (Wright, 1996a; 1996b).

If the basic role of language is to enable us to express inner experience rather than describe states of affairs in the world then the realistic question of how such experience relates to external reality becomes sidelined. The fact that we feel good about ourselves becomes more important than whether or not we understand the world correctly. Being a contented pig is preferable to being a discontented philosopher.

This is especially so in the field of religion. Liberal religious education tends to favour an experiential-expressive model of religion in which religious language is concerned to express spiritual experience rather than describe the way things are in the world. As a result religious doctrines are important not as cognitive truth claims but merely as expressions of religious piety. This is reflected in liberal classrooms, with religious teaching concerned more with the stimulation of the child's capacity for spiritual experience than with issues of realistic religious truth (Wright, 1996b).

The widespread use of the experiential-expressive model has lead many liberal religious educators to adopt by default a specific universal theology. Here all religious traditions are seen as embodying equally valid expressions of a common religious experience. Doctrinal differences are mere accidents of culture, possessing no inherent cognitive significance. The liberal indoctrination of children into this particular theology is supported by the liberal commitment to the twin principles of freedom of belief and tolerance, one effect of which is to locate religious dogma within the subjective sphere of private belief, effectively withdrawing it from public discourse. It is at this point that liberalism ceases to function as an interim ethic intended to facilitate dialogue between contrasting traditions, and takes on instead the form of a closed ideological world-view into which pupils are indoctrinated (Wright 2000b).

CRITICAL RELIGIOUS EDUCATION

The negative critique of liberal religious education leads into a positive attempt to construct a critical theory of religious teaching.

The attempt begins with the recognition that there are viable alternatives to the mind-set of liberalism: an anthropology in which identity is formed via communal relationship rather than introspection; a model of language in which words function in a critically realistic manner to engage with external reality; a theology concerned with questions of ultimate truth; an education concerned with equipping pupils to explore conflicting world-views rather than inducting them into a single paradigm.

Critical religious education has no interest in a return to confessional modes of teaching. The shift to a liberal agenda is welcomed as a positive move, and the basic concern is with the consolidation and refinement of liberalism (Wright, 2000a). Here there are two possible paths forward. The first is to adopt a post-modern agenda, an option rejected on the grounds that to shift from a liberal to a post-modern framework will simply replace one ideology with another (Wright, 1996c). The second possibility is to draw on the resources of critical realism.

Critical realists seek to uphold the humanistic commitment to reason and thirst for truth first established by the Enlightenment. They recognise, however, that modern western culture has been guilty of abusing the ideals of the Enlightenment. Critical realism thus rejects the quick-fix approaches of scientism, emotivism, positivism and absolute idealism in favour of a more patient engagement with, and interrogation of, reality. For the critical realist the truth is indeed out there, but is larger than our ability to comprehend it. The appropriate response to this is neither scepticism, nor fundamentalism, but instead a contingent rationality: "This is the best sense we can make of reality at present, now let's see if we can achieve anything better".

To date the attempt to construct a critical theory for religious education has been developing in two directions. The first is in relationship with the hermeneutical tradition running from Schleiermacher through Dilthey, Husserl and Gadamer to Habermas (Wright 1997c, 1998a). The second is through the Spiritual Education Project itself, and it is to the basic findings of the project that we now turn.

2. The Research Report: Spiritual Pedagogy

Spiritual Pedagogy represents the heart of the Spirituality Project, consequently this section will concentrate on providing a basic summary of its main themes.

Survey: the contemporary consensus

The first section of the report identifies a basic liberal consensus regarding the rationale for spiritual education in the classroom. In the 1980s many religious educators had perceived the need to move beyond merely teaching pupils 'about' religion, and support the spiritual development of their pupils by encouraging them to learn 'from' religion. This process became dependent upon the adoption of an experiential-expressive model of religion, in which religious dogma and culture are seen as the external secondary expressions of internal primary religious experience. Effective spiritual education, it is suggested, must penetrate beyond the external core of religious expression and embrace its inner experiential heart.

As a result spirituality is linked with our capacity for inner experience and the cultivation of our spiritual sensibility. Spirituality has to do with exploring the 'inner space' of our minds. Such exploration is seen as constituting a means of enabling pupils to transcend ordinary everyday existence, since spiritual experience has to do with the extraordinary rather than the ordinary. Further, this capacity for spiritual experience is universal, common to all humanity. We are all spiritual beings, even though the capacity for spiritual awareness is more developed in some than others. Spiritual experience is not cognitive, it does not provide us with information about the world. it is, however, the source and ground of ultimate meaning and value. Spiritual awareness draws us to the fundamental mystery at the heart of the universe.

The question of the connection between spiritual experience and the actual way things are in reality is unanswered in the literature. Spiritual sensibility may be linked with specific religious traditions, with forms of universal theology embracing all religious systems, and with various types of atheism and agnosticism. Spiritual experience has little to do with truth, and all to do with personal integrity. It is better, within this framework, to hold a false belief in an appropriate manner than a true belief in an inappropriate way. This ambiguity about the connection between experience and truth is not perceived as a problem in the literature. The primary role of spiritual education is to enhance pupils' freedom to create their own personal world-views. The criteria for authentic spiritual experience is its ability to enhance self-understanding and self-acceptance rather than to relate individuals appropriately to the world they indwell.

Critique: flaws in the consensus

The second major section of the report attempts to deconstruct this liberal consensus. It does so in two stages. In the first place it undermines the claim that the understanding of spirituality adopted by liberal religious education is universally valid across all cultures and traditions. In the second place it demonstrates, through a case study of Trinitarian Christianity, that alternative spiritual traditions exist which are incompatible with that adopted in contemporary education.

The contemporary spiritual consensus is dominated by an ongoing tension between rationalism and romanticism. Rationalism, with its stress on objectivity and its simplistic faith in the power of science and technology to solve the fundamental problems faced by humanity is challenged by the counter-tradition of romanticism, with its stress on the significance of feeling and emotion and commitment to the realms of aesthetics, morality and religion. Modern western culture has been shaped by the polarity between rationalism and romanticism, fact and value, science and art, reason and emotion, sense and sensibility. It is here that the roots of the liberal understanding of spirituality are to be found.

The spiritual resources of Trinitarian Christianity begin not with inner subjectivity, but with the objective reality of God the Father, Son and Holy Spirit. The roots of this Trinitarian spirituality lie not in human experience but in divine revelation. Since God has chosen to reveal himself through creation, history, scripture and the teaching office of the church, our identities are dependent upon the nature of our relationship with this Trinitarian God. Sin distorts our relationship with God, leading to a false spirituality. It is in the public worship of the Christian community, in which sacramentally the divine realm breaks into the immanent realm of creation, that the possibility of an authentic relationship with our creator becomes a reality. For Trinitarian Christians genuine spirituality has little to do with introspective experience, and all to do with our developing relationship with an objective deity.

This particular Trinitarian spiritual tradition is clearly at odds with the liberal consensus. It is offered not as an alternative to liberalism, since critical religious education is not concerned with the re-establishment of Christian confessionalism in the public sphere of education. Rather it is offered as one example of a range of spiritual traditions that are incompatible with the predominantly western, white, male, middle-class, academic liberal spirituality presently imposed on the majority of our children.

Reconstruction: towards spiritual literacy

The third section of the report offers a framework for a critical spiritual education. It begins with a general definition of spirituality. This definition does not propose a common universal spirituality, but rather a deliberately broad backdrop within which specific spiritual traditions can be placed without compromising their distinctive identities.

> Spirituality is the developing relationship of the individual within community and tradition, to that which is – or is perceived to be – of ultimate concern, ultimate value and ultimate truth.
>
> (Wright 1998a, p.88)

Education is never neutral or value free, and will always nurture children into a specific spiritual tradition. The problem of liberal education is not the fact that it nurtures, but that it fails to acknowledge what it is doing. The choice of spiritual tradition ought to be the responsibility of the local school and community in accordance with its particular foundation. This process of spiritual nurture constitutes the first phase of spiritual education.

> Education will inevitably nurture children into a particular world view. the question is not whether this will happen, but how: consequently a primary task of spiritual education is to ensure that the spiritual tradition in which children are nurtured is appropriate, and that the process of nurture is effective.
>
> (Wright 1998a, p.95)

Any school that limits its task to that of nurturing pupils into a single spiritual tradition – whether this be Christian or Islamic, atheistic or agnostic, romantic or post-modernism – will offer no more than a confessional education. In an open democratic society good education needs to move beyond nurture and introduce a critical element into the classroom. This process of cultivating spiritual literacy constitutes the second phase of spiritual education.

> In addition to nurturing pupils within a particular spiritual tradition the school also has the duty of allowing them critical access to alternative traditions so that informed insight and wisdom may flourish through the development of spiritual literacy.
>
> (Wright 1998a, p.97)

An effective spiritual education will combine a hermeneutic of nurture with a hermeneutic of criticism. A good school will unashamedly induct children into the spiritual values and world-view which it considers to be of greatest worth, as well as insisting that children explore alternative possibilities.

PEDAGOGICAL PRINCIPLES

On the basis of the report, and of subsequent writings, it is possible to isolate five key pedagogical principles.

1. Critical religious education seeks to do justice to the horizon of religion

The major move in recent religious education has been a shift from a curriculum dominated by a broadly conceived Protestant Christianity to one dominated by (what are assumed to be) the 'big-six' major world faiths. This shift however achieves only a *quantitative* pluralism in which a plurality of religious traditions are presented within a common phenomenological framework, with the implication that they a generically related and compatible with one another. To do justice to the horizon of religion a *qualitative* pluralism is necessary, one which reflects the genuine diversity of religious and secular perspectives on religion, and accepts the ambiguous, controversial, and conflicting nature of theological truth claims.

Within a qualitative pluralism account must be taken of tensions within specific religious traditions. A presentation of Christianity, for example, will need to recognise the distinctions between fundamentalist, traditionalist, liberal and radical versions of the faith. Account must also be taken of differing attempts to understand the inter-relationship between religious traditions, reflecting a spectrum that runs from extreme sectarian exclusivism through to an all-embracing universal theology. Account must also be taken of the strength and authority of atheistic criticisms of religion on intellectual, moral and aesthetic grounds.

Justice can only be done to the various horizons of religion if the curriculum invites pupils to engage with an adequate range of contrasting and conflicting perspectives.

2. Critical religious education must do justice to the horizon of the pupil

Traditional confessional Christian religious education shifted from an assumption that pupils are embryonic Christians requiring no more than an ongoing nurture into their faith to an assumption that pupils are implicitly religious, lacking in explicit Christian belief and practice but retaining the capacity to have their innate religious potential unleashed by effective teaching. The shift to a liberal curriculum tended to perpetuate this latter approach. Pupils were approached as possessing the innate potential for religious and spiritual sensibility. Common to all these approaches is the tendency to view the religious horizon of children in terms of future potential rather than present reality. This leads to an increasingly idealised and abstract understanding of pupils' religious horizons. This in turn was exacerbated by the increasing assumption that children should learn to be neutral and unbiased in their approach to religious traditions other than their own. All this reflects an ongoing failure to take seriously the concrete horizon of the individual pupil.

Critical religious education operates on the assumption that children come to the classroom with an already developing religious world-view. It will almost certainly have been adopted from the significant adults and peers in each child's life. Such religious presuppositions will not necessarily be stable or internally coherent. The religious sentiments expressed in these emerging world views will not necessarily be positive and affirmative of religion. If theology is simply 'god-talk' then every child is a theologian. It is impossible for any individual to avoid a particular religious stance, whether that be of faith and commitment, rejection and derision, or ignorance and agnosticism. It is vital to effective education that children are given the freedom and encouragement to recognise and articulate their emergent religious beliefs and attitudes without constraint or manipulation, and that the horizons of the pupils – whatever their material content – become a conscious and integral part of the learning process.

3. Critical religious education seeks to equip pupils to recognise and respond appropriately to power structures inherent in religious and educational discourse

One of the implied claims of liberal religious education is that it provides a neutral vantage point from which religion can be explored without prejudice. It is now generally accepted that such a privileged perspective is unobtainable. The way to constrain the imposition of ideological bias is not to pretend that it does not exist, but rather to draw it to the surface and openly acknowledge it. This is something that Christian educators have (at times painfully) begun to learn to do, and a path which liberal religious educators urgently need to learn to tread.

Given that ideological power structures are unavoidable, even in the most 'open' of liberal settings, it is imperative not only that teachers learn to recognise and admit to their underlying presuppositions, but that pupils do so as well. Here critical religious education seeks to avoid two extremes. The first is a traditionalist subject based pedagogy which proceeds by pre-packaging the subject to be taught within a particular ideological framework and then develops ways of encouraging and enabling pupils to swallow the entire package. The second is a progressive child-centred pedagogy which retreats from the imposition of pre-packaged knowledge on children by insisting on their freedom to assimilate knowledge in any way they choose, without rule, guidance or restraint. Such an anarchic pedagogy is no less an immersion into an ideological world-view, in which personal preference is offered as the basic criteria of truth, than the traditionalist model. A critical pedagogy will seek to avoid both extremes by insisting on the primary importance of providing pupils with the skills, knowledge and wisdom through which they can identify and explore both their own ideology and the various ideologies presented by religious and secular traditions.

4. Critical religious education seeks to enable a critical dialogue between the horizon of the child and the horizon of religion

Learning takes place, critical religious education claims, when the horizons of the pupil and of religion are brought face-to-face. As these horizons interact two dangers must be avoided. The first is the colonisation of the child's horizon by any one particular religious horizon. The second is the colonisation of the horizon(s) of religion by the unchecked horizon of the child, driven by the child's untutored prejudice. An instinctive acceptance or rejection of religion that immediately closes down the possibility of conversation is not supportive to effective learning. Critical education demands the cultivation of intelligent conversation between the two horizons, in which the religious horizons of the child encounters a range of religious perspectives and options, and uses this encounter as a means of further clarifying, enriching and developing the child's religious beliefs.

5. Critical religious education seeks to develop in pupils a religious literacy rooted in attentiveness, intelligence, reasonableness and responsibility

The coming together of the horizons of pupil and religion will result both in convergence and dissonance. At least some aspects of one or more of the horizons of religious meaning are likely to be familiar and acceptable to the pupil. However other aspects of alternative horizons will appear strange, difficult to comprehend, and even fantastical. Both the recognition of compatibility and of dissonance provide a stimulation for further reflection, conversation and study. What is important for the educator is not what is believed by the child, but the manner in which they come to own their particular belief systems. A belief can be held through ignorance, or through sensitive reflective. It is better, whether one espouses atheism, agnosticism or religious belief, to be attentive, intelligent reasonable and responsible than lazy, ignorant, immoderate and irresponsible in assimilating and developing one's ultimate beliefs systems and commitments. It is pupils' ability to take part in an informed, critical, sensitive and ideologically aware conversation about the nature of ultimate reality, and of their relationships to this reality, that marks the heart of religious literacy, and the fundamental aim of the pedagogy of critical religious education.

PEDAGOGICAL STRATEGIES

The series of pedagogical principles outlined above do not demand any one specific teaching methodology. What is offered in this section is simply an example of one possible way in which the principles of critical pedagogy may be applied in the classroom. It is rooted in a spiral rather than linear model of learning. In spiral learning pupils continually circle around a series of topics, periodically returning to an issue to review it in ever increasing depth. The model described here involves three spirals of learning. In each of the three turns pupils return to the same topic with a new agenda which enables them to develop their learning in ever increasing depth. The first turn is concerned with exploring the horizon of the child, the second with the horizons of religion, the third with the cultivation of dialogue across horizons with a view to enhancing religious literacy *viz*:

A PEDAGOGY FOR CRITICAL RELIGIOUS EDUCATION

Phase One: The Horizon of the Pupil

(i) basic introduction to the topic

(ii) open exploration of the topic

(iii) articulation of initial beliefs

Phase Two: The Horizons of Religion

(i) presentation of a spectrum of conflicting religious and secular perspectives

(ii) location of pupils' positions within this spectrum

Phase Three: The Engagement of Horizons

(i) Development of critical thinking skills

(ii) conversation across and between horizons

(iii) re-articulation of pupils' initial position

Phase one: the horizons of the pupils

Every pupil brings with them to the classroom an emergent theology. The first stage of learning begins with enabling them to recognise and initially articulate their developing belief systems. Thus, for example, a series of lessons on the existence of God might begin simply by introducing the class to the concepts 'atheism', 'theism' and 'agnosticism'. Once the topic is introduced pupils will need to be encouraged to explore the range of possible responses to the topic and begin to identify and evaluate reasons why a particular belief might be held. Thus small groups might be encouraged to brainstorm as many reasons as they can find for and against belief in God. Once the range of possible responses to a topic has been opened up in this way the first phase may be drawn to a conclusion by inviting pupils to articulate their own particular stance on the topic, together with a provisional justification for their adopted position. Thus the first spiral of learning begins with pupils being open and honest in their engagement with the topic.

Phase two: the horizons of religion

In phase two attention shifts from a concern to provide pupils with the freedom to articulate their own personal world-views to an attempt to allow them the freedom to encounter a range of perspectives within the religious horizon(s) of the topic under consideration. Here, inevitably, the teacher will need to be selective, since it is clearly not possible to place every perspective on the table. However the crucial issue here is that a range of contrasting perspectives are indeed brought before the pupils. A *quantitative* religious pluralism, such as that reflected in much liberal teaching, will do no more than introduce pupils to a plurality of religious tradition within a common interpretative framework. What is required is a *qualitative* presentation of religious horizons which enable pupils to encounter a range of perspectives that may well be conflicting and incompatible.

To continue with the previous example, once pupils have provisionally identified themselves as atheist, theist or agnostic they may now be invited to explore the concepts in greater depth. This might proceed via a sociological examination of the rich spectrum of religious beliefs, attitudes and practice in contemporary Britain. As well as providing important information about the prevalence of religion in Britain this will crucially enable pupils to locate their own particular religious faith and practice within this panoramic picture. This presentation of religious horizons will need to go deeper than a mere sociological description of the religiosity of the United Kingdom. It will need to introduce pupils to the reasons and justifications for being an atheist, an agnostic or a theist.

Phase three: the horizons engaged

The presentation of a diverse range of religious horizons of meaning in phase two, if taught well, ought to set up dissonance in the minds of pupils. They will be forced to recognise both the tension between the various perspectives presented to them and also the tension between their own horizon and the various religious horizons. This is a good thing since dissonance, when properly handled, plays a key in the learning process. The focus in phase three is on the cultivation of the skills needed to engage in a reasonable and responsible conversation within and between the various horizons. Pupils must be taught how to think theologically and philosophically as they embark on the task of discovering meaning within dissonance and ambiguity.

Thus a series of lessons on the existence of God will need to move beyond a mere description of the theistic, atheistic and agnostic contours of contemporary society, and engage with the question of which particular account of 'God' is true. The rational and moral arguments of secular atheism will need to be placed alongside post-modern agnosticism, rational philosophical arguments for the existence of God, and arguments for belief in God rooted in religious authority and faith commitment. It is not enough that pupils simply affirms their particular religious belief and stop there. Nor is it sufficient to introduce children to the full range of beliefs about God on a 'choose-for-yourself' basis if the criteria for selection is no more than personal preference and inclination. Only when pupils learn to engage in informed conversation about their beliefs, and the beliefs of others, can authentic religious literacy emerge.

EVALUATING THE PROJECT

In its short time in the public domain the *Spiritual Education Project* has been the subject of widespread interest, attracting a mixture of enthusiastic support and deeply felt – and occasionally vociferous – opposition. It is currently the focus of the research of a number of doctoral students at King's College. This section offer a summary of some of the main oral criticisms made of the project, together with an indication of possible directions for future research.

The reality of the classroom

It has been asked whether *Spiritual Pedagogy* gives an accurate picture of actual classroom practice. The simple answer to this is that such information is not currently available: the empirical research, though much needed, has yet to be carried out. The report offers a survey of the academic literature and assumes a relatively close connection between theory and practice.

For some the proposals put forward by the project are impracticable and too difficult for pupils to achieve. The concept of religious literacy appears to place too high a demand on children's cognitive skills. The counter-argument is that religious education has consistently under-estimated the conceptual abilities of pupils, and that one of the main reasons why children fail to engage with religion in the classroom is the failure to offer appropriate intellectual stimulation. There is certainly much work to be done in this area. My colleague Ann-Marie Brandom is currently undertaking research at King's into the development of religious literacy with special reference to thinking skills and programmes of accelerated learning.

By far the most frequent response to the project are requests for support and guidance for teachers who wish to introduce a critical dimension into their teaching. A number of approaches to teacher education at PGCE and INSET level are currently being explored. The philosophy of critical religious education is reflected in the editorial policy – though not necessarily by individual contributions – of the introductory primer *Learning to Teach Religious Education in the Secondary School* (Wright & Brandom, 2000). There remains an urgent need for curriculum materials and learning resources to be produced and made available.

Spirituality across the whole curriculum

Historically religious education has always been the Cinderella of the curriculum, seeking permission from more powerful partners to take part in the enterprise of secular educational. The model of critical spiritual education derives in part from the recognition by some religious educators that plural education in a democratic context must entail a process of empowering children to becomes responsible and literate. This approach is transferable from religious education to the whole curriculum. For once religious educators find themselves in the unusual position of being able to give a lead and direction to education as a whole.

Much contemporary educational debate is mesmerised by an unnecessary dualism between subject-centred education and child-centred education. Educational debate frequently descends to the level of a political scrap between conservatives and progressive, with both factions competing for the right to impose their particular ideology in the classroom. Critical education constitutes an attempt to rewrite the ground rules of educational debate. Good education is not a matter of fighting for the right to impose a particular truth on children, but of providing future generations with the skills, insight, wisdom and literacy to enable them to make a better job of flourishing in a plural society than the present generation. The exploration of the implication of a critical religious education for the whole curriculum are explored in *Spirituality and Education* (Wright, 2000c).

A Reactionary Programme?

For many the major flaw in the project lies in its supposedly reactionary nature. Some advocates of liberal and post-modern forms of religious education find in the project a neo-confessional attempt to recover a Christian world-view. This is not true. Opposition to the contemporary consensus is not driven by the fact that it excludes the particular religious tradition of the current author, but that it excludes *all* spiritual traditions apart from the liberal one. The fundamental opposition is to the resurgent confessionalism and indoctrination currently rife, if unrecognised, in many liberal classrooms.

It is increasingly clear that some readers have understood the references to Trinitarian spirituality in the second part of Spiritual Pedagogy as prescriptive rather than as a descriptive case-study. The lack of careful attention to the basic argument of the report reflects the somewhat disturbing rise of an 'evangelical' – and even on occasions 'fundamentalist' – liberalism that is all too quick to spring to its own defence, and struggles to apply the principles of critical thinking to its own fundamental assumptions.

The question of spiritual truth

A final common complaint is that critical religious education misunderstands the nature of religion in making the question of realistic truth primary.

Any response to this must begin by affirming the historical reality that at least one theological tradition, Christianity, quite clearly and unambiguously understands its credal and dogmatic statements to refer to real events and a real God. To suggest, as happened at a recent conference, that 'Christianity makes no truth claims' is simply a historical untruth. It is, of course, true to say that there is a certain post-modern nominalistic philosophy currently in fashion that denies *a priori* that there has ever been any such entity as Christianity. It is also true to affirm that within Christianity there is a small radical group who espouse non-realistic versions of the tradition. However, to privilege these two discourses above the centuries long self-understanding of both grass-root Christianity and official Christian documents constitutes yet another case of intellectual colonisation.

Both the traditionalist Christian, radical Christian and post-modern narratives concerning Christianity demand a hearing, and should be given one in the classroom. To begin to make sense of the conflict between them is, inevitably, to embark on a search for truth, whether that truth be realistic or non-realistic in nature. A critical religious education will allow children to sit at the feet of traditionalist Christians, radical Christians and advocates of a post-modern deconstruction, and learn to be intelligent about all three, and about their own response to the various truth claims involved.

Summary And Conclusion

It has only been possible to offer a flavour of the work currently being carried out in the field of critical religious education in general, and spiritual education in particular. At its heart is a fairly basic thesis: Curriculum debate in religious education has all too often been limited to an ideological battle for control of the hearts and minds of children amongst conflicting and contrasting religious and secular ideologies. No education can avoid being ideological. Critical religious education, with its commitment to enabling children to achieve appropriate levels of spiritual and religious literacy, simply offers the most appropriate ideological framework for religious education, since its basic ideology is that of the empowerment of children to learn to be responsible and wise as they encounter the vitally important, though extremely dangerous, horizon of religion.

REFERENCES

Wright, A. (1993) *Religious Education in the Secondary School: Prospects for Religious Literacy*, (London: David Fulton).

Wright, A. (1996a) 'The Child in Relationship: Towards a Communal Model of Spirituality' in, R. Best (ed.) *Education, Spirituality and the Whole Child*, (London: Cassell), pp. 139-149.

Wright, A. (1996b) 'Language and Experience in the Hermeneutics of Religious Understanding', *British Journal of Religious Education*, 18:3, pp. 166-180.

Wright, A. (1996c) 'Postmodernism and Religious Education: A Reply to Liam Gearon', *The Journal of Beliefs and Values*, 17:1, pp. 22-28.

Wright, A. (1996d) 'Myths of Emancipation, Narratives of Redemption: An Educational Reflection on the Epistemological Roots of the Contemporary Ecological Crisis in the West', *The Journal of Beliefs and Values*, 17:2, pp. 22-28.

Wright, A. (1997a) 'Mishmash, Religionism and Theological Literacy. An Appreciation and Critique of Trevor Cooling's Hermeneutical Programme', *British Journal of Religious Education*, 19:3, pp. 143-156.

Wright, A. (1997b) 'Embodied Spirituality. The Place of Culture and Tradition in Contemporary Educational Discourse on Spirituality', *The International Journal of Children's Spirituality*, 1:2, pp. 8-20.

Wright, A. (1997c) 'Hermeneutics and Religious Understanding. Part One:The Hermeneutics of Modern Religious Education', *The Journal of Beliefs and Values*, 18:2, pp. 203-216.

Wright, A. (1998a) *Spiritual Pedagogy. A Survey, Critique and Reconstruction of Contemporary Spiritual Education in England and Wales*, (Abingdon: Culham College Institute).

Wright, A. (1998b) 'Hermeneutics and Religious Understanding. Part Two:Towards a Critical Theory for Religious Education', *The Journal of Beliefs and Values*, 19:1, pp. 59-70.

Wright, A. (1999) *Discerning the Spirit. Teaching Spirituality in the Religious Education Classroom* (Abingdon: Culham College Institute).

Wright, A. (2000b) 'Religious Education, Religious Literacy and Democratic Citizenship' in Astley, J., Francis, L.J. and Robbins, M. (Eds). *The Fourth R for the Third Millennium*, Dublin, Lindisfarne Books.

Wright, A. (2000c) *Spirituality and Education. Master Classes in Education Series*. (London: Falmer Press).

Wright, A. & Brandom, A-M. (Eds.) (2000d) *Learning to Teach Religious Education in the Secondary School* (London: Routledge).

CHAPTER 10

THE CHILDREN AND WORLDVIEWS PROJECT:
A NARRATIVE PEDAGOGY OF RELIGIOUS EDUCATION

Clive and Jane Erricker

INTRODUCTION

The Children and Worldviews Project began in 1993. Initially it was funded by three higher education institutions: University College, Chichester, King Alfred's College, Winchester and La Sainte Union College, Southampton. The collaborating researchers were Clive Erricker, Jane Erricker, Danny Sullivan and John Logan. With the demise of La Sainte Union College in 1996-7 the Project continued funded by the first two colleges. Cathy Ota was, by then, a member of the Project team, having joined it in 1994.

The impetus for the Project derived from the conviction that education and religious education was too content led and paid insufficient attention to the capabilities and experiences of children and young people. This conviction was a result of a number of influences. The first was based on the previous teaching experiences of the Project team. Religious Education, since the 1970s, had been considerably changed and enhanced by employing a phenomenological model of enquiry and a broader curriculum based on the study of 'world faiths'. Thus it was a mirror of what had become religious studies in higher education. This sufficed as an exciting academic discipline but, when translated into the school curriculum, paid insufficient attention to the experiences of the learner as part of the model of enquiry. This was exacerbated by the fact that most learners had secular worldviews, rather than religious ones, and tended to be suspicious of, rather than interested in, the subject of religion.

The second influence was that of educational theory and policy. During the 1980s and early nineties education was, and still is, dominated by a

188

'competencies model. This determines that skills, knowledge and understanding are the measure of learning. However, such terms are firmly wedded to a notion of curriculum subjects by which they are circumscribed. This results in the idea of 'attainment'. Such a model emphasises what the learner has 'learnt' in relation to what the subject demands. It is content and skills specific and thus marginalises what the individual can bring to their learning. It over-emphasises what the subject has to offer to the detriment of the larger learning experience and development of what has been called 'the whole child'. Since religions were, ostensibly, concerned with 'whole people' this is somewhat ironic, although the history of religious education has never had a sound pedagogy in this respect.

The third influence, and perhaps the most vital, was the experience of relating to children and young people. Whilst it is clear to teachers of some experience that trust, respect and a willingness to listen are important professional qualities, these tend to be seen as pre-requisites for good classroom relationships rather than as a vehicle for learning. In other words, they are understood as pre-requisites for good curriculum learning to take place rather than *the* site of learning and development. The nature of this distinction was brought home to us forcibly by the youngest child of two of the authors.

At this time P. was seven years old. Her grandfather died shortly after she was born. He had met her in the first two weeks of her life but she of course could not remember him. In family conversations stories about him were told by her older brother and sister and parents. He was part of their world but excluded from hers. As a result, in trying to rectify this situation, she would ask what had happened to him and where she could find his grave. He was cremated and there was no place to go where she could find evidence of him having lived. There was no concrete way whether via memorial or memory in which she could share in his life. For P. this resulted in a sense of separation or exclusion from the family story and one to which she often referred. In consequence she is particularly concerned about her remaining grandparents and wishes to stay in close touch with them. It also influenced her attitude towards death and especially in relation to anyone in her family carrying donor cards. She believes that making one's body available for medical use after death will result in a similar lack of memorial to that of her grandfather; in other words, an incomplete story.

However, in relating this story, much is left unsaid, particularly in relation to the circumstances within which it was related. It resulted from a chance remark made by P. when driving past a crematorium. She spotted the memorials erected in the grounds and asked the question 'Has Umpy (her grandfather) got one of those?' What ensued was a conversation about cremation, wills and the question of an afterlife (Erricker C., Erricker J. ,1994). The salient points to note are that this conversation, the mutual learning that ensued and the 'knowledge' that derived were driven by her existential enquiry and took place contingently within what Shotter has called 'the disorderliness of everyday life' (Shotter, 1992, 69).

The main point to note in reflecting on this incident is that, had the conversational process of enquiry not been pursued, ad hock, by closing it down with a 'suitable' and safe 'answer', mutual ignorance would have ensued. Pedagogically speaking, what was required was attending to the nature of the question asked, seeking to explore its relationship with the experience from which it derived, and working through the issues that needed to be addressed as the subject matter of enquiry. At a theoretical level this is what Newman and Holzman refer to as 'the performance of conversation' (Newman F. and Holzman L. 1997, 105-113).

If this incident were offered as a solitary anecdotal tale it would have only tangential relevance to pedagogical practice in the classroom setting. However, it was an impetus for the Project to research with children in school employing the above principles and procedures. Put simply we set out to research what mattered in children's lives and, using conversational technique, explore the issues that they raised. An account of this is given in a report on the Project's research in this first phase (Erricker C, Erricker J, Ota C, Sullivan D, Fletcher M.,1997). The findings of this research confirm Theodore Roszak's observation that:

'We all bring into school a wholly unexplored, radically unpredictable identity. To educate is to unfold that identity – to unfold it with the utmost delicacy, recognising that it is the most precious resource of our species, the true wealth of the human nation.'

(Roszak 1981)

Our own research, conducted on the principles of Grounded Theory (Glaser and Strauss 1967), identifies an area of enquiry and an original research question, then works toward the construction of a theory from the data collected. This is the reverse of how we normally construct what we call a curriculum. Thus the educational principles behind the research design were the opposite of those employed in curriculum design. In other words by matching our findings against curriculum requirements the distinctions would amount to what curriculum leaves out of education. Thus we could arrive at a reconsideration of the principles and procedures for pedagogical practice on the basis of the research process and findings. As we wrote at the time when we published our findings:

'The evidence, approach and conclusions of our research suggest that when listening to children's accounts of their experience and imaginative play with concepts we are forced to reconsider what it is we undertake in the business of education, A fundamental question such as 'What are schools for?' springs to mind. How do we deal with this question and what evidence is there that we should reconsider our professional role? The central issue appears to be the delivery of the curriculum. The term 'deliver' is the clue to our dilemma. If we regard listening and responding to children as central to our educational endeavour then this delivery is an aspect of, but not the sole driving force behind our work. However, the curriculum then becomes less content led.'

(Erricker C. and Erricker J. in Erricker C. et. al., 1997, 186)

This confirmed conclusions derived from other research, notably that of Gordon Wells into language development. He stated that:

'No two children – and no two adults, for that matter – are identical. Each is unique as a result of his or her particular combination of genetic inheritance and individual experience. The recognition of this unique quality of every individual is essential, of course, as a basis for our personal dealings with them.'

(Wells 1987, 125).

Applying these conclusions to the question of what constitutes a sufficient pedagogical design for religious education results in a radical reconsideration of not only how we teach but also of what is to be learnt and how learning take place. It is these considerations that will be the subject of the next section.

PEDAGOGICAL PRINCIPLES

Here the influence of two key contextualising factors must be addressed in relation to the delivery of religious education, educational aims and curriculum design. The first is that the history of modern western education and curriculum construction is dominated by rationalist and empiricist conceptions of knowledge that developed during the period of the Enlightenment; two key figures and works in this period being Immanuel Kant (Kant, republished 1960) and David Hume (Hume, republished 1975). This has had two significant consequences. The first is that any defence of a curriculum subject must be on the basis that it has a body of knowledge. Both religious studies and religious education have suffered criticism on this account, being charged with having a non-rational and non-empirical character. In response both have sought to defend their status on rational and empirical grounds. By and large they have been successful to a sufficient degree (Waardenberg 1973; Otto 1927; Smart 1973; Jackson 1997; Wright 1998; Erricker 1999). However, there has been a pedagogical cost as far as religious education is concerned.

The predominantly descriptive character of phenomenological enquiry, when translated into the context of religious education has tended to accentuate the importance of knowing the subject of study rather than the reflexive character of engagement. At its worst this has been understood in the classroom as knowing the 'facts' and exterior manifestations of religious behaviour rather than existential issues related to faith and spirituality. The latter, of course, are susceptible to criticism from a rationalist and empiricist perspective. Both phenomenological and theological approaches to religious education have also recoursed to the idea that the subject is one of studying belief systems. These can be understood as metaphysical ways of explaining the world and the meaning of human existence in a rational, if metaphysical, manner. The concern then becomes one of truth claims. Again this provides a defence against the insufficiency of the subject but at the cost of emphasising its rational and objective character (Wright 1998).

The second consequence of the influence of rationalism and empiricism is that education is understood as a secular enterprise. The curriculum, with the exception of religious education, is entirely secular in purpose and design. The secular basis of education reflects the institutional secularisation of society generally. As a result the teacher of religious education is often attempting to address the learning of pupils whose own worldviews are secular in character. Pedagogically the inclusion of the learner's experience within a subject that, by definition of its content, has an opposing frame of reference, can often result in unproductive learning. The teacher is trapped between the exclusivity of the content matter of the subject and the issues of interest to the learner. This is not because there are not issues of interest to the learner within the teachings of religious traditions but because those issues have to be addressed in relation to, or within the frame of reference of, the traditions. In other words the enquiry has to have a religious character.

The second contextualising factor is as follows. It could be argued that the reason for maintaining religious education within the curriculum in England and Wales is not primarily due to the robustness of the defences as to religious education's intrinsic worth as a subject of study, but rather because of extrinsic, historic and social, purposes. Largely these amount to an underlying recognition that it maintains the presence of moral education (historically understood as moral instruction), and affirms the importance of Christianity as an aspect of our cultural heritage. Initial evidence for this can be found in the emphasis placed on Christianity, in this respect, in the wording of the 1988 Education Reform Act and the subsequent circular 1/94 (DFEE 1994), and in the argument presented in the opening speech by Nicholas Tate, chief executive of the Qualifications and Curriculum Authority (QCA) (Tate 1996; Erricker C. 1997). The latter heralded the inception of Education for Adult Life, under the banner of which spiritual, moral, social and cultural education were to be addressed. The pedagogical issue at stake here is whether we are taking seriously the experiences, issues and thinking of young people with diverse cultural backgrounds and in differing family and community contexts-which in turn operate with different values, or whether we are seeking to enculturate them into a particular mono-communitarian model of national identity which incorporates a normative code of morality (Bauman 1999, xlvff).

Having outlined these two contextualising factors it should be clear that the Project's approach to pedagogy calls into question the educational sufficiency of them both. In response the issue is not a matter of fine tuning the present provision but asking for a radical re-assessment of the pedagogical principles we employ to achieve a different educational purpose. This begins by questioning what we mean by 'knowledge' and how we go about 'knowing'. According to rationalist and empiricist design knowledge is objective. This also leads to creating the difference between secular, that is scientific, and religious truth claims. This divide is wholly unhelpful for a number of reasons. The most important are that it denies subjectivity, thus it does not permit the importance of the 'affective': relating to emotions and individual experience, as a way of 'knowing'. Also, this model of knowledge does not concern itself with relationships, what we may call relational knowing, knowing from within a group or community (Newman and Holzman 1997, 105ff). An alternative approach is to speak of knowing as narrative knowledge. Narrative knowledge or what Lyotard terms 'narrative pragmatics' (Lyotard 1984) has the following characteristics: it is relative; relational and process oriented. These features will be addressed below in explaining the principles and procedures of a narrative pedagogy.

A Narrative Pedagogy

The first principle that underpins a narrative pedagogy is that all 'knowledge' is relative. Relativism posits that there is no absolute or objective knowledge, in effect 'there is no "contrary" to place in opposition to relativism (Smith 1998, 25). This is because we must recognise that the 'When we speak of a picture of nature...we do not actually mean any longer a picture of nature, but rather a picture of our relation to nature' (Heisenberg in Hazelrigg 1995, ix). In other words, to put it another way, 'we have 'no God's eye view' (Putnam 1981 in Smith 1998, 26). This argument is elaborated in detail in Lyotard's classic text (Lyotard 1984) but to a different conclusion. Smith argues that the value of relativism is that it enables seeking for consensus; for Lyotard this is an unachievable aim, and anyway denies difference. For him the process is one of paralogy, to undermine from within any attempt to produce a grand narrative (or orthodoxy of view) that silences small narratives. This distinction effectively divides relativist from postmodern positions. For our purposes this distinction is not the central issue. Pedagogically the principle question is whether learning is measured according to our knowledge and understanding of grand narratives; in the case of religious education these would be the belief systems of Christianity, Islam, Buddhism, Hinduism, etc. or whether we understand them as constructions with political purposes, in the context of which they make truth claims. The decision we make on this issue also has a radical effect on the pedagogical process.

If we wish to take the 'small narratives' of learners seriously and put them at the centre of this process we cannot also put learning these belief systems at the centre. The result of doing the former will engage us, as teachers, with constructing a process that enables the learner to express, reflèct on and converse across the narratives presented in the context of the classroom community. The result of doing the latter will be first to ensure that learners know, can communicate and respond to understanding the truth claims presented. Any attempt to balance these two objectives must fall down on one side or the other because they operate according to opposing epistemological and pedagogical principles. This cannot be rectified by attempting to employ a pedagogical process that apparently hides this radical difference.

For this reason the attempts that have been made, from the attainment targets in the SCAA Model syllabuses of Learning About and Learning From (SCAA 1994), through to introducing the idea of a 'New Style' phenomenology (Jackson 1997), are pedagogically insufficient. This is not because the subject matter is inappropriate, it is because the idea of subject matter is wrong in itself. In terms of the relationship between curriculum content and pedagogical practice we find ourselves operating across two incommensurable paradigms. This is the case even if we seek to represent religions as 'faith traditions' with 'membership groups' (Jackson 1997). Presenting religions in this way offers an admirable and sophisticated model that takes account of cultural pluralism. But it cannot extend to cultural plurality (Bauman 1999, xxix ff.), within which it is the voices of individuals that have to be heard, rather than individuals speaking as representatives of membership groups belonging to faith traditions.

PEDAGOGICAL PROCEDURES AND STRATEGIES

When we translate this into the principles that facilitate the relational process in the classroom we can present it as attending to the following five issues, in order to allow children and young people to speak freely and responsibly:

- Attending to the means by which meaning can be articulated;

- Attending to the degree of security provided;

- Attending to the degree of negotiation required;

- Attending to the degree of freedom and independence desired (cognitively, spiritually and emotionally);

- Attending to the balance of authority and authoritative statements.

The aim of this process is to encourage narrative response.

As well as these specific 'attendances' within a particular conversation, the teacher needs to have developed a relationship with the child that encourages trust. These conversations are self-revelatory, and the usual power relationship between teacher and pupil may well preclude the kind of narrative response required in this type of practice. The type of relationship needed is that defined by McGuiness (1998), when speaking of the counselling relationship, as having the following core dimensions:

- Empathy
- Unconditional positive regard
- Genuineness
- Immediacy

This demands sophisticated skills from the teacher. But the whole point is that the teacher develops these skills in order to teach in such a way that his or her learners are encouraged to develop them also. One vital aspect of this pedagogical practice is the capacity to analyse the conceptual relevance and the affective significance of a particular response. It is important not to separate these out as though the conceptual and affective are distinct categories (as rationalism would have us believe). Here we can take an example from a seven year old child.

The stimulus used prior to this response was a poem by Brian Patten, 'Looking for Dad'. The subject was parental separation and Dad leaving home.

V.'s response was prefaced by another child, J. explaining that she thought Dad had gone to heaven. V. then picked up this idea and elaborated on it in relation to the death of her grandmother.

Q.   Where do you think Dad has gone?

J.   up in heaven.

Q J. tell me what happens when you go up to heaven.

J.   You see God and that.

V. I think that in heaven you can ride a white pony and have marshmallows. Before my Nan died she told me lots of things because she knew she was going to die and she told me about all the things she was going to do and she said she was going to send me a postcard. Before she went she gave me a piece of paper and stuck a photograph on it. I've still got it.

She said she would be happy and she wanted me to be happy when she died. On that day she got a picture of her and all the family, stuck it on a postcard and wrote on the back, "I'll see you in your heart". Now she's always with me. Now I talk to her all the time. I talk to her when I'm lonely. When I've argued with my friends I go and sit on the wall and think about her and talk to her. When I get fed up I sit there and talk to her about my friends. She tells me that she's riding on things. She says she's having a really nice time. She says she's going to ring me up. She says things in my head, she rings up my brain and talks to me. When she went up in heaven she took one of her special secrets. She took it with her and she can just ring me up, it's clever. This special secret makes her able to do that.

I keep on wanting to tell people things but they don't understand. I know everyone's in heaven who has died. Grandma tells me. She works in a cleaners. She washes all the clouds in heaven. She's got lots and lots of friends in heaven. She hopes we'll stay alive a long time but she wants me to go up there to see her. I'd like to go and see her but if you go up there you've got to stay there. You can't go unless you've died. Heaven is high, high in the sky, it's higher than space.

I've never worried about these things. I just keep it in my heart. It's not a problem. It makes me quite sad they [people] don't believe. But when God talks to them they will know. We are very, very lucky that just some people care in this world. Like me and my friends and everybody in this school, I hope, we care, we keeps this planet going. I think heaven is part of this planet.

My Nan was burnt when she died, cremated. I think that's better than worms coming into your coffin.

V.'s response is interesting for a number of reasons, as follows:

• Because she took the concept of loss and translated it into her own experience;

- because she was prepared to make such a personal statement in the presence of an adult and other children, not just her own friends;

- because she makes it with conviction. She is committed to an interpretation of her grandmother's death that is more than a fanciful idea;

- because of the metaphorical language she uses which is necessary to an interpretation and communication of her experience, which includes making use of objects which are given symbolic significance and ritual;

- because through this explanation she clearly gains empowerment;

- because the explanation necessitates further reflection on metaphysical ideas related to her grandmother's continued existence. So, God and the world, and the sustaining power of love become important;

- because child-like and rather Disneyesque imagery becomes used for and functions to provide a vehicle for a more profound personal purpose; to locate the possibility of her continued relationship with her grandmother beyond death;

- because it points to the significance of a particular traumatic experience in generating and utilising a child's reflective capabilities in a way that would not have focused them otherwise;

- because her explanation does not depend on a use of any overtly religious or Christian doctrine or imagery to substantiate her views, other than the utilisation of an afterlife, suggesting that a formal nurture in explicitly Christian ideas has not been necessary to the creation of her own explanation.

The analysis of children's stories, such as that quoted above, has resulted in the identification of particular themes that the children find important to talk about, such as relationships, secret places, ethnic identity, religious affiliation, death, separation, and the environment. As explained above, the analysis has also revealed the process that the children go through as they attempt to verbalise what they think and feel. The process not only involves finding the right words or metaphors to express complex and deeply felt issues, but also the verbalisation is a part of the process of the child's self understanding. As the children express themselves their feelings are made clearer to themselves and this self-discovery is evident in what they say. Sharing these feelings and the process of discovering them allows the children to find that other people have these feelings too, revealing and facilitating the development of empathy and understanding as the children discuss and help each other. (Erricker et al 1997)

As the children narrate, they can be said to be constructing their worldviews, a process that can be expressed diagrammatically.

The Construction of Worldview

worldview

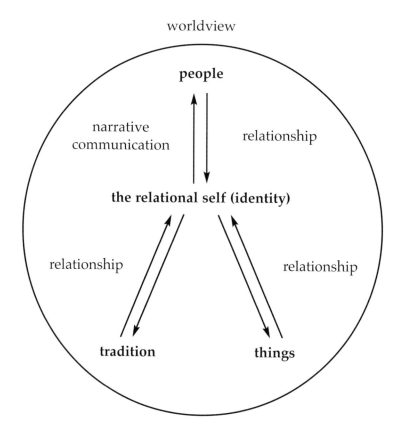

The whole process represented is dynamic, with no end point envisaged where the 'worldview' is a finished product, and with no sense of 'development' except change.

This summary of the results of using the narrative process allows us to begin to practically develop the relationship of this process to religious education. If we are removing conventional subject knowledge from consideration and replacing it with a process, then what are the skills that we are expecting the children to develop when engaging in narration? Analysis of transcript data has enabled the identification of certain skills that the children are practising as they engage with each other and with each other's experiences. These are:

1. reflection on one's own emotions;

2. self knowledge (understanding why one does something);

3. understanding of consequences;

4. self criticism (according to one's own recognised principles);

5. self control;

6. reflection on the emotions of others;

7. empathy;

8. criticism of others (according to one's own recognised principles);

9. understanding why others do things;

10. recognition of relationship;

11. recognition of difference;

12. recognition of the complexity of social discourse.

These skills can form the basis of what religious education can be understood to be.

In the development of these skills the rules and regulations by which a life is led are self-determined and self imposed, there is no conforming to specified values. It is not about knowing, or being told, about how one should be or how one should behave. Instead, the recognition and practise of the skills should result in a recognition of the complexity of social discourse, a recognition of one's own agency within it and one's responsibility for its successful functioning.

This is not to deny the possibility of conforming to a set of values or a spirituality derived from a religion, if that is what the individual wants and needs, only that that course of action should be pursued mindfully, in the knowledge that this is a choice and a positive decision that one is free to make. We suggest that religious education must include developing these skills.

When teachers in primary schools tried out this method of teaching and learning we produced some guidelines to help the teachers with this methodology. A more detailed account of this work can be found in a chapter in *New Perspectives in PSHE*, edited by Ron Best (Erricker, J.1999). The guidelines suggested the following to the teachers:

- When the children raise an issue, allow them to talk freely even if they appear to be going off the point. The most valuable reflections often come unexpectedly. Allow them to talk about their own experiences and how they feel about them.

- Try not to jump in with judgements about their expressed positions, but allow them to express themselves fully, to explain their positions, and to be challenged by other children before being challenged by you as teacher.

- Discussion between the children is much better for their development than a conversation between teacher and pupil.

CRITICAL REFLECTIONS

Working with the teachers has revealed problems that the teachers have in adjusting to a novel pedagogy.

In asking the teachers to value the children's narratives we are asking them to act in opposition to the demands increasingly made by curricula to concentrate on objective knowledge and instead to value subjective knowledge in the form of the narratives, or stories that the children tell. The teachers are not used to this and to differing degrees they found it difficult to adjust their working practices, and to identify clear learning objectives beyond those that normally derive from the 'objective' knowledge paradigm.

This quote from one of our teachers shows the conflict for them. While working on a Maths topic one child 'poured her heart out':

'I then asked myself... why feel guilty about going with the mood and needs of the group and abandoning a core subject!!'

(Teacher G, log, May 1998)

As well as demanding a valuing of, and commitment to, objective knowledge, the National Curriculum also demands the valuing of the purveyor of that knowledge, the 'one who knows', that is, the teacher. Thus by asking teachers to shift their commitment to a particular knowledge paradigm we are also asking them to yield their position of power and authority within the classroom. We are suggesting that children can be allowed to know as much or even more than the teacher, can publicly claim the position of the repository of that knowledge and have it acknowledged by the former holder of that exalted rank – the teacher.

If 'objective knowledge' is an inappropriate category to use when developing emotional literacy then the transmission model of teaching is no longer appropriate either. This meant that the teachers working with us had to learn a different way of relating to the children in what could be called a 'teaching' situation and this was difficult for them.

Some found it more difficult than the others because of their personalities, their experience and their confidence. Some found it difficult to relinquish the control and their position as the powerful one in the classroom. It took about nine months for all of them to be comfortable with the way of working that we were suggesting. They eventually reported that they felt comfortable with it and they thought that the children were benefiting. The exact nature of that benefit will be the subject of a future longitudinal study. The teachers also felt that they themselves had benefited as the following statement shows:

> **Teacher C** .'It's been really enjoyable to do with the children and I feel that I've developed skills in the kind of interviewing, trying not to direct it too much. You know, stepping back as we've discussed before, not being, you know, knowing exactly the way something's going to go, you plan all the outcomes, with this it's letting go of that, and it's quite liberating to do that for a session... let the children take it where it's going.
>
> (Teachers' meeting 20/5/98)

When we discussed the method with them, they were committed to the idea of child-centred, child-led education, but in practice they found it hard to do. Their role as teachers was to be in control, to guide the lesson and to achieve the learning objectives. However they believed that the children learned best when education was in their (the children's) control. There appeared to be a tension between the method that was best for teaching and that best for learning. In other words they believed that teaching is best done by control but learning is best done by facilitation. Put another way, learning is something children do for themselves, with help. This contrasts with the paradigm underpinning parts of the RE agreed syllabuses, that of learning being knowing what you have been taught.

Thus our teachers had to work through the stresses of working in a different paradigm from that required of them in their normal teaching, but one which they felt was right for their children. The comments of teachers at the last teachers' meeting show that they can do so:

> **Teacher C**: You don't need them (the stories) in a way. You can start at any point. It takes shape all on its own. We need to learn that you can't always ensure the outcome. We need to be open to any outcome

> **Teacher N**: You don't stop playing because you grow old, you grow old because you stop playing. And this is playing with talk. You have to have a certain confidence and reflection to be able to do it and that's maybe why our colleagues don't want to do it. We're the enlightened ones.

CONCLUSION

Narrative pedagogy in the context of religious education throws into light certain tensions that, we would maintain, have always been present and limited the effectiveness of the subject. The first is the relationship between the aims of the subject and their relevance to the learning experience of the child and young person. If narrative replaces 'knowledge' then narratives within different faith traditions can be valuable for the learner to relate to, but that is not the same as *learning about* and *learning from* as presently conceived. Teachings within religious traditions are most obviously reflections on experience, but theologies are meta-narratives that systematise such teachings to construct knowledge. This marginalises the learner in the classroom in so far as his or her narratives are concerned. Ironically, we may say that 'faith' is replaced by 'ideology' and yet, at the same time, 'faith' becomes a concept exclusively appropriated by religion. It is by releasing the grip religion has on faith that the subject can achieve its pedagogical potential. At the same time we have to transform the subject into something broader than religious education. As a beginning toward this end we may say, from a narrative perspective, that faith is wholly subjective, there is no object of faith, it involves a subject relating to another subject. The same is true of values, values are not objects but means of relating. In short religious education has to reject its exclusivist epistemological justifications and construct inclusive ontological ones.

If we attempt to place this approach within the current framework for provision, related to the teaching of world faiths and Christianity in particular, we must recognise the important issue as being that young people are introduced to the struggles and joys of faith, the difficulties and successes of constructing values and community without recourse to simply presenting them with the sanitising ideological platitudes of religious tradition. Young people, as with all of us, recognise the difference between the authenticity of the individual voice and the rhetoric of ideological pronouncements. If we attend to the former and avoid the latter we shall gain their interest and engagement and advance their learning and development.

REFERENCES

Bauman Z. (1999) *Culture as Praxis*, (London, Sage).

DFEE (1994) *Circular 1/94* (London, HMSO).

Erricker J. (1999) 'A Collaborative Approach to Researching Teacher Work in Developing Spiritual and Moral Education' in R. Best (ed.) *New Perspectives in PSHE* (London, Cassell).

Erricker J. (1998) 'Teachers Developing Spiritual and Moral Education', *Conference paper*, Conference on Education, Spirituality and the Whole Child, Roehampton.

Erricker, C. (1998) 'Spiritual Confusion: a critique of current educational policy in England and Wales', *International Journal of Children's Spirituality* 3 (1), pp. 51-64.

Erricker, C. and Erricker, J. (1994) 'Metaphorical awareness and the methodology of religious education', *British Journal of Religious Education* 16 (3), pp. 174-184.

Erricker, C., Erricker, J., Ota, C., Sullivan, D. and Fletcher, M. (1997) *The Education of the Whole Child* (London, Cassell).

Erricker, C. (1999) 'Phenomenological Approaches to the Study of Religion', in P. Connolly (ed.) *Approaches to the Study of Religion* (London, Cassell), pp. 73-104.

Glaser, B. D. and Strauss, A. K. (1967) *The Discovery of Grounded Theory* (Chicago, Aldine).

Hazelrigg, L. (1995) *Cultures of Nature* (Tallahassee, Fl., Florida State University Press).

Hume D. (1975) *Enquiries Concerning Human Understanding And Concerning The Principles Of Morals* (Oxford, Oxford University Press).

Jackson R. (1997) *Religious Education: an interpretative approach* (London, Hodder and Stoughton).

Kant I. (1960) *Religion Within The Limits Of Reason Alone* (New York, Harper Row).

McGuiness J. (1998) *Counselling in Schools: New Perspectives* (London, Cassell).

Newman, F. and Holzman, L. (1997) *The End of Knowing: a new developmental way of learning* (London, Routledge).

Otto, R. (1923) *The Idea of the Holy* (London, Oxford University Press).

Putnam, H. (1981) *Reason, Truth and History* (Cambridge, Cambridge University Press).

Roszak, T. (1981) *Person/Planet* (London, Granada).

SCAA (1994) *Model Syllabuses for Religious Education* (London, SCAA)

Shotter, J. (1992) 'Getting in touch: The meta-methodology of a postmodern science of mental life', in S. Kvale (ed.), *Psychology and Postmodernism* (London, Sage), pp. 58-73.

Smart, N. (1973) *The Science of Religion and the Sociology of Knowledge* (Princeton, Princeton University Press).

Smith, J. (1998) 'Learning to Live with Relativism', in P. Hodkinson (ed.), *The Nature of Educational Research: Realism, Relativism or Post-modernism?* (Crewe, Manchester Metropolitan University), pp. 25-36.

Tate, N. (1996) *Introductory Address, Conference on Education for Adult Life* (London, SCAA).

Waardenburg, J. (1973) *Classical Approaches to the Study of Religion* (The Hague, Mouton Publishers).

Wells, G. (1987) *The Meaning Makers: Children Learning Language and Using Language to Learn* (London, Hodder and Stoughton).

Wright, A. (1998) *Spiritual Pedagogy* (Abingdon, Culham College Institute).

Bibliography of selected publications by the Children and Worldviews Project.

Erricker J. (1998) 'Teachers Developing Spiritual and Moral Education', *Conference paper*, Conference on Education, Spirituality and the Whole Child, Roehampton.

Erricker J. (1999) 'A Collaborative Approach to Researching Teacher Work in Developing Spiritual and Moral Education' in R. Best (ed.) *New Perspectives in PSHE* (London, Cassell).

Erricker, C. (1999) 'Spirituality and the Market Place of Education', *Panorama* 18 (2) (forthcoming).

Erricker, C. (1998) 'Journeys through the Heart: the effect of death, loss and conflict on children's worldviews', *Journal of Beliefs and Values* 19 (1), pp. 107-118.

Erricker, C. (1998) 'Spiritual Confusion: a critique of current educational policy in England and Wales', *International Journal of Children's Spirituality* 3 (1), pp. 51-64.

Erricker, C. (1999), 'Phenomenological Approaches to the Study of Religion', in P. Connolly (ed.) *Approaches to the Study of Religion* (London, Cassell), pp. 73-104.

Erricker, C. and Erricker, J. (1994) 'Metaphorical awareness and the methodology of religious education', *British Journal of Religious Education* 16 (3), pp. 174-184.

Erricker, C. and Erricker, J. (1997) 'Hindsight and Foresight in Religious Education: Opening Pandora's Box or Oedipus' Eyes' in Nils Holm (ed.) *The Familiar and the Unfamiliar in the World Religions: Challenges for Religious Education Today* (Turku, Abo Academi University).

Erricker, C. and Erricker, J. (2000) *Children's Spirituality and the Transformation of Religious Education* (London, Routledge).

Erricker, C., Erricker, J., Ota, C., Sullivan, D. and Fletcher, M. (1997) *The Education of the Whole Child* (London, Cassell).

Erricker, J. (1999) 'Representation in Research' in R. Gardner (ed) *Values and Curriculum* (London, Kogan Page) (forthcoming).

Erricker, J. and Erricker, C. (1995), 'Children speaking their minds', *Panorama* 7 (1), pp. 96-109.

Ota, C. (1997) 'Learning to Juggle – the experience of Muslim and Sikh children coping with different value systems', *Journal of Beliefs and Values* 18 (2), pp. 227-234.

Ota, C., Erricker, C. and Erricker, J. (1997) 'The Secrets of the Playground', *Pastoral Care in Education* 15 (4), pp. 19-24.

CHAPTER 11

CONSTRUCTIVIST PEDAGOGIES OF
RELIGIOUS EDUCATION PROJECT:
RE-THINKING KNOWLEDGE, TEACHING AND LEARNING IN
RELIGIOUS EDUCATION

Michael Grimmitt

INTRODUCTION

In the last decade there has been a swing in emphasis in government-related guidelines on RE in England away from a process-oriented view of RE to a content-centred or a content-led one. There are a number of reasons for this and I have given an account of these in the introductory chapter of this book. While these trends could serve to undermine the broader educational concerns of RE by encouraging the subject to concentrate on instructing pupils in religious knowledge, it cannot be denied that any view of RE, however liberal and radical, must necessarily involve pupils *learning about religion and religions*. How this is best achieved, however, is controversial. In an attempt to highlight the limitations of the *instructional model* **(1)** which, if by default, continues to be widely employed in teaching about religions, I propose to try and demonstrate in this chapter how *constructivist theories of learning* provide a more acceptable basis for the development of pedagogical procedures and principles appropriate to the concerns of RE. I will do this by describing my experience of teaching a single item of religious content – *Shiva as Nataraja* – to a small group of young people aged 14 or 15 years. I see this description as exemplifying an approach which is transferable to any item of religious content from any religious tradition. Finally I will indicate, very briefly, some of the implications that a constructivist approach to learning and teaching has for the training of RE teachers.

CONSTRUCTIVIST MODELS OF LEARNING AND TEACHING

Constructivism is a theory (or more accurately a meta-theory) about knowledge and learning which incorporates several different philosophical positions. At root it identifies knowledge as a human construct which is a consequence of the way in which individuals and communities order their experience. As such, what is conceived of as 'knowledge' does not and cannot reflect some 'objective', ontological reality because that is unknowable. Human knowledge, as a consequence, reflects the way in which individuals and communities order and organise their experience of the world, using concepts which fit the situations which they encounter. A characteristic of human knowledge, whatever the field or discipline, including religious knowledge, is that it is subject to multiple interpretations or 'constructs' and is controversial or problematic by nature.

For the purposes of this discussion we can distinguish between *Piagetian constructivism, social constructivism, emancipatory constructivism* and *radical constructivism.*

Piagetian constructivism does not deny the existence of an objective world but stresses that it is only possible to know that world through experience. Consequently knowledge is not passively received but actively built up by the individual. This process of building up knowledge involves the individual assimilating new knowledge and ideas within their existing cognitive structures or 'schemas' which, as a result, accommodate the new knowledge and are subject to change and development. It is this process which Piaget divided into four distinct stages, each representing a qualitatively different and more complex understanding of the world. **(2)** Development concludes when 'formal' or 'abstract' operations emerge and the individual is able to move from egocentric interpretations of experience to an 'objective' viewpoint. Piaget saw this as the *ultimate end and purpose of cognitive development*, namely moving from a self-centred interpretation to objective or rational thought. Another way of expressing this idea is to say that Piaget's view of cognitive development involved the individual moving from *situated* thought to *decontextualised* thought.

Social constructivism is a term which derives largely from the work of Vygotsky. **(3)** Whereas Piaget talked about the active construction of knowledge through action on the world of objects, for Vygotsky the construction of knowledge occurs through *interaction* in the social world.

In other words, while Piaget believed that learning results from children's actions related to their own external world and that teaching has no place in this, Vygotsky stressed the importance of the teacher's intervention in this process. Unlike Piaget, Vygotsky stressed that there is a *dialectical relationship* between the individual and their social context. As a consequence, the (socially) situated individual actively builds knowledge through the process of internalising social knowledge. An important concept in Vygotsky's work is that of the ZPD or 'zone of proximal development'. In Vygotsky's own words, the ZPD is:

> 'the distance between the actual developmental level as determined by independent problem solving and the level of potential development as determined through problem solving under adult guidance, or in collaboration with more capable peers.' **(4)**

In positing the ZPD, Vygotsky gives more significance than Piaget to the teacher's intervention in enabling pupils to move beyond their natural levels of conceptualisation to higher levels of conceptualisation. But to do this effectively the teacher needs to understand something of the pupils' conceptual structures. Indeed, the process that Vygotsky is advocating is one whereby the teacher is aware of the pupils' constructions and deliberately seeks to build upon, extend and challenge them with alternative ways of responding to the subject matter being studied.

Vygotsky, in pursuing his notion that knowledge is socially constructed, gave particular attention to the effects of small group processes upon the way in which individuals learn. Typically he investigated the effects of collaborative work between *dyads* – a child and an adult or a child and a more advanced peer – upon learning. He found that when performing tasks collaboratively, a child can be more successful than when working alone. A metaphor which is commonly used by social constructivists to describe this process of collaboration and partnership in learning is *scaffolding*. One of Vygotsky's colleagues – Leont'ev **(5)** – described the process of the individual building knowledge through this form of social interaction as *appropriation* in contrast to Piaget's explanation of *assimilation*. Such a view clearly has implications for both pedagogical and organisational decisions that a teacher might make about how best to support pupils' learning.

Emancipatory constructivism has arisen from considering the implications of learning being situated within and derived from a sociocultural context (that is, from accepting what is sometimes called *sociocultural constructivism*)**(6)**. If individuals acquire knowledge through their interactions within a social and cultural context – simply because they are *situated* or *contextualised* individuals – does this mean that they must accept uncritically knowledge which is mediated and legitimated through those social structures? Social structures reflect the *relationships of power and privilege* within a society, not least in relation to *class, race* and *gender*. If teachers do not problematize and question existing knowledge and social structures, and it does not occur to pupils to do so, cultural assumptions and beliefs become 'taken for granted truths' and are appropriated by pupils uncritically. As we will see later, any attempt to address this involves the development of a pedagogy and a style of learning and teaching which are in sharp contrast to those of the instructional approach.

Radical constructivism is principally associated with the work of von Glaserfeld **(7)** and has been developed, so far, mainly in the field of mathematics teaching. His work serves to highlight the tension among constructivists with regard to the relation between what one *knows* and what is *real*. Whereas some constructivists, Piaget included, acknowledge the existence of an external reality composed of entities called objects but maintain that these objects can never be known directly, von Glaserfeld maintains that knowledge is 'exclusively an order and organisation of a world constituted by our experience' and not a reflection of an objective ontological reality.' **(8)** In a recent paper entitled, *'Why constructivism must be radical'* **(9)** von Glaserfeld reiterates his position by contrasting the traditional view that human knowledge can provide a 'true' representation of an independently existing, or ontological reality with his view that the relationship between knowledge and reality can at best be described as 'viable'. What he means by this is that a 'viable' concept or theory can never be true in an ultimate sense, but only so far as it is useful in accomplishing a task or in achieving a goal that one has set oneself. By implication, when a concept or theory fails to do this it is no longer viable and should be abandoned. Here von Glaserfeld's radical constructivism is synonymous with pragmatism and resonates with the post-modern concept of *performativity*, as proposed by Lyotard **(10)**.

A key element in von Glaserfeld's view of constructivism is the role played by *language*. He is wholly critical of the traditional view that language is a means of conveying knowledge from one person to another, for example from teacher to pupil. This is because he holds that 'the meaning of words… must be constructed by each user of the language individually, and this construction is based solely on the subjective experience of the particular person.' **(11)**. His conclusion is:

'If knowledge cannot be transmitted, but must instead be constructed by each student individually, this does not imply that teaching must dispense with language. It implies that the role of language must be conceived differently. We can no longer justify the intention of conveying our ideas to receivers (as though ideas could be wrapped in little packages by means of words). Rather, we will have to speak in such a way as to "orient" students' efforts at construction… This means that it is absolutely necessary for teachers to have some notion of their students' conceptual networks.' **(12)**

CONSTRUCTIVISM IN PRACTICE:
TEACHING AN ITEM OF RELIGIOUS KNOWLEDGE IN
RELIGIOUS EDUCATION

Identifying the content to be taught and learnt.

In this section I intend to show how a constructivist approach to teaching and learning about religions in RE differs from an instructional approach. I will do this by taking a typical item of religious content and by identifying the different pedagogical strategies that a teacher might adopt. The content I have chosen to identify is the meaning and significance of Shiva as Nataraja – part of a unit of work on Hinduism which pupils of 14 or 15 years of age may be required to be taught in RE, perhaps as part of a GCSE Religious Education Short Course.

Here is a list of the *background knowledge* that pupils might reasonably be thought to need to understand in order to place their study of Shiva as Nataraja within a context of Hindu belief and practice.

1.   That Shiva (or Síva) is one of the main deities of Hinduism (for example, he is

    one of the three Hindu deities which form the ancient Vedic Tri-murti – Brahma, Vishnu and Shiva – and one of the most popular gods that Hindus worship today);

2. That he is shown as having different aspects to his character (for example, as an ascetic *yogi* meditating on the Himalayan Mountain, as Lord of the Beasts, and as the god of procreation in the form of the Lingam);

3. That Shiva as Nataraja depicts Shiva performing his cosmic dance;

4. That in his dance he simultaneously creates and destroys the universe (or the worlds that comprise the universe) so that he can create it again.

Shiva as Nataraja
(Lord or King of The Dance)

The process of understanding concepts and information in isolation from each other is difficult because religious knowledge (like any other kind of knowledge) consists of a complex but coherent system of interlocking concepts and categories which are combined in accordance with certain fundamental principles expressed through and embedded in particular vocabulary and a distinctive form of language. In terms of this example, in order to begin to understand Shiva as Nataraja pupils will, therefore, need to acquire some understanding of:

- Hindu conceptions of deity;

- how and why some Vedic gods survived into the modern period;

- the difference between a deity like Vishnu who is believed to descend to earth and take different 'forms' (such as the *avatars* Rama and Krishna) and a deity like Shiva who does not;

- the technical meaning of *asceticism*, the practice of *yoga* and the nature of fertility rites and symbols in Hinduism;

- Hindu beliefs in *maya, karma, samara,* and *moksha* (both as key concepts but also as theological organising principles which give coherence to the belief system).

In order to understand the *symbolism* implicit within the representation of Shiva as Nataraja and the *meaning* that this has for Hindus, pupils would need to learn that:

1. *Nata*, in Sanskrit, means dancer and *raja* means king. *Nataraja* is another name for *Shiva* and means *Lord or King of the Dance*.

2. The classic representation of Shiva as Nataraja or as Lord of the Dance (going back to at least the 13th century CE, and possibly as early as the 9th century CE) graphically depicts Shiva's five cosmic acts of:

    *   creation

    *   preservation

    *   destruction

    *   unveiling of illusion (*maya*)

    *   the liberation of the soul (the achievement of *moksha* – the passing beyond the cycle of birth and rebirth).

The symbolism represents each of these actions as follows:

3. Shiva has four arms and four hands:

    *   in his upper right hand he holds a drum whose beat, (a) provides the rhythm of his dance, (b) reproduces the primordial sound of creation, and (c) gives the rhythm of creation and calls into being the renewal of the universe;

    *   in his upper left hand he holds the flame which symbolises, (a) the fire by which he destroys the universe in order to recreate it, and (b) that birth and creation inevitably lead to death and destruction;

    *   the gestures (called *mudras*, or *messages*) from the two lower hands represent the idea that life and death are held rhythmically in a state of balance. His lower right hand expresses the gesture of reassurance and safety ('Have no fear'), suggesting his continuous action of preserving the universe and of protecting the world and his devotees. With his lower left hand he points to his raised left foot.

4.   His left foot, coming forward from the circle, represents *moksha* (salvation or release from *samsara* – the cycle of birth and rebirth); it signals that all who approach Shiva with devotion may find protection at his feet.

5.   With his right foot Shiva treads (or dances) on the back of a dwarf demon named Apasmara. The demon, representing ignorance and forgetfulness, symbolises how humanity's efforts to reach a perfect understanding of reality (i.e. *moksha*) are constantly thwarted by ignorance and illusions. Shiva symbolically offers his followers the hope that they can escape life's illusions, thus leading to the liberation of the soul.

6.   Through the dance steps Shiva both creates and destroys the universe. He dances on one spot, at the centre of the universe which is also the human mind-heart (*atman*). The dance of Shiva takes place in every minute particle of matter; it is the source of all energy (*shakti*).

7.   The circle of flames represents the endless cycle of birth and re-birth. It also represents the universe which is brought into being and then destroyed by the rhythm of Shiva's dance. All life must be destroyed in order for it to be recreated, so enabling it to move ever closer to its fulfilment through absorption into *Brahman* – Ultimate Reality.

8.   Other symbolism includes the flowing of the Goddess of River Ganga from Shiva's matted hair; the protective presence of the Cobra; the Skull – symbol of the ascetic; the Third Eye – symbol of wisdom and power but with one blink it can bring mass destruction; one male and one female ear-ring (in the form of the *swastika*) because Shiva combines the attributes of both sexes; the Sacred Thread; the *dhoti*, the garment worn by an ascetic.

9.   The name Shiva means *benign* or kindly. The posture and gestures depicted in the statue of Shiva as Nataraja reflect the 108 basic postures of classical dance, *Bharata Natyam*, which have been performed since at least the second century BCE

   While this may seem a formidable list of content for pupils to learn, it is fairly typical of the kind of knowledge about religions which is now assumed to be a necessary part of RE by compilers of contemporary syllabuses and writers of classroom textbooks.

Applying an *instructional* approach to the task of teaching this content, one can envisage a teacher making use of an artefact of Shiva as Nataraja to point out the symbolism and to explain it, requiring pupils to research the information from textbooks, showing a video in which the process of how the figure is crafted is explained, and, possibly, how Shiva is represented and worshipped in other forms. Follow up activities to reinforce the learning might include:

- giving pupils a Shiva as Nataraja artefact and asking them to explain its meaning and religious significance to each other;

- asking pupils to draw a picture of Shiva as Nataraja and label the items of symbolism, i.e. drum, flame, third eye, skull, demon of ignorance, circle of flames, etc.;

- providing pupils with a printed description of Shiva as Nataraja but with the symbols and their meaning left as blanks to be filled in;

- asking pupils to write a description of the meaning of each of the symbols against a list given;

- organising a quiz or competitive game requiring teams of pupils to compete against each other in answering questions about Shiva as Nataraja and other related concepts (such as *maya, karma, samsara,* and *moksha*).

Applying constructivist theory to teaching and learning in RE.

In contrast to the instructional approach, the pedagogical implications of applying constructivist theories of learning to RE, especially emancipatory and radical constructivism, are far reaching and require a major re-orientation and re-thinking of current theory and practice. Before suggesting how a constructivist approach might be applied to the teaching of Shiva as Nataraja, it is important that I attempt to identify some of the essential principles of constructivism that need to be addressed when doing this. In terms of constructivist theories pupils might be said to learn effectively:

- through engaging in enquiry and reflection which encourages the interaction of thought and experience;

- through making links between their own experiences, needs, interests, questions and beliefs and the content being studied;

- through constructing their own meanings, coming to their own conclusions and being able to describe how they reached them;

- through interacting with and being challenged by the views of others, including responding to the interventions of other pupils and teachers;

- through engaging in collaborative and co-operative problem-solving;

- through reflecting critically on their own knowledge, belief and value assumptions (i.e. as situated or contextualised individuals) and contrasting them with those of alternative cultural perspectives;

- through recognising that language and vocabulary conveys meanings and interpretations which represent the self-interests and values of different groups, be they cultural, religious, social or political, and that these meanings can be re-interpreted or *deconstructed* to yield new meanings which serve and express the self-interests and values of alternative groups.

I suggest that a *three stage pedagogical strategy* may be derived from these principles.

1. Preparatory Pedagogical Constructivism (PPC)

In the first stage of the strategy pupils are engaged in an enquiry into and reflection upon their own *experience* in order to *prepare* them conceptually and linguistically for an encounter with the item of religious content. The teacher contributes to the pupils' enquiries and reflections through questions and interventions which may include practical, group-focused activities.

2. Direct Pedagogical Constructivism (DPC)

In the second stage of the strategy pupils are confronted with the item of religious content *directly*, but without explanation and instruction, so that it becomes the stimulus for them to begin to construct their own meaning and understanding of it by using observation, formulating hypotheses, and drawing upon their own experience and that represented in the group. The teacher and pupils may contribute to the process through questions and interventions. (**13**)

216

3. Supplementary Pedagogical Constructivism (SPC)

In the third stage of the strategy pupils are provided with additional or *supplementary* information about the item of religious content (i.e. as listed earlier) which enables their constructions to become more complex and embrace alternative perspectives. It is important, however, that this process is seen as inviting pupils to continue to be *constructivist* in their response to such new information. In other words, pupils do not abandon their interpretations in the face of some 'objective' knowledge which the teacher provides but continue to engage in an *interpretative process* in which new knowledge is considered *critically* and may or may not be accommodated within their own understanding. The teacher plays a significant part in the process by providing information and supporting pupils in their attempts to consider if and how they might accommodate this within their own meaning structures.

It should be noted that the most important constructivist principles of learning which this three stage pedagogical strategy embodies are:

- that the item of religious content is *always* brought into a dynamic relationship with critical and reflective thought which pupils undertake as situated or contextualised individuals;

- that any communication of information about the item of religious content on the part of the teacher is *always* related to the constructions that pupils are using, applying and articulating;

- that the sequence of learning is *always* from encouraging egocentric interpretations of experience within *situated thought*, through *alternative contextualised interpretations* (as represented by interventions from pupils or the teacher), to *evaluative judgements* about the interests which each interpretation serves and expresses.

Applying Preparatory Pedagogical Constructivism (PPC) to Shiva as Nataraja.

What follows is a verbatim account of a *conversation* between myself and some young people of 14/15 years. They were unaware of my agenda to introduce them to Shiva as Nataraja and to the Hindu concept of the cycle of rebirth. They had not previously studied Hinduism. *My questions and interventions are in italics.* The conversation focuses upon exploring the relationship between birth and death and the concept of fulfilment in life.

How might the idea of being born be related to dying? Can you see any connections between these two events?
Birth is the beginning of life and death is the end of life; being born and dying are the starting and stopping points of life; they are the fixed points in between which you experience life; they are the two most important events in your life when you are least conscious of what is happening to you and which you are unable to remember; once you are born you begin to die; you have the longest life expectation at birth than you ever have again because each day you live is a day closer to dying; living is also dying, but if you're lucky it takes a long time to get to death itself!

If you are always dying and moving towards death, what is the point of living?
Life is a challenge to make you become what you want to be; it makes each person into an individual different from everyone else; there is always something more to achieve; your ideas of achievement change during life but you will continue to regret that you may not achieve everything you want to.

Is there a solution to the problem of not being able to achieve what you want in life before you die?
Yes, eternal youth! It would be great if you went on and on until you achieved everything that you wanted to achieve – and never got older! But you can't get this so you just have to achieve as much as you can and accept that you'll always be disappointed. Not achieving something might make someone a better person – more accepting and having lower expectations of what you can achieve. *Can you think of any other solutions?* Life after death! If you don't achieve something in this life you can believe that you will achieve it in a life after death – that's a solution for some people. *Is that a solution for you?* I'm not sure; I don't think so. There is the idea that you can be reborn in another life and have another go so that next time you might get closer to achieving your goals – or you might change your goals and adopt less optimistic and more realistic ones.

Does the idea of being reborn and living lots of lives appeal to you? Do you think it is a good solution to the problem of not achieving what you want to in a lifetime?
I think it is quite a good idea, but you could get racked off when you never achieve what you want to do. It would mean that you could find out how to achieve things and when you didn't you could always do it differently next time. But you could get very fed up – bored, I mean. Continually dying at seventy or whatever is not very appealing, you would want to look for a way of not starting it all again. I think life is a puzzle and if you finally cracked it you would be happy for ever and ever.

What would happen if you suddenly cracked it? Where would you be?
What would you do?
Once you had cracked it you would either be annihilated, totally gone for ever, or you would live for ever entirely fulfilled with no death! That would be nice, but I still think it would be boring!

Other ideas that were explored included:

What is the relationship between creation and destruction or between creating something and destroying it?
I would only want to destroy things that were evil, not things that were good and even then I don't like the idea of destroying anything that is living. If you could improve on something you had made (like drawing a better picture, or making a better model) it would be all right to destroy an earlier effort, but even then you can't expect perfection. *Why not?* Human being aren't perfect and never will be; only God is perfect; we have to accept our limitations and faults and live with them. It is a dangerous idea that anything less than perfect should be destroyed or replaced; it could lead to euthanasia of children who are born with a handicap or when old people get ill. Life is about having a mixture of good and evil, things which are perfect and things that aren't, some good things and some bad things.

What causes things to get worse or better for human beings?
Some people are just lucky; everything goes well for them; other people are just unlucky, everything goes wrong for them. *How could you change this so that what happens to you isn't just a matter of luck?* You can work hard to make sure that you are successful; people who fail often don't work hard enough or don't want something badly enough. *Why not?* A lot of people don't get the help they need. *What sort of help?* From parents and teachers. *What about from God?* If you think God is on your side that can help. But in the end it is about believing in yourself and keeping on trying.

Applying Direct Pedagogical Constructivism (DPC) to Shiva as Nataraja.

The photograph of the Shiva as Nataraja statue was shown to the young people and they were asked to say what they thought it was. Their verbatim questions and responses follow. *My questions and interventions are in italics.*

It's some religious type thing. What are those spiky things round it? What is it made of? Is it expensive? What is she or it doing? Why has it got three (four) arms? Has it got wings? What is it holding in its hands? *There is a drum in one hand*. Is a drum a sign of dancing? Is it dancing? Is it standing on an animal or a baby or something? Why is it in a circle? Has it got a snake in its hand? Which religion is it from? *It is from Hinduism*. Is it a god? What type of god is it? Is it male or female? It looks like a female. *It is a male god called Shiva*. He is standing in a ring of fire. Is he dancing in a ring of fire? Does it symbolise a god who can go through anything, you know, the four elements – earth, fire, wind and water? Who is the little guy at the bottom? Look at her hair – is that hair? It looks like the snakes that came from Medusa the Gorgon.

What has this statue got to do with our earlier conversation about birth and death?
The circle is eternity, it goes on for ever and ever. Is that how we treat people on our way through life – by standing on them? How many eyes has she got? Is that a crown with an eye in it? She is a goddess of life. Is she wearing any clothes? *Let's go back to our earlier conversation*. Is she dancing? Is she celebrating life and death? Why is it dancing? Because it has to? Is it the god of dance or celebration? Is this how it always is? Can you get other statues of this god doing something else or in a different form? Is he always dancing? Are there stages in his life – one dancing and celebrating and one when he is dying? He has got fire in his hand and he has got four hands!

I want you to think back to our conversation about birth and death and tell me if looking at this statue suggests any of the ideas we talked about.
Do all the hands represent a different life? The circle is the circle of life, and there are stages in life. Do the flames round the circle represent the stages? The circle is everlasting; there is no start and no end; it just keeps going for ever. The circle says life goes on for ever? What is that little thing at the bottom? Is it an angel or something? *It is a demon*. Is the circle about good and bad? That horrible little thing is stopping something which is good. The god is trying to tread him out of the circle. *What sort of demon is he? What does he represent?* He is death. Are all the bad things that you come across in your life, all the disappointments rolled into this little guy? *He is the demon of ignorance*. Is the god trying to get rid of ignorance so we can all have a better life? It's the ignorance which is stopping our life from going on and on for ever. We don't live for ever because we are ignorant? *Perhaps, but it could be the opposite of this*. What is the opposite? In getting rid of ignorance we do go on and on? No (laughter) that's the same! Is it saying that if we get rid of ignorance our life does **not** continue on and on? *Yes, that is exactly what it is saying! Overcome ignorance and you won't be reborn*. But why doesn't the god want us to go on and on?

Why, do you think, doesn't the god want our lives to go on and on?
Because there are too many people in the world already? Because he wants us to suffer? – if you get old you suffer more. To give more people a chance to achieve what they want? – the fewer people there are the more likely you are

to achieve your goal? (Another young person) Does he want us to be as perfect as possible so we can be like him? *How can we do this?* We need to know perfectly, to know the truth, then we can be like him. Ah! If we know the truth perfectly throughout our life, that's it – we would become perfect first time and we would not need to keep going on and on or coming back again.

So what is the truth? The truth about what? *What is the truth about human life?* I've got it! You go round and round being reborn until you are perfect and when you are perfect you are released from this world and become a god. You need to keep being re-born because getting to the truth takes a long time. Once you have got there you become a god and can guide other people there. We are training to become gods!

So what gets in the way of us finding this truth? Ignorance! Fantasy! Living in our own dreamland. Illusions! We have to know the difference between what is false and what is real. We have to know the difference between what is evil and what is good. The god helps us to find truth – that's why he is stamping on the demon of ignorance; he's stamping on our ignorance. He's making us free from having to be reborn so that we can find truth and be fulfilled in a single lifetime.

Applying Supplementary Pedagogical Constructivism (SPC) to Shiva as Nataraja.

This session concentrated on exploring links between aspects of the earlier discussion (during both PPC and DCP) and the Hindu concepts of *maya, karma, samsara,* and *moksha.* Space only permits a brief summary of key issues which were raised about these concepts, either by myself or the young people.

Maya: not everything is illusion, if it was nothing would be real: we create illusion: it is to do with seeing what we want to see and not what is really there: life would be too hard if we couldn't have our fantasies and daydreams, but we usually know when we are fantasising and daydreaming: people who mix up fantasy with reality are mentally ill or sick. *What part does maya play in helping us to know what is true?* It probably doesn't help at all – that's why Hindus want to get rid of it. *So do you agree or disagree with them about getting rid of illusion and seeing things as they really are?* I agree with some of it, but I still think a bit of fantasising doesn't hurt you.

Karma: it is true that you can't get away from what you do: it's a bit like the conscience – it keeps reminding you of the bad things you've done. (Another young person) Do Hindus believe in forgiveness? Can the gods forgive people? Can you have your karma forgiven? Carrying all your bad deeds around with you for your whole life is scary – it's like a punishment, a life sentence! No wonder Hindus want to escape from being reborn, you know, *samsara*. (Another young person) But that's what we have to do – live with the things we do. We have to learn from our mistakes. I don't believe in all this forgiveness stuff: you can't change what someone has done by forgiving them: they learn faster if they're not forgiven: that's why I think *karma* is true.

Samsara: I can see now why Hindus don't want to be re-born; when we first started talking about being reborn again and again I quite liked the idea, but I don't now. I prefer to believe that you have one life and that's it. *And not have a life after death?* It makes you wonder what it would be like to have a life after death – what if it was like *samsara*? You know, believing like Christians do in going to heaven but when you die you find out that you come back here to do it all over again! Not nice! *How could you begin to find out which one is true?* You can't, unless someone comes back from the dead and tells you! Oh! (laughter), that's what the Bible says Jesus did! *Hindus have their own sacred scriptures which tell you about this.* It's all a matter of belief, of faith and that; it can't be proved to be true.

Moksha: this is about getting out of the circle, being released from going round and round for ever; but how do you do it?: do you have to believe everything that's in the scriptures without having any doubts? *You can achieve it through loving devotion to god and through practising yoga.* Yoga is good for you, it makes you fit; even if it doesn't lead to *moksha* it's a good idea to do it. *But not just as a hobby but as a way of life?* Are you serious! You couldn't do much else if you just did yoga. *But that's the point – doing what is important, going for what is real.* I don't think I could ever take religion that seriously!

THE STRENGTHS OF CONSTRUCTIVISM IN PROMOTING THE EDUCATIONAL CONCERNS OF RELIGIOUS EDUCATION

While there may be a place for an instructional approach to some learning and teaching in RE (for example, breaking down complex religious concepts into small, logical steps in order to support pupils' progress towards acquiring basic information about religions and some understanding of religious ideas, etc.), the overall aims of the subject are unlikely to be achieved by means of this approach to learning and teaching. This is because the mechanistic basis of the theory underlying instruction (stimulus/response/reinforcement) is unable to promote learning which enables pupils to:

- enter imaginatively and empathetically into the subjective consciousness of religious adherents in order to become aware of and understand the interpretative process that is a feature (a) of formulating personal faith, and (b) of participating as a member in the life of a faith community (i.e. *inter-subjective understanding*);

- make connections between their own feelings, acts and experiences and the content being studied in order to use these (a) as a basis for understanding religious concepts, beliefs and practices, and (b) as a means of encouraging critical reflection upon their own beliefs and values (i.e. *intra-subjective understanding*).

It is because constructivist theories of learning do promote these more complex and sophisticated forms of learning – and others – that their principles are well placed to underpin an effective pedagogy for use in RE and provide some guidance in the choice and treatment of religious content. The example of applying *preparatory, direct* and *supplementary pedagogical constructivism* to Shiva as Nataraja given earlier serves to illustrate some of the characteristics of constructivist learning theory and how it can address some of the essential concerns of RE. The particular strengths of these characteristics and their implications for teaching and learning in RE can now be summarised as follows:

- constructivism emphasises the importance of encouraging pupils to explore ideas and issues for themselves and arrive at their own conclusions.

It has still to be appreciated by most RE teachers that the process of teaching pupils about an item of religious content within a religious tradition (such as a belief, a practice, or a value) can never result in some uniform, unequivocal meaning being conveyed to each pupil so that they all share a common understanding. Just as religious adherents within a single faith tradition interpret commonly held beliefs, practices and values within a broad spectrum of meaning reflecting the particularities of their personal experiences, so pupils, coming from diverse cultural, social and religious backgrounds, will interpret and understand the same religious ideas in an even greater variety of ways. Far from being a problem in the understanding of religion and religions, the fact that each and every pupil is engaged in this form of *interpretation* does not undermine the educational experience of RE but enhances it. One of the fundamental concerns of the subject is to enable pupils to participate consciously and critically in the process of meaning-making as a characteristic activity of being human. RE enables pupils to do this through considering the inescapable, ultimate questions that arise from reflecting upon the human condition. Merely conveying to them pre-packaged meanings (although constructivism shows this to be an impossibility) does little to engage them in such reflections or convince them of the need to do so.

- constructivism stresses the influence of the individual's social and cultural circumstances upon the way in which they respond to and interpret their experiences.

While this is a factor in the development of every individual's understanding of themselves and of their beliefs and values, it is also a factor in their experience of learning in the classroom. RE teachers can, therefore, use the social, cultural and religious environment of the classroom to provide individual pupils with the support – *scaffolding* – for exploring their ideas and articulating them to others, perhaps for the first time. Equally these circumstances can be used to promote their development through challenge and stimulation, often by the provision of further information or, as in the examples given earlier, through strategic (and sequential) questioning on the part of the teacher. The importance of discussion in pairs or groups and of providing differentiated activities to extend pupils' understanding across their ZPDs and address individual differences is affirmed by constructivist theories. In contrast, whole class teaching is almost exclusively the province of an approach to teaching and learning which places an undue emphasis on instruction and an unfounded belief in its efficacy.

- constructivism, while not being incompatible with methods drawing upon phenomenology and ethnography, enables religious knowledge and understanding to be problematized and its language and meanings related to power and privilege to be deconstructed.

Despite the considerable attention in recent years which writers from many different disciplines have given to the issue of the sexist and racist nature of religion, most religious educators and many RE teachers remain peculiarly impervious to being influenced in their pedagogic practice by such a concern even if they are sympathetic to it. *Emancipatory constructivism* offers a promising basis for the development of a pedagogy which encourages pupils to be sensitive to the positive and negative effects of religion upon human life, including its intrinsic sexism and racism. Thus, in place of the uncritical, descriptive approach of a pedagogy applying only phenomenological method and making extensive use of instruction, an *emancipatory pedagogy* would place all items of religious content within a critical framework. Such a framework would, perhaps, consist of a set of exploratory or investigatory questions designed to assist pupils to *deconstruct* and *reconstruct* traditional and formal religious interpretations and meanings in the light of their own experience and alternative perspectives. For example: *How does this religious text, belief, practice or value present the possibilities of being female and male? From where or from whom does it derive and for whom is it intended? To whom does it give power and privilege? To whom does it deny power and privilege? etc.* Such a framework would fit within the third section of the pedagogical model proposed earlier, that is as part of supplementary pedagogical constructivism (SPC). Putting such an emancipatory pedagogy into effect would prevent RE from furthering the hegemony of cultural and social reproduction involving the perpetuation of injustice, inequality and oppression and would challenge concepts and practices which have become *reified* by tradition and which may no longer be worthy of support or toleration. It would also represent a significant advance in ensuring that RE has a direct effect on sensitising pupils to matters of social and political concern in a pluralistic democracy.

IMPLICATIONS OF ADOPTING A SOCIAL CONSTRUCTIVIST PEDAGOGY OF RELIGIOUS EDUCATION FOR THE TRAINING OF RE TEACHERS

Constructivism highlights the necessary involvement of the learner, as a situated and contextualised individual, in the construction of knowledge. The theory of learning and teaching which we have been considering is a natural by-product of this view of epistemology. As we have seen, there is a range of interpretations within constructivism from acceptance of the existence of an objective world enabling 'truth' to be known through experience, to a view that truth, at best, can be no more than the *viability* of certain culturally and individually determined *beliefs*. It follows that the application of constructivism to learning and teaching in RE must impact upon our conceptions of religious knowledge – its epistemological nature, form, mode of expression and status as a claim to ultimate truth.

It would be unfortunate, however, if RE teachers' theological assumptions were the major determinant of how they responded to the challenge that constructivism makes to the central task of teaching, namely, ensuring effective learning on the part of their pupils. The successful accomplishment of this central task is dependent upon relating the process of teaching to how pupils, coming from a wide range of social, cultural, and religious backgrounds, learn. The pedagogical principles that constructivist theory supports are a direct challenge to any process of teaching which over-relies upon the use of a simple transmission model of knowledge to achieve its aims. Similarly, constructivist theory challenges teachers to recognise that the process of teaching also demands that they are constantly involved in adapting their own knowledge to the needs of their pupils. How teachers have acquired their own religious knowledge does not provide an adequate model for teaching RE **(14)**. Inspecting trainees' knowledge of the contents of the Model Syllabuses for RE really has very little reliability as an indicator that they know how to teach it successfully. As RE teachers they need to subject their own religious knowledge to the same processes of deconstruction and reconstruction that constructivism advocates as a basis for pupils' learning. Teaching trainees how to transform and transmute their own religious knowledge within a wider pedagogical focus continues to present the major challenge to teacher trainers, especially when working in a very tight time scale and when much of their teaching experience in schools can still be limited to applying an instructional model.

END PIECE

Conversations with young people along the lines described in this chapter have convinced me of the importance of trying to build new pedagogical strategies to further a constructivist approach to knowledge and learning in RE. These early experiments have shown that, when motivated, interested and challenged to engage in critical reflections, and supported in their efforts, pupils begin to move rapidly towards far more sophisticated and profound constructions of meaning and thought than is ever the case when they are merely expected to receive and replicate pre-packaged information. The pedagogical strategies that are here described for the first time will, no doubt, undergo review and revision as the project develops. If, in the meantime, any readers feel inclined to try them out I would be very interested to hear about their results **(15)**.

Notes And References

1. It would be more accurate to use the term **behaviourist model** and to locate **instruction** within the behaviourist theory of learning through stimulus, response and reinforcement. However, in current practice in teaching RE in England, instruction is an appropriate term for describing the way in which the 'phenomenological approach' is applied by many teachers – as a narrowly descriptive, information conveying approach devoid of any pedagogical sensitivity.

2. See Piaget . J. (1950) *The Psychology of Intelligence* (London, Routledge and Kegan Paul) in which he distinguishes between the sensori-motor stage, the pre-operational stage, the concrete operations stage, and the formal operations stage.

3. See Vygotsky, L.S. (1962) *Thought and Language* (Cambridge, USA, Massachusetts Institute of Technology).

4. See Vygotsky, L.S. (1978) *Mind in Society: The Development of Higher Psychological Processes* (Cambridge, USA, Harvard University Press), p.86.

5. See Leont'ev, A.N. (1981) *Problems of the development of mind* (Moscow, Progressive Publishers).

6. The term *emancipatory constructivism* is first used in: O'Loughlin, M. (1992) 'Engaging teachers in emancipatory knowledge construction,' *Journal of Teacher Education*, Vol 43, No 5, pp.336-346.

7. See von Glaserfeld, E. (1995) *Constructivism: A way of knowing and learning* (London, Falmer Press).

8. See Watzlawick, P. (Ed.), (1984) *The invented reality: How do we know what we believe we know?* (New York, Norton) p.24.

9. See Larochelle, M, Bednarz, N and Garrison J. (Eds.) *Constructivism and education* (Cambridge, UK, Cambridge University Press) pp. 23-28.

10. See Lyotard, J.F. (1984) *The postmodern condition: A report on knowledge,* (Minneapolis, University of Minnesota Press) pp. 47-53.

11. Larochelle et al. (Op.cit) p.27.

12. Ibid, p.27.

13. See Grimmitt, M. et al (1991), *A Gift to the Child: Religious Education in the Primary School,* (Cheltenham, UK, Stanley Thornes, Ltd,) pp. 8-15 for an earlier and similar view, but not underpinned by constructivist learning theory.

14. See Williams, A. (1998) *The Career Value of Qualifications in Religious Education and Theology, unpublished research study* (Oxford, The Farmington Institute of Christian Studies, Harris Manchester College, Oxford) pp. 24-25.

15. My address for correspondence is: The School of Education, University of Birmingham, Edgbaston, Birmingham B12 2TT, UK: e-mail: M.H.Grimmitt@bham.ac.uk

CONTRIBUTORS

ALAN BROWN is Deputy Director of The National Society and Director of the National Society's Religious Education Centre. Following undergraduate studies at Leeds University in theology and postgraduate studies in Christian-Hindu dialogue he held posts in higher education and as Schools Officer for the Church of England. He has been both Chair and Secretary of the SHAP Working Party on World Religions in Education, President of the Inter-European Commission of Church and School, and Chair of Feed the Minds. He has been influential in advising both Government and the Church of England Board of Education on matters relating to Religious Education, including the formulation of the religious clauses of the 1988 Education Reform Act. He has a particular interest in the religious education of pupils with special educational needs and has written widely on many aspects of Religious Education for the National Society.

DR TREVOR COOLING is Head of the Stapleford Centre, an independent educational charity founded by the Association of Christian Teachers (ACT) in 1997. He began his teaching career as a biology teacher while also contributing to some teaching of Religious Education out of personal interest. After completing a University of London Diploma in Theology at the London Bible College he became a full-time Religious Education teacher for seven years and completed an MA in Religious Education at King's College, University of London. While acting as Director of Stapleford House he undertook a Ph.D. in Religious Education in the University of Birmingham. He has acted as adviser to the NCC, SCAA and QCA and is course leader for the distance learning courses for RE teachers validated by the University of Nottingham where he is a Special Lecturer.

CLIVE ERRICKER is Reader in the Study of Religions at University College, Chichester. Previously he taught at the University of Warwick, King Alfred's College, Winchester, and in a sixth form college and secondary schools. His interests lie in children's spirituality and religious education, holistic education and post-modern theory and philosophy.

JANE ERRICKER is Research Officer and Science Co-ordinator in the School of Education at King Alfred's College, Winchester. Previously she taught in a sixth form college and secondary schools. Her principal interests are emotional literacy, post-modern theory and philosophy, and inter-disciplinary education. With Clive Erricker, she is co-editor of The International Journal of Children's Spirituality and Co-director of The Children and Worldviews Project. (113)

DR MICHAEL GRIMMITT is Reader in Religion in Education in the University of Birmingham. Following posts in secondary schools and a lectureship in Divinity at the C.F. Mott College of Education in Liverpool, he became Founder Director of the Religious Education Centre in Westhill College, Birmingham, where he directed the Christians Today Project, out of which The Westhill Project developed. In 1979 he moved to the University of Birmingham where he co-directed the Religion in The Early Years Project and the Religion in The Service of the Child Project. He was Reviews Editor of the *British Journal of Religious Education* for 24 years. In 1997 he was seconded as an Additional Inspector to the Office of Her Majesty's Chief Inspector of Schools in England with responsibility for contributing to the inspection of Religious Education Teacher Training. He has lectured widely on RE in the UK and abroad and his writings on RE are available in a number of languages, most recently in Danish and Finnish.

DR DAVID HAY is Reader in Spiritual Education in the University of Nottingham. Following graduate and post-graduate studies in zoology he entered school teaching and after some years was appointed Lecturer in the Education Department of Nottingham University. An interest in the work of the zoologist Sir Alister Hardy at the Religious Experience Research Unit in Oxford University led to collaboration in research into religious experience, including directing several national and in-depth surveys of reports of religious experience in the United Kingdom. In 1985 he was appointed Director of the Religious Experience Research Unit in Oxford University. He was also recipient of the Templeton UK Prize in the Study of Religion. A Roman Catholic layman, he has continued to make a major contribution to the on-going debate about the nature, aims and methodology of contemporary religious education in non-denominational schools.

PROFESSOR JOHN. M. HULL is Professor of Religious Education in the University of Birmingham. An Australian by birth, he is a graduate of the Universities of Melbourne, Cambridge and Birmingham. He was Editor of the *British Journal of Religious Education* for twenty-five years, the joint founder and General Secretary of the International Seminar on Religious Education and Values, and President of the National Christian Education Council. He is on the Board of Directors of AbilityNet which assists disabled people with computers. In 1992 he received the William Rainey Harper Award of the Religious Education Association of the United States and Canada, and in 1995 had the honorary degree of D.Theol. conferred upon him by the University of Frankfurt for his contribution to Religious Education. His autobiography was published in 1979 by One World in Oxford under the title *On Sight and Insight: A Journey into the World of Blindness*.

PROFESSOR ROBERT JACKSON is Director of the Warwick Religions and Education Research Unit in the Institute of Education at the University of Warwick. He has directed a range of funded research projects, including several on the religious upbringing of children in Britain from different ethnic and religious backgrounds. He was Co-Director of the Warwick RE Project, a curriculum development project using ethnographic data as source material for religious education. He belongs to a number of research networks in Europe and beyond, including the International Seminar on Religious Education and Values, the Norwegian Network for Research in Culture, Religion and Identity in a Multicultural Context, the International Research Symposium on Inter-religious and Inter-cultural Education and the International Association for the History of Religions. In 1996 his work received the Templeton UK Institutional Award for 'promoting understanding of other faiths'. He is Editor in Chief of the *British Journal of Religious Education* and serves on the editorial boards of several international journals.

DR JOHN RUDGE is an independent Religious Education Consultant and an Additional Inspector appointed to the Office of Her Majesty's Chief Inspector of Schools in England with responsibility for contributing to the inspection of Religious Education Teacher Training. Following experience as a Religious Education Teacher and Head of Department in schools in Manchester, he was appointed to the staff of the Religious Education Centre, Westhill College, Birmingham in 1980. He contributed to a number of the Centre's publications, including *The Westhill Project*, and made a specialist contribution to the development of assessment in Religious Education. In 1995, as Director of the Westhill Religious Education Centre, he acted as consultant to the Birmingham Agreed Syllabus of Religious Education.

DR ANDREW WRIGHT is Lecturer in Religious and Theological Education at King's College, University of London, where he is currently Programme Director of the MA in Religious Education and co-ordinator of Religious Education doctoral research students. He has been responsible for the PGCE RE courses at King's College, the Roehampton Institute and the London Institute of Education. Prior to his move into Higher Education he was Head of Religious Education in three contrasting secondary schools. He was responsible for directing the research project into Spiritual Education commissioned by the All Saints Educational Trust and continues to publish widely on many aspects of Religious Education.

Author Index

Subject Index